Nano Nagle and an Evolving Charism
A Guide for Educators, Leaders and Care Providers

Nano Nagle

AND AN EVOLVING CHARISM
A Guide for Educators, Leaders and Care Providers

Edited by Bernadette Flanagan,
Mary T. O'Brien and Anne M. O'Leary

VERITAS

Published 2017 by
Veritas Publications
7–8 Lower Abbey Street
Dublin 1, Ireland
publications@veritas.ie
www.veritas.ie

ISBN 978 1 84730 781 1

Copyright © Union of Sisters of the Presentation of the Blessed Virgin Mary, 2017

10 9 8 7 6 5 4 3 2 1

A catalogue record for this book is available from the British Library.

Designed by Heather Costello, Veritas Publications
Printed in the Republic of Ireland by SPRINT-print Ltd, Dublin

Veritas books are printed on paper made from the wood pulp of managed forests. For every tree felled, at least one tree is planted, thereby renewing natural resources.

Dedication

To all who have been inspired by the charism of Nano Nagle.

Contents

Foreword   9

Acknowledgements   15

Introduction   17

Part One: Context

The Nagle Family: Supporters of a Catholic Faith
under Siege in Penal Ireland
Máirín MacCarron   25

Portrait of a Foundress: Nano Nagle and
Catholic Education in Ireland
Catherine Nowlan-Roebuck and Deirdre Raftery   33

Part Two: Sources of Inspiration for Nano Nagle

'Zeal' in the Writings and Life of St Paul and of Nano Nagle
Mary T. O'Brien PBVM   53

Nano Nagle and St John of God: Parallel Lives
Anne M. O'Leary PBVM   65

'For the Greater Glory of God': A Reflection on
the Jesuit Influence on Nano Nagle
Mary T. O'Brien PBVM   79

'You Did it to Me' (Mt 25:40): The Religious Motivation of Catholic
Philanthropy in Eighteenth and Nineteenth-Century Ireland
Frank Steele   93

Part Three: Presentation Vision

'Consider the Mustard Seed': From Nano's Humble Beginnings
to Disproportionate Growth
Mary T. O'Brien PBVM   107

Edmund Rice and the Presentation Sisters
Beth Hassel PBVM   119

The Presentation of Mary: Returning to the Protogospel of James
Anne M. O'Leary PBVM   127

Presented in the Temple of God's Glory
Mary L. Coloe PBVM   141

'God in our Midst': A Theology of Indwelling
Anne M. O'Leary PBVM   151

Church – 'Home and School of Communion' –
Enriched by Presentation Charism
Anne M. Codd PBVM   163

Part Four: Evolving Charism

Presentation Charism in a Latino Context
Gloria Inés Loya PBVM   177

Stewardship and the Charism of Nano Nagle
Anne M. O'Leary PBVM   189

Missionaries on the Prairie
Margaret H. Preston   203

Nano Nagle and Everyday Leadership
Bernadette Flanagan PBVM   213

The Song Must not Stop with Us: Investing in
the Future of Presentation
Mary T. O'Brien PBVM   223

List of Contributors   235

Select Bibliography   239

Index   247

Foreword

Henry Ford famously remarked that 'History is bunk' and he set its value out in raw financial terms: 'it is not worth ten cents'. While few who pick up a book like this would openly espouse such cultural barbarism, the sentiment is widespread. The simplest form is the seemingly irrefutable wisdom of 'not crying over spilt milk' and proclaiming: 'the past is past; it is where we are going now that matters'. This truism conveniently ignores that we start our journey into the future from a very distinct situation – our now – and we can only know the location of our now, with all its nooks and crannies, by retracing our steps; which, in the case of this book, is the original energy of Nano Nagle's charism.

But Henry Ford's vision also seems to fit with the Christian 'big picture'. Our desire is the establishment of the eschatological 'Kingdom' (probably the most complex image in our whole religious imagination) and its approximation through our engagements in the world around us – our work to establish a culture of justice, truth, love – is always in the future. Jews and Christians look to the future as the destination towards which they journey in hope, rather than pining for a lost Golden Age to which they might happily return. This *is* the big picture within which the essays in this collection are set. Moreover, the instinctive conservative (and conservatism is a default setting in human religious sentiment), who rises each morning hoping to wind the clock back a little from the secular present to a more pious past, is in conflict with that basic thrust of faith which is towards the future and is dedicated to finding God's presence in the evolving now.

But if Judaism and Christianity are future-oriented, they also spend a vast amount of their resources on recalling the past. The basis of Jewish prayer is the recollection of the mighty works of God – most of 'the [Old Testament] scriptures' are unashamedly written as history – which in turn is the basis for blessing and thanking God now, and so asking him to bless us as we move into the future. This is also the kernel of Christian prayer: we recall God's mighty works and his sending us the Christ; hence we are now blessing the Father, asking for our daily bread which will empower us to move forward in time knowing that the kingdom, the power and the glory is his now and forever.

So we live with a paradox: we are focused on the evolving future but cannot move without recalling the historical charism of Nano Nagle. Is this so? The simplest demonstration of the relationship of the future and the past is that no liturgy takes place (or, at least, should take place) at which we do not recall the past through reading the Scriptures, and it is the remembering (history is an activity) of Jesus that tells us who we are, why we are doing what we are doing, and which acts as a lamp for where we are moving. We do not exist simply in 'the present' (which is a 'good place' if you like to think of yourself as a 'progressive' or a 'bad place' if you consider yourself a 'conservative') but in a constant motion of tumbling forward from roots deep in the past towards a dimly evolving horizon. But in the constant movement we seek to walk as disciples – there are right and wrong ways of walking which are revealed to us through conscientious examination of the path before us – and there is the presence of the Spirit which allows us to see a light beyond the horizon of our human vision. The people who are on 'The Way' (Acts 9:2) are those who have, collectively, chosen the Way of Life (Deuteronomy 31). The People of God are, and have been since the time of our father Abraham, a history-obsessed group going forward. Presentation Sisters are rightly concerned with the undiscovered treasures of their charism. History is worth a lot more to us than ten cents.

History and Community

We can approach the relationship between a historical charism and an evolving future in another way. If *I* were to ask where do *I* want to go or what do *I* want to do – seeing myself as a wholly autonomous individual in the classic modern view of the isolated ego – then I can ignore history. I can imagine that my past is irrelevant to my life: only my now and my future concern me. However, once the question moves to being one about a community – 'where will *we* go?' or 'what will *we* do?' – then history cannot be avoided because that 'we' is constituted by our shared past, the charism lived by Nano Nagle. A community is a community by what it shares and at the heart of this lies memory: memory of what drew us together, draws us together, our ups and downs, and the factors external to us that have shaped us and buffeted us, what we have built together – and, sadly, also our shared stupidities and failures.

If it is because we have a past together that there is an 'us' who can ask questions about a common future, then looking at that past, the gift of the charism, is both inevitable and important. The depth of any community's identity is a direct function of their awareness of a common path that has brought them to where they are: shared experiences, trials, tasks, concerns, and friends, as well as shared myths, images, icons and dreams. This is true for good or ill: a shared memory of discrimination and abusive behaviour can resurface in a community – irrespective of the size of the community, be it a nuclear family, a religious community or a Church – with a virulence that defies the logic of those who live only in the present; while a shared memory of care, courage and endurance can empower people in their present difficulties and encourage them to tackle massive challenges undaunted.

This principle is true for large groups and very small groups: the common rituals of a family or religious community are as indelible for them as the rubrics of the Roman Missal. And it is true whether we like it or not: our past is like the path which has delivered us to where we are and it will have some high points, some courageous acts of witness and wisdom, and some moments when we were 'ahead of the game' and of which we are justly proud. The past will also have its darker side and shameful moments when we have betrayed trust, acted in a short-sighted way, or acted from selfish motives. When history turns to these things – and none of us likes looking at our darker side – it reveals part of who we are and this truth about ourselves can be both shocking and liberating.

But inevitably, engaging in a re-appreciation of the historical gift of charism is painful: it reveals that our identity is not that of a shining jewel, it shows the limitations that we once laboured under, and it poses awkward questions. So perhaps it is best to avoid history altogether? This is certainly a path that has been taken by many religious communities in the last two hundred years – and it is worth observing this process of ignoring history (the process to which we give the name 'obscurantism') because it shows us *both* a feature of contemporary Christianity *and* the importance of historical enquiry.

The most startling case is that of addressing the early Christian documents which we usually refer to collectively as 'the [books of the] New Testament'. Faced with the fact that these did not present us with the clear-cut answers of later theologians – of whichever Church – many decided that the critical study of history was either optional, spiritually unrewarding, or merely the work of those who lacked faith. The effects of such obscurantism are manifold: the past expression of a charism may be seen so simply that it can be presented as the source of certainties for today and tomorrow. Such an approach does not acknowledge that every human situation is limited in its cultural understanding; and not to accept this is to imprison oneself in one's immediate past.

Similarly, just because one chooses to ignore the awkward questions the past throws up does not obliterate those questions, but rather generates an atmosphere of bad faith among those who refuse to ask the questions and a suspicion of a cover-up by outsiders. Moreover, in an increasingly secular world the general impression is that everything to do with religion is simply irrational and that when it is subjected to clear observation then the emperor will indeed appear without clothes. To a group who look back – as part of the history of their charism – to the Presentation of Mary in the Temple, such a process can be exceptionally difficult, but it is only by facing these questions that history throws up that we can see where we really stand today. Moreover, the questions are always larger than the immediate community which asks them, so the questioning by any one group is also a contribution to the questions of a larger community. This book does not merely serve the community of Presentation Sisters then, but also the wider Church.

But history is not just about the past – only someone who is fully committed to living in the present and the future can be an historian. It is about recounting in depth who we are now: it is *anamnesis* – remembering who we are. This too is not to be confused with nostalgia: the uncritical emotion of longing for an imaginary time when things were 'good' and which serves to blot out from our minds everything that needs attention right now. Anamnesis is life-giving: it brings us – sometimes drags us – to the core of our identity and forces us to restate our most basic questions and beliefs in the manner in which they make sense in our situation. The act of anamnesis which these essays represent is an intrinsic part of renewal.

While some Christian groups have made obscurantism into a fetish – we tend to label these with imprecise names such as 'fundamentalists' or 'conservatives' forgetting that it is a constant temptation – others have adopted another history-denying strategy. This is the approach of those who stress 'continuity' so that the differences between our situation and some fixed time in the past is imagined as minimal. This latter approach is usually far more self-conscious of the past than that of those who ignore history as simply awkward, and these questers for continuities often give themselves the name of 'traditionalists' or seek to characterize their approach as a simple rational option. In fact, such an approach is one of romanticizing the past so as to avoid both facing the questions that the present throws up and struggling with the fears that are part of any set of decisions which must be made in the face of an evolving future. Traditions, such as charism, are not a single phenomenon endlessly repeated, but rather the procession of a community through time, and its vicissitudes, that brings it from the past and into the present. Reflection on that process can illuminate possible futures. Tradition, as Picasso once remarked, is having a baby rather than wearing your grandfather's hat!

Remembering and Forgetting

Christian communities are always remembering – that is obvious – but they are also always forgetting: sometimes *we need to forget* some practices that we have carried out for centuries, and sometimes *we have simply forgotten* why we are doing something and so lose our bearings in the present. The disciplined remembering that is *critical history* gives us an additional level of insight into these processes. It shows us why and what we are remembering, helps us to identify those positions and activities that we need to allow to pass from us and disappear, and it can help us to recover those aspects of our past we should never have let slip from our consciousness. Critical history is, therefore, a part of any renewal process. It can show how a community may have been in collusion with unjust systems and that this involvement may have been invisible to them in its evil.

Good people have often been unwittingly tied into some of the greatest crimes of history. The most startling example for Christians is the acceptance of slavery from the earliest times – from Paul's time before we were even called 'Christians' until the last decades of the nineteenth century. Indeed, formal Catholic moral theology never caught up with this problem or its evils, and the questions in theology books simply became redundant because secular society had rejected slavery: a case of the larger society being more moral than those in the Church who claimed to be the preachers of morality to that society. Likewise, the notion that women were essentially subservient to men has gone unquestioned for most of Christianity's past, as has the corporate thinking in the notion that the good of the whole group or 'the institution' or 'avoiding giving scandal' was more significant than the good and safety of the individuals that make up the group.

Yet now even the most 'conservative,' perhaps unwillingly, has had to admit that these are unacceptable positions. Today we see these legacies of the past not only as problematic but, in themselves, scandalous; and it is critical historical study that seeks explanation of how that which seems so abhorrent to the Gospel could have been, and perhaps in places still is, accepted. Historical retrieving of a charism, when done well as in these essays, is always eye-opening. And perhaps may even help us see the blind spots of the present.

So Why the Retrieval of the Charism and Why this Book?

At a time when most communities of vowed religious in the Western world are undergoing massive change: communities getting older, with little prospect of new members; tasks once considered central to the group's identity being no longer needed; communities having to apologize for their skeletons, and paths to the evolving future very unclear, then to devote a book to the historical source of a congregation – to use precious human resources on speculative explorations – might seem a digression or even a waste. To anyone who would assert this I offer two reflections.

The first is based on the nature of our human condition as creatures in time. We search our sources to resource our experimenting for the evolving future. We recreate the past in its time so as to liberate ourselves from being imprisoned by the past and so gain a new understanding of where we are today and where we can go tomorrow. Indeed, when we fail as communities to reflect on our past iconic sources, we lose our identities.

The second answer can be verified empirically: read this book, note what it says about where the Presentation Sisters came from and how they moved through time creatively with ever-new imaginative responses, and then admit that as a result of explorations of charism presented here that you now have a far better grasp of Presentation identity in the present, the problems that face Presentation Sisters now, and also of the possibilities that can lie ahead for all those in whom the charism lives today. The first premise of all history is that the present is always different from the past, and so the future will be different again: tomorrow is another day. And for Christians this is not simply optimism: it is the hope that fullness of life lies in the future rather than in the past. We as the People of God, and each smaller community within that People, 'press onwards towards the goal for the prize of the heavenly call of God in Christ Jesus' (Phil 3:14).

Professor Thomas O'Loughlin
Professor of Historical Theology, University of Nottingham
President of the Catholic Theological Association
of Great Britain

Acknowledgements

The inspiration for this volume came during a Presentation Spirituality and Charism retreat directed by Mary T. O'Brien PBVM and Anne M. O'Leary PBVM at the invitation of the Presentation Sisters, Dubuque, Iowa, in July 2012. This was the third such major retreat led by Anne and Mary in the United States, the earlier retreats having taken place at Presentation Centre, Los Gatos, San Francisco, 2008; and at the Presentation Convent, Aberdeen, South Dakota, 2010. Invited to publish the papers of the 2012 retreat by the Sisters in Dubuque, Anne and Mary wondered about 'widening the tent' in relation to this invitation: 'What if we engaged with Presentation Sister-scholars or scholars associated with Presentation Sisters across the world in relation to a book project?' To support the vision further, they invited Bernadette Flanagan PBVM to co-edit the project to add another lens and area of expertise, that of spirituality, to the work of editing.

Several years in the making, the vision has now become a reality. We, the Editors, hope it will be a helpful resource toward fanning the flame of the charism of Nano Nagle as we mark the tercentenary of her birth in 2018.

We wish to express our gratitude and deep appreciation to the Sister-contributors from the international community of Presentation Sisters, who collaborated with us in creating this publication. We also appreciate the contributions of other scholars associated with Presentation and Nano Nagle who shared their unique expertise to enrich this collection of essays.

Much support was received from the Congregational Leadership Team of the Presentation Sisters Union at Monasterevin, Ireland – not only financial but also in terms of friendship and prayer. The editorial guidance of the copy editor, Catherine KilBride, was invaluable. We express sincere gratitude to Analee Garciano PBVM who linked with the former students of Binalbagan Catholic College, Negros, Philippines to solicit their permission for the use of their beautiful artwork for the cover of this book. The dream would not have come to pass without the commitment and dedication of Donna Doherty, Commissioning Editor, and the staff at Veritas Publications, Dublin. To all of you, we are truly indebted.

Finally, we wish to pay tribute to all the Presentation Sisters, Presentation Brothers and Christian Brothers who have sought over the centuries to bring the charism of Nano Nagle alive in new ways in new settings. Thanks to you, and to all who today – as Associates, Friends of Nano, collaborators, partners-in-mission and co-workers – continue to expand and evolve the expression of the charism of Nano Nagle in new and exciting ways.

There are other aspects in relation to the evolving charism of Nano Nagle that have yet to be written about or recorded in some way. Therefore, we truly hope that this project will inspire many other creative projects (in term of writing or otherwise) which will be the fruits of collaboration between members of the Presentation Family, along with others, who care about a future full of hope for all peoples and for our shared home, planet Earth.

Bernadette Flanagan PBVM
Mary T. O'Brien PBVM
Anne M. O'Leary PBVM

Introduction

> My views are not for one object alone. If I could be of any service in saving souls in any part of the globe I would willingly do all in my power.[1]

The words, written by Nano Nagle at the age of fifty-two, capture the theme which this book addresses. In its construction this book could be described as a patchwork quilt. Different writers give us an insight into the motivation, energy and inspiration behind the global vision which Nano possessed; while other writers paint the details of settings in which the vision took shape and form. This book is being published in anticipation of the tercentenary of the birth of Nano Nagle (1718–1784) and strives to illustrate how the Nagle family motto – 'Not words, but deeds' – was enacted through the power of Nano Nagle's utter reliance on the loving-kindness of God (Hb., *hesed*).

At the source of this book then is the spiritual journey of one woman – Nano Nagle. Honora (Nano) Nagle was born in 1718 in the townland of Ballygriffin, near the village of Killavullen, in the beautiful valley of the Blackwater in County Cork. Her parents, Garret (d. 1746) and Ann (nee Mathew, d. 1748), were relatively wealthy Catholic landowners. Ireland at that time was in the grip of Penal Laws, a series of laws imposed by the then Established Government the United Kingdom in an attempt to force Irish Roman Catholics and Protestant dissenters (such as Presbyterians) to accept the Anglican Church. The laws included many restrictions on the Catholic population. They denied Catholics the right to property, to education, to entry into the professions – even the right to own a horse! Edmund Burke (1729 1797), the famed author, orator and parliamentarian was a cousin of Nano Nagle's and had spent some of his childhood with her parents. He described the Penal Laws as, 'a machine of wise and elaborate contrivance, as well fitted for the oppression, impoverishment and degradation of a people, and the debasement in them of human nature itself, as ever proceeded from the perverted ingenuity of man'.[2]

It is not surprising then that some branches of the Nagle family had embraced the Protestant faith in order to escape the rigour of the Penal Laws and to secure succession rights for their children and descendants. Nano grew up knowing that many of her closest relatives were adherents of the established Protestant faith. Others had been forced to emigrate. Two of Nano's brothers departed Cork to go and live in the more peaceful setting of Bath, England. Many of her cousins had made their homes in France and elsewhere in mainland Europe.

From what is known of Nano's childhood, it seems to have been happy and carefree. By the standards of the day it was privileged. She and her siblings received a basic education at home and in a nearby hedge-school. We glean from tradition and a number of records that at age ten, she was sent to a Benedictine convent school in Ypres, Flanders (then French territory) where the Nagle family had many relatives. On leaving there at age sixteen she continued her education in Paris, moving in courtly circles there – 'creating a stir' as a charming debutante with a wonderful singing voice. It is documented that she was presented at the Royal Court of Louis XV at Versailles. Wealthy, beautiful and talented, with all the right connections at court, Nano immersed herself in the social scene in Paris.

An event occurred, when Nano was in her early twenties, which was to change the course of her life. One morning, returning in her carriage from an all-night ball, she saw a group of poor people waiting at a church door for early morning Mass. It was a turning point. The contrast between her life and that of the poor, whose riches were of another kind, left a lasting impression on her. She resolved to take action. Returning to Ireland and defying the Penal Laws, she eventually secretly set up a cabin-school in Cork's Cove Lane (now Douglas Street), initially enrolling a class of thirty-five girls. From there the project grew. Soon she had schools in other parts of Cork city. She employed teachers at her own expense to teach basic literacy and life-skills, while she travelled each day on foot to teach the catechism and to prepare her pupils for the sacraments. At night she would visit the poor in their homes, travelling the unlit lanes and dangerous, unprotected quays, offering what help she could. One of her biographers noted that 'there was not a garret in Cork that she did not know'. Nano became affectionately known in the city as 'The Lady of the Lantern'.

On Christmas Eve 1775, after many trials and challenges, she established the Sisters of Charitable Instruction of the Sacred Heart, later to be known as Presentation Sisters, to continue 'the work of God' she had begun. On the 26 April 1784, Nano died of tuberculosis. Her message to the Sisters gathered around her as she lay dying was 'Love one another as you have hitherto done'.[3] The profound depth of her commitment as a woman of faith received formal ecclesial recognition in 1994 when she received from the Vatican the designation, 'Servant of God' a title given to a person when the Pope gives permission for the opening of the cause of his/her sainthood. More recently, Nano Nagle was declared Venerable by Pope Francis on 31 October 2013. This is the second step on the path to canonical sainthood and it takes place when it is established that the person had practised virtue to a heroic degree.

In sustaining her zeal and commitment Nano Nagle was supported by a close circle of friends, collaborators and family. Of particular note, was the contribution of Teresa Mulally[4] (1728–1803), who appears in eleven of the chapters of this collection of papers. Maria Teresa Mulally was born in October 1728, the only child of Daniel and Elizabeth Mulally in Pill Lane (Chancery Street) Dublin. Her father was a 'provision dealer', perhaps a grocer and the family lived in financial security. Teresa received a good education, probably at the Dominican Sisters' fee-paying school in nearby Channel Row. When Teresa was seven years of age her father retired from business and the family moved a short distance to Phrapper Lane (Beresford Street), within the Parish of St Michan. As time passed the financial circumstances of the family declined and they were obliged to take paying guests into their home. In early adulthood, Teresa, set herself up as a self-taught milliner in the front parlour of the family home. Shortly afterwards, she won a few hundred pounds sterling in the State lottery and this enabled her to expand her business and keep her parents in comfort until their death (c. 1761).

Teresa was a most devout Catholic and was known to spend many hours in prayer. Being now free from family duties Teresa considered her future and seriously considered entering Religious Life. There were two small Religious Communities living quietly in her locality – the Dominicans in Channel Row and the Poor Clare Sisters in North King Street. However, the sight of the poor, helpless children whom she encountered on the streets, as she moved from home to Chapel, pulled at her heart strings and disturbed her quiet reflective moments. When, in 1763, Fr James Mulcaile SJ returned to Mary's Lane Chapel in Teresa's Parish of St Michan on the suppression of the Jesuit Order in France she found a soul friend for her discerning her way forward.

Teresa was also influenced by the fact that she had begun to hear of the work being done in Cork by Nano Nagle. Teresa Mulally was a family friend of the Fitzsimons Family of St Michan's Parish, Dublin. In 1767, when the twenty-eight year old Eleanor Fitzsimons had left Dublin to join the Sisters of the Visitation in France, Teresa, then aged thirty-nine, must have followed her progress with great interest.

When in Paris Eleanor met Rev Dr Moylan who had just negotiated the acceptance of Irish candidates into the Ursuline novitiate at Rue St Jacques, Paris. He pleaded the cause of the poor children of Cork and outlined the benefits already achieved by the schools set up there by Nano Nagle. Eventually, Dr Moylan persuaded Eleanor to reconsider her intention to enter a French Convent and to become the first volunteer for Nano's Ursuline foundation in Cork. This change of plan must have caused some anxiety among Eleanor's family and friends in Dublin and a demand for information about Nano Nagle and her work in Cork. Favourable testimony was readily available. Mrs Mary Burke, lived with her son, Edmund, the aforementioned cousin of Nano, at twelve Arran Quay, Dublin. She was formerly Mary Nagle of Ballyduff, near Ballygriffin.

Throughout the years 1771–1774, Teresa and Nano continued to plough a lone furrow in their service of God through the poor and abandoned members of society. Dr Moylan, the Parish Priest of St Finbarr's Church, Cork, was the common link. He was a friend of Fr Mulcaile, perhaps through his uncle Fr Doran SJ, and through him he came to know Teresa Mulally. Dr Moylan told of Nano's intention to find someone to establish a new Institute freed from the limitations of enclosure.

Teresa became aware that in January 1775, Nano Nagle had invited two of her teaching assistants, Elizabeth Burke and Mary Fouhy, and later Mary Ann Collins, to join her in beginning her Religious Institute and consequently had found a solution to the dilemma of the continuity of her schools. Later that year, Dr Moylan was appointed Bishop of Kerry and consequently direct contact with Nano was curtailed. This was probably the incentive for Nano and Teresa to begin a correspondence in September 1776. There are nine extant letters from Nano Nagle to Teresa Mulally. These cover the years 1776–1783 as Nano's Institute of Charitable Instruction was evolving and struggling for survival.

Through this collection of papers the aim is to offer a window on how women like Nano and Teresa lived within an energy stream of the Spirit i.e., a charism. This charism is a way of being and an energy for life. In the papers we will see that the charism impelled all who have been caught up in it to respond to the great projects toward ensuring a dignified life for every human being. This charism invites those it touches to discover where the face of God is seeking to smile on people; to live, with clarity and compassion, in an unjust, torn and violent world and; to interpret the unique signs of the Spirit at work in diverse settings. May you be touched by this energetic and renewing Spirit as you 'take and read' this book.

Endnotes
1. Letter to Miss Fitzsimons, 1770, Par 14.
2. John Savage, *Fenian Heroes and Martyrs: Edited with An Historical Introduction* (Boston: Patrick Donahoe, 1869), 16.
3. William Hutch, *Nano Nagle: Her Life, Her Labours and Their Fruits* (Dublin: McGlashan and Gill, 1875), 90.
4. Roland Burke Savage, *A Valiant Dublin Woman: The Story of George's Hill, 1766–1940* (Dublin: M.H. Gill & Son, 1940)

Part One
Context

The Nagle Family: Supporters of a Catholic Faith under Siege in Penal Ireland

Máirín MacCarron

Nano Nagle (1718–1784) lived through a period of profound change and development in Irish history.[1] She was born during one of the darkest times for Irish Catholics, and died as confidence and hope were beginning to be restored. During her lifetime, Ireland witnessed the repression of Catholics under the Penal Laws, which brought about a significant reduction in Catholic land ownership, political influence, educational standards and social mobility among the professional classes.

Despite all the obstacles, legal and otherwise, placed in her path Nano succeeded in establishing Catholic schools and convents, and thereby played a role in the Catholic revival. This chapter will discuss the situation for Catholics in eighteenth-century Ireland in order to place the life and work of Nano Nagle in context.

Ireland in the Eighteenth Century

Ireland was unique in post-Reformation Europe as the only country where the majority of the population followed a different creed from that of their rulers. From the mid-seventeenth century onwards it had become apparent that two separate societies were developing in Ireland which were distinguished by religious rather than cultural factors.[2] By the early 1700s Catholics represented about 75 per cent of the population but were excluded from public office and had no role in the civil structures and organisation of their country. They paid the price for their support of James II and the Catholic Cause in the Williamite Wars. The successive defeats at the Boyne, Aughrim and Limerick in 1690–1691 signalled the end of any realistic hope for the return of a Catholic monarch, and from the reigns of William of Orange and Mary onward, the British throne remained in resolutely Protestant hands.

In Ireland, the defeats of 1690–1691 marked the last in a series of significant reversals during the seventeenth century which included the Battle of Kinsale in 1601 and the devastation caused by Cromwell's New Model Army, 1649–1653. The final defeat of the Jacobites was followed by the departure of thousands of Irish soldiers from these shores never to return; these men subsequently distinguished themselves on the battlefields of Europe and came to be known as the Wild Geese. Nano Nagle's family had personal experience of such exile as her father's uncle, Sir Richard Nagle, and his family left for France and the exiled court of James II in 1691.

The tumultuous seventeenth century had left both Catholics and Protestants in Ireland scarred, apprehensive, and mistrustful of each other. The Catholic landed class resented that there was no land redistribution during the Jacobite reign (as had been promised in 1649) which would have returned much of the land that Catholics had lost. The failure of the Dublin government to ratify the Treaty of Limerick of 1691, contrary to the wishes of William of Orange, was an enormous betrayal of their trust. On the other hand the burgeoning Ascendancy class, the post-1690s élite, who had been established by the land redistributions of the seventeenth century, feared the potential power of the majority Catholic population, remembering the 1641 rebellion and the much-publicised massacre of Protestant settlers.[3] It was against this background, with memories of betrayal on both sides, that the Penal Laws were introduced to Ireland.

The Penal Laws were enacted in the first quarter of the eighteenth century. The intensity with which they were applied to Irish Catholics varied considerably over time and in different localities. They were less stringently applied as the century progressed and began to be repealed from the late-eighteenth century onwards. The efforts of Daniel O'Connell and the Irish Repeal Movement finally brought about Catholic Emancipation in 1829. However, as long as the legislation remained on the statute books, the laws could be enforced at any time leading to continued fear and uncertainty for Catholics.

The Penal Laws were a legislative means of restraining the Catholic presence in Irish society, and maintaining the Protestant Ascendancy, by formally excluding Catholics from participation in most areas of public life.[4] John Bowes, Chief Baron of the Exchequer, declared in 1759 that 'the laws did not presume an Irish Catholic to exist except for the purposes of punishment'.[5] While the laws were religious in character, there is general agreement that their actual target was Catholic wealth rather than Catholic piety, particularly Catholic landed property as land was the basis of political power. The Ascendancy greatly feared that Irish Catholics might succeed in recovering their estates. The legislation limited the inheritance rights of Catholics and their rights to secure leases. Catholic estates were split up by the legal insistence on inheritance by gavelkind (which meant that a Catholic estate had to be divided between all a landowner's sons, thereby reducing the size and, therefore, the influence of Catholic landed estates), rather than primogeniture (where the eldest son inherited the estate intact). However, a son who conformed to the Established Anglican Church could inherit the whole estate and certain enactments rewarded sons who conformed during their father's lifetime.[6] Catholics were also precluded from buying and selling land.

Even before the penal code was enacted, Catholics had been prevented from holding seats in parliament, as oaths that denied the doctrines of transubstantiation and papal power were imposed on Irish MPs from the 1690s. Sir Richard Nagle, Nano's great-uncle, had been speaker in the Irish parliament of 1689.[7] In 1729 the right to vote was specifically removed from all Catholic freeholders. This meant that the Irish parliament represented only Protestant opinion, both in its membership and in its electorate. The Irish parliament held limited powers and was committed to the link with Britain and the Protestant faith.[8]

Under the Penal Laws Catholics were also excluded from the professions, such as law. Through denying Catholics access to the legal profession, they were also excluding them from one of the major routes to acquiring landed wealth.[9] Enactments were passed to regulate marriage between Catholics and Protestants, although these were similarly motivated by property rights as the legislation ensured that any settlement would support the Protestant interest.[10] Catholics were also prohibited from bearing arms. The Penal Laws even extended to forbidding a Catholic to own a horse worth more than £5: a restriction that was a factor in the death of Art Ó Laoghaire in 1773 as recalled in the famous lament by his wife, Eibhlín Dubh Ní Chonaill, *Caoineadh Airt Uí Laoghaire*.

Catholics were also prevented from setting up in manufacture by certain enactments, but no major effort was made to exclude them from trade. Many Catholic families built up considerable wealth in this area, especially from trade in provisions.[11] This enabled the Catholic merchant classes to retain their authority in the towns, especially in the port cities of Cork, Galway, Limerick, Waterford and Wexford where their trade links with continental ports led to an increase in commercial activities. These new commercial ventures also enabled access to major European centres of learning. These towns and the surrounding areas led the Catholic revival; it is no coincidence that the establishment of small communities of nuns, such as Nano Nagle's foundations, were connected to these concentrations of wealth.[12]

The Penal Laws that specifically targeted religious practice were considerably more difficult to enforce, but greatly disrupted Catholic devotions when they were rigorously applied. Acts of the late-seventeenth and early-eighteenth centuries attempted to control and ultimately remove all Catholic priests from Ireland. An Act of 1704 required that all priests must be registered but was explicit that no new registrations would be accepted, the consequence of which would be the erosion of the Catholic priesthood within a generation. An attempt was also made to force priests to take an oath of abjuration of the Stuarts, who hoped to reclaim the throne of England, and those who refused lost the benefits of registration and faced banishment from Ireland. Professional discoverers, who came to be known as 'priest-catchers', attempted to hand priests over to the authorities; however, such individuals were often despised equally by Protestants and Catholics. The persecution of Catholic clergy was sporadic and was ultimately unsuccessful in preventing the re-establishment of the Catholic mission in Ireland.[13]

Although Catholic schools were illegal under the penal legislation and Catholics were forbidden to teach, many parishes had schools of one sort or another, while the children from wealthy Catholic families were sent to Europe for their education. Nano Nagle was educated in France, along with many others of her generation. The launch of the Anglican Charter School movement in 1731, which attempted to bring the children of the poor to Protestantism, only encouraged the Catholic clergy to devote more time and energy to teaching.[14] The hedge schools developed early in the era of the penal code and itinerant school masters were frequently prosecuted, though many escaped simply by moving on. The Catholic education system was reformed during the eighteenth century and, by the second half of that century, a Catholic parish school system was in existence in much of the country.[15] However, despite the growth and development of Catholic schools and church structures in this period, they existed outside the law and lived under the shadow of potential persecution at all times.

The religious character of the Penal Laws aside, it is clear that the provisions most aggressively enforced over the course of the eighteenth century applied to property and wealth rather than devotional practices. During the late seventeenth century, the authorities came to the conclusion that a mass conversion of Catholics was economically undesirable.[16] The nineteenth-century historian, Lecky, wrote:

The penal code, as it was actually carried out, was inspired much less by fanaticism than by rapacity, and was directed less against the Catholic religion than against the property and industry of its professors. It was intended to make them poor and to keep them poor, to crush in them every germ of enterprise, to degrade them into a servile caste who could never hope to rise to the level of their oppressors.[17]

Indeed, in terms of targeting wealth and property, the consequences of the Penal Laws were staggering. Among the most startling statistics from seventeenth and eighteenth century Ireland are the figures for land ownership. The Catholic share of Irish land was approximately 59 per cent in 1641; this had dropped to 22 per cent in 1688; to 14 per cent in 1703; and to 5 per cent by the 1770s.[18] However, the majority of the population remained Catholic during this period. This was also at a time of dramatic population growth in Ireland. While the figures are uncertain, there is general agreement that the population of Ireland had probably doubled by the end of the eighteenth century, reaching a total of nearly five million in 1800.[19] The population was growing but the opportunities for Catholics were greatly reduced. This was the Ireland in which Nano Nagle lived and worked.

The Nagle Family

Wealthy Catholic families like Edmund Burke's, and his cousins, the Nagles, the 'depressed gentry', suffered most during the Penal Laws as they lived permanently in 'a zone of insecurity'.[20] The Nagles certainly experienced the pressure of the Penal Laws. On the death of Nano's grandfather, David Nagle, the large fortune that he had amassed was gavelled between his two sons, Garret (Nano's father) and Joseph, and they lost some of their land when it was publicly revealed that they were practising Catholics.[21] Garret Nagle was a merchant, who presumably travelled frequently, and in 1733 was accused of acting as the agent of James II (referred to as 'the Pretender') in Flanders, though there is no clear evidence for this charge.[22] In addition Nano's uncle, Joseph, was in a precarious position as he was a lawyer who had been admitted to Gray's Inn in 1696, prior to the enforcement of laws prohibiting Catholics from practising law.[23]

Joseph Nagle was regarded as a leader of the Catholic laity in Cork and Nano described him to a friend 'as the most hated Catholic in Ireland'.[24] He devoted his legal skills to assisting the bishop and laity in their efforts to circumvent the legal measures against Catholic ownership and succession. Despite the significant reduction in Catholic land ownership, Joseph succeeded in retaining substantial land holdings in Cork. There is much reference to Protestants assisting their Catholic friends in evading the property laws, and Joseph Nagle appears to have engaged in such behaviour. According to T.J. Walsh, between 1718 and 1749 he engaged in sales and transfers to non-Catholics which may have been 'simply a smokescreen' intended to conceal Catholic ownership through arrangements with friendly Protestants.[25]

On his death in 1757, Joseph Nagle's estate was divided between members of his family. He died intestate, which was a method adopted by Catholics to ensure that property remained in their family's hands. Instead of making a will, a deed of trust was drawn up amongst immediate relatives who pledged to administer the estate according to directions. The evidence suggests that James Nagle made such an arrangement with his nieces and nephews, which provided Nano with the financial support for her poor schools in Cork. She subsequently wrote that she received the best part of her fortune from him.[26]

Conclusion

Nano Nagle lived through one of the darkest times for Irish Catholics. She was born when the Penal Laws were most aggressively enforced and members of her family suffered exile and loss of property under the regime. Although the laws were relaxed as the eighteenth century progressed, a renewal of persecution was an ever-present fear for Irish Catholics. Nano's working life in Ireland was spent outside the law as she engaged in activities, such as opening and teaching in Catholic schools, which were specifically prohibited by the Penal Laws. She followed her calling despite the dangers and lived to see the beginnings of the repeal movement and the Relief Acts which began to restore rights and legitimacy to Irish Catholics. The opportunities for Catholic women to participate in public life in Ireland were practically non-existent in the eighteenth century, and the 'outstanding exception was Honora (Nano) Nagle, founder of the Presentation Sisters'.[27] Her courage and her commitment to the poor were an inspiration in her own time and her influence continues to endure today.

Endnotes

1. I am very grateful to Dr Margaret Curtis-Clayton and Dr Ciarán Wallace for their comments.
2. Nicholas Canny, 'Early Modern Ireland, c 1500–1700', in R.F. Foster (ed.), *The Oxford Illustrated History of Ireland* (Oxford University Press, 1989), 104–60 at 143.
3. There is considerable debate over the numbers that were killed by both sides during the 1640s. However, it is generally accepted that the memory of the event had a significant impact on the Protestant population's attitude to their more numerous Catholic neighbours.
4. R.F. Foster, 'Ascendancy and Union', in *The Oxford Illustrated History of Ireland*, 161–211 at 164.
5. See Patrick J. Corish, *The Catholic Community in the Seventeenth and Eighteenth Centuries* (Dublin: Helicon, 1981), 73.
6. ibid.
7. T.J. Walsh, *Nano Nagle and the Presentation Sisters* (Dublin: M. H. Gill and Son, 1959), 27.
8. Foster, 'Ascendancy and Union', 163–4.
9. Ian McBride, *Eighteenth Century Ireland* (Dublin: Gill and Macmillan, 2009), 131.
10. Corish, *The Catholic Community*, 74.
11. ibid.
12. McBride, *Eighteenth Century Ireland*, 230.
13. Corish, *The Catholic Community*, 76–7.
14. Corish, *The Catholic Community*, 79–80 and 102; McBride, Eighteenth Century Ireland, 58.
15. Corish, *The Catholic Community*, 79.
16. Corish, *The Catholic Community*, 55.
17. W.E.H. Lecky, *A History of England in the 18th Century*, Vol. 1 (London: Longmans, Green and Company, 1878), 288.
18. See Corish, *The Catholic Community*, 74.
19. Foster, 'Ascendancy and Union', 172.
20. Conor Cruise O'Brien, *The Great Melody: A Thematic Biography of Edmund Burke* (London: Sinclair-Stevenson, 1992, repr. 1993), 12–13.
21. Walsh, *Nano Nagle*, 28–9.
22. McBride, *Eighteenth Century Ireland*, 131 and 230; Walsh, Nano Nagle, 30–1.
23. Edmund Burke's father, Richard, was also a lawyer who subsequently conformed in Cruise O'Brien, *The Great Melody*, 7–10.
24. Walsh, *Nano Nagle*, 28; McBride, Eighteenth Century Ireland, 131.
25. Walsh, *Nano Nagle*, 29.
26. Walsh, *Nano Nagle*, 30; Mary Pius O'Farrell, Nano Nagle. Woman of the Gospel (Cork: Cork Publishing, 1996), 36–7.
27. McBride, *Eighteenth Century Ireland*, 150.

Portrait of a Foundress: Nano Nagle and Catholic Education in Ireland

Catherine Nowlan-Roebuck and Deirdre Raftery

Few Irish people have left to their nation as great a legacy as that of Nano Nagle (1718–1784). Known internationally as the mother foundress of the Presentation order of women religious, she laid the ground work for what would eventually make a global contribution to the education of girls and women, while also articulating a mission to the poor. Nano's legacy to Presentation schooling is the main focus of this chapter, which also provides an outline of her life, examining how she established schools in Ireland during a period of Catholic repression and widespread poverty.

Even as women religious grow fewer in number in global education, their presence as subjects of scholarship is increasing.[1] Over the past ten years, Ireland has begun to catch up on North America in developing critical histories of the women who educated the Irish masses, and sent tens of thousands of Sisters into the international mission field.[2] This burgeoning interest in the contribution of women religious to education will, doubtless, see Nano Nagle accorded a prominent position in the history of education, of women, and of Ireland.[3]

Early Life and Early Influences
Nano Nagle was born in 1718 in Ballygriffin County Cork, the eldest of Garret and Ann Nagle's seven children. They were a wealthy Roman Catholic family, whose ancestry has been traced back to the Norman invasion of Ireland in 1169.[4] Like many children from a similar background, Nano was sent to the continent to complete her education in 1731, contrary to the laws forbidding foreign education.[5] The education landscape at home cannot have escaped Nano's attention; it was a time when Catholics paid heavy penalties

for pursuing education – at home or abroad – as a consequence of the Penal Laws that prevailed. Irish schools followed the model of the English charity schools. Anglican clergymen were actively involved in their establishment, and most schools were funded by public subscription. The Protestant Society for the Promotion of Christian Knowledge successfully established one hundred and sixty-three schools by 1725, while in 1733 the Incorporated Society for Promoting English Protestant Schools in Ireland (Charter Schools) was founded. These types of school were openly proselytising, and poor Catholics who did not want to send their children to such schools usually turned to the illegal system of 'hedge schools'. Wealthier families, such as the Nagles, could quietly send their children abroad to Catholic schools in England, Spain and France. This education would give Nano the wherewithal to educate her own people.

When her schooling was finished, she stayed in Paris where she was joined by her sister, Ann. The Nagle family had a number of relatives living among the exiled community there, and the two sisters lived a carefree life among them until their return to Dublin in 1746. The death of their father in that year altered the family circumstances both in Ireland and France, and Nano and Ann Nagle came to live with their mother on Bachelor's Quay in Dublin. They became involved in visiting the homes of the poor in the city and the distribution of alms. Their mother died in 1748, and some time after 1749 Nano suffered another loss with the death of her sister Ann.[6] This event marked the turning point in Nano Nagle's life. Ann's charitable and compassionate disposition had a profound impact on Nano, which was described in a letter to Dr Coppinger from Mother Clare Callaghan thus:

> … But being so soon after called home on the death of her father and living with her mother and sister in Dublin, she was one day requesting her sister to get made up a splendid suit of silk which she had brought for that purpose from Paris; and she was both astonished and edified when her sister disposed of the silk to relieve a distressed family. Such an action, with the death of that sister soon after and her uncommon piety before it, wrought much on the heart of Miss Nagle and served to disengage it from the fashionable world which she had tasted and enjoyed until then …[7]

Nano left Dublin and joined her brother David in the old family home at Ballygriffin. During this time she witnessed the poverty, ignorance and superstition of the poor people around her. It was how these conditions affected the people that impacted upon Nano the most, as described by Mother Clare Callaghan:

> ... It was in such favourable dispositions that being in the country she was afflicted to discover the ignorance of the poor, which she principally perceived in one of the servants of the house whom she had conversed with on some points of religion. It is then she resolved that had she thousands she would dedicate them to the poor ...[8]

Overwhelmed by the hopelessness of the situation, she resolved to enter the religious life on the continent. However, her stay there was brief and she did not reach the stage of religious profession. It was a time of spiritual torment for Nano, which culminated in the advice of her director, a Jesuit priest, to return to Ireland to instruct Irish children.[9] In one of her letters to the first Irish Ursuline, Nano confided that 'Nothing would have made me come home but the decision of the clergyman that I should run a great risk of salvation if I did not follow the inspiration'.[10] At the invitation of her sister-in-law she returned to Cork to live with her brother Joseph and his wife Frances, on some family property at Cove Lane (now Douglas Street) in the southern part of the old city in the early 1750s.

Nano Nagle's First Schools

At this time the conditions under which the vast majority of the Irish people lived were characterised by poverty and deprivation. During the eighteenth century, the port of Cork had established favourable trading connections not only with France, Spain, and Portugal, but also with the American colonies, Newfoundland and the West Indies. The mercantile families, who amassed fortunes on this trade, lived in town houses or spacious villas in the suburbs.[11] In 1764 the traveller Bush described Cork as the most flourishing city in Ireland and expressed his pleasure in the 'modern part of the city ... houses really magnificent and superb, that at the same time exhibit the wealth of their owners and are an ornament to the city'.[12] The large preponderance of the labouring class, however, was confined to a patchwork of lanes and alleys in the northern, central and southern part of the city. The homes of the poor were generally airless and unsanitary mud-walled cabins, with thatched roofs. Of the towns he visited, Bush noted 'the long string of despicable huts, or cabins, that most of them are prefaced with ... a whole street of which might be built for 150l, for absolutely the material and workmanship together, of many of them, are not worth twenty shillings'. Such primitive conditions gave rise to begging, assaults, robberies, bull-baiting in the streets and murders, which were matched with severe forms of public punishment.[13]

Apart from the social conditions around her, Nano had other difficulties with which to contend. Until the death of her uncle Joseph Nagle in 1757 and the financial security his legacy afforded, Nano had no great personal wealth. Her health was frail. She was also aware that, as a Catholic, she was exposing herself and her immediate family to serious legal risk by opening and running a school for Catholic children.[14] In spite of all these difficulties she opened her first school in a little cabin in Cove Lane, near her brother's residence. The schoolhouse was a rented mud cabin that had two earthen-floored rooms, a garret and a thatched roof.[15] Nano described the opening of this school to Miss Fitzsimons:

> ... I kept my design a profound secret, as I knew, if it were spoken of, I should meet with opposition on every side, particularly from my immediate family as in all appearance they would suffer from it. My confessor was the only person I told of it; and as I could not appear in the affair, I sent my maid to get a good mistress and to take in thirty poor girls ...[16]

It was some months before her brother Joseph and his wife accidentally discovered that she was conducting a Catholic school. Initially he strongly opposed the venture, pointing to the 'bad consequences' he felt sure would follow. However, he was soon reconciled to it, and along with their uncle Joseph became a benefactor.[17] Although taking children in '... by degrees', within nine months a second cabin was secured to cater for the two hundred children who were attending the school. This success resulted in a request to establish schools in the northern part of the city. Nano agreed to this on the understanding that these schools would receive local financial support. Within a similar timeframe, two hundred children were accommodated in a disused warehouse in Philpot Lane (Clarence Street). This meant that over a period of two years Nano's schools were catering for more children than the other known schools combined.[18] Initially, Nano's intention was to cater for girls only, but at the insistence of her sister-in-law Frances she obtained another cabin in Cove Lane and paid a master to teach forty boys there. As the promised local finance for the schools in the north of the city did not materialise, Nano supported all the schools from her own resources until the death of her uncle in April 1757. Under the administration of Joseph Nagle's estate, Nano received considerable assistance.[19]

By 1769 Nano Nagle had opened seven schools, five for girls and two for boys. Although she may have drawn on a variety of influences in devising a daily programme for the schools, the one on which she settled owed much to the French *petites écoles*, of which she would have been aware from her time in France.[20] She outlined the daily programme in the schools to Eleanor Fitzsimons:

> … At present I have two schools for boys and five for girls. The former learn to read, and when they have the Douai catechism by heart they learn to write and cypher. There are three schools where the girls learn to read, and when they have the catechism by heart they learn to work. They all hear Mass every day, say their morning and night prayers, say the Catechism in each school by question and answer all together. Every Saturday they all say beads, the grown girls every evening. They go to Confession every month and to Communion when their Confessors think proper. The schools are opened at eight, at twelve the children go to dinner, at five o'clock they leave school. The workers do not begin their night prayers until six, after the beads …[21]

Responsibility for teaching the secular subjects was left to lay mistresses and masters, whilst Nano explained the catechism in one school or another every day and prepared the children for the sacraments of Confession and Communion. She instructed and prepared a group in each of the seven schools twice a year, an arduous task that extracted a toll on her health and on which she commented '… being obliged to speak for upwards of four hours and my chest not being as strong as it had been – I spat blood; which I took great care to conceal for fear of being prevented from instructing the poor'.[22] Doctor Coppinger described how, having overcome her early terror at the wickedness displayed by the children, she would study their disposition, assess their capacity and adapt her instructions accordingly.[23]

Nano Nagle did not confine herself to working with the children in the schools. After the hours at the schools were finished, she visited and tended the sick, the aged and the poor in their homes and in the North and South Infirmaries before she returned to her brother's house.[24] In his address, Coppinger pointed to the frequency with which Nano could be seen on the streets of the city, '… returning through the darkness of night, dripping with rain, mingled in the bustling crowd, moving thoughtfully along by the faint glimmering of a wretched lantern withholding from herself … the necessaries of life to administer the comforts to others.'[25] The importance of this work to her mission was reflected in several references to care of the sick poor and the elderly, particularly women, in the Constitutions of the Sisters of Charitable Instruction of the Sacred Heart, drawn up *circa* 1775. Whilst her hopes of providing a refuge for prostitutes who wanted to give up that way of life did not materialise, Nano built a home for old women the year before she died in 1784.[26]

The Need for Change

Nano Nagle was fortunate that between the mid-1750s and 1771, the authorities made no attempt to interfere with her work in relation to Catholic education. The informality of the schools and their obvious social advantages, may have been seen as the philanthropic experiment of a lady from a good family. Greater difficulties were caused by Roman Catholics who were opposed to the work that Nano was doing. In choosing to work actively with, and for, the Catholic poor she took a different view from those who followed a policy of conciliation and appeasement to their Protestant rulers in the hope of achieving rights for Catholics. Their opposition was based on the belief that her disregard of the Penal Laws would provoke repressive action, and took the form of misrepresentations and insults.[27] In the years 1763–1764, Nano was in serious financial difficulty and the survival of the boys' schools was in doubt. At her request some Catholic gentlemen collected contributions towards the schools, but this proved inadequate. Under these circumstances, and unusually for a woman of her background, Nano took it upon herself to go begging, an activity – described by Coppinger as 'disgusting solicitation' – that continued to be part of her work up to the last weeks of her life. The donations were not only used for the poor schools, but also for the widows, orphans, reduced housekeepers and retired tradesmen.[28]

During the 1760s a number of circumstances arose which convinced Nano that it was necessary to introduce a religious institute to secure the future of her work. Over the years she had gradually broadened the focus of her mission from education to the wider needs of the poor, immersing herself in their world and becoming part of it.[29] Hitherto, she had managed her schools alone and paid lay teachers to work in them. However, the work of the paid assistants was not always satisfactory, and the need for more organised control and staffing became apparent. She also came in contact with Francis Moylan, a young priest who had recently returned from France, as had his uncle Patrick Doran. Nano and Moylan shared a common zeal for education and he became an important figure in her subsequent efforts.[30] Finally, in 1761 her two brothers David and Joseph, along with their wives, left Cork to live in Bath. One outcome of their departure was that Nano received a generous settlement on their uncle Joseph Nagle's estate. This meant that by 1767 she was in a sufficiently strong position financially to meet the costs that were necessarily involved in the introduction of a religious institute to Cork.[31]

The Coming of the Ursulines

Nano Nagle's work was making a major contribution to Catholic education. However, under the circumstances that pertained, her schools could have no permanence beyond Nano's lifetime. In the hope of ensuring this permanence and continuity, Nano resolved to introduce a religious congregation to Cork.[32] In 1788 Francis Moylan described this decision in a letter to the Archbishop of Dublin, Dr Troy:

> ... She prudently foresaw, however, that a work of this extensive charity could not long subsist, unless the persons charged with the Instruction considered it as a duty, and attended to it, not for a salary, but from motives of religion and zeal for God's glory ... [33]

On the suggestion of Patrick Doran, Nano, assisted by Moylan, began the long process of establishing a foundation of the Ursuline Order in Cork. She already had connections with the order through her cousin Margaret Butler, a professed nun at its convent in St Denis.[34] At the time that Nano began this venture, the existing orders of Poor Clares, Dominicans and Carmelites carried out their work under various pretexts. They dared not wear the religious habit or maintain the externals of religious observance.[35] Clearly the risks and difficulties that surrounded the establishing of a foundation of nuns were great. In addition, Nano had definite reservations about the discipline of foreign religious orders. In a letter to the first novice for the Cork foundation, Eleanor Fitzsimons, she wrote '... I think religious discipline would be too strict for this country, and I own I should not rejoice to see it kept up ...'[36]

At the beginning of 1767 Nano went to the Ursuline convent of St Denis, north of Paris, which her cousin Margaret Butler had entered in 1763, to receive training in the exercises of the novitiate and improve her knowledge of French. Having spent seven months there Nano left Paris for Cork on 28 August. She was accompanied by her cousin, who had been given permission to begin the establishment of an Ursuline convent, with Nano as foundress, by Christophe de Beaumont, Archbishop of Paris.[37] In the summer of 1767, Dr Moylan made the first approach to the Ursuline convent in the Rue St Jacques to send Sisters for a foundation in Cork. However, at this time French families were reluctant to allow their daughters to come to Ireland. As there was no response to his initial request, Moylan appealed to the superiors to extend the facilities for religious training to volunteers presented to them from outside the convent. When they agreed to this proposal he set about finding postulants for the proposed foundation.[38] Among the Irish community in Paris, Moylan met Eleanor Fitzsimons, daughter of a Dublin merchant, who had gone there with the intention of joining the Sisters of the Visitation. He persuaded her to volunteer for the Cork foundation, and on 19 November 1767 she was presented to the Ursuline superiors as its first postulant.[39] The venture suffered a setback in 1768 when Margaret Butler returned to St Denis on 9 August. Having spent almost a year in Cork, it appears that she was unable to adapt to the demands of the apostolate.[40] Nearly two years after entering the convent on Rue St Jacques Eleanor Fitzsimons was joined by Elizabeth Coppinger and Margaret Nagle, a cousin of Nano's, in September 1769. A year later Mary Kavanagh, the fourth aspirant, entered the novitiate.[41] Just as she did when she opened her first school, Nano waited until the plans for the new foundation were well advanced before she informed her family of her intentions. Her reasons for this action were described in one of the letters to Miss Fitzsimons:

> ... when I began my schools my own immediate family knew nothing of it. So the same method I resolved to take [now], as I was sure they would be the first to oppose me. Never said I one word to them till I saw things had such a prospect of succeeding, which I was sure I never could have persuaded them of if they did not see it.[42]

In Cork, she set about a large building programme in preparation for the new foundation. The cottage in which she was living was a small cabin, situated on the street-front and unsuitable as a religious house. She built the new convent on a nearby site owned by the family. Situated to the rear and therefore more remote from the street, it was more suited to the purposes of a convent.[43]

In Paris, the novices were experiencing difficulties with the superiors of the community. Whilst Margaret Nagle proved a cause of concern to them, the question of appointing a superior to the new foundation was a greater worry. Canon law required that a religious foundation had to have at least one professed religious to act as superior. However, the superiors in the Rue St Jacques did not want Eleanor Fitzsimons, or any other Irish novices, to be professed in their community as this would leave them responsible for the Cork foundation. Neither were they willing to allow a professed Sister from the community to act as temporary superior, even though one member had volunteered to do so. In spite of the efforts of Patrick Doran and Francis Moylan, the superiors in the Rue St Jacques refused to give way.[44] Finally Dr Moylan consulted the Superior of the Irish College in Paris, Dr Lawrence Kelly, who suggested an approach be made to Mother Margaret Kelly of the Visitation in the Ursuline convent at Dieppe. Under a directive of obedience issued by the Archbishop of Rouen, within whose jurisdiction Dieppe fell, Margaret Kelly agreed to travel to Ireland in the capacity of superior of the Cork foundation.[45] Accompanied by Moylan the four novices and Margaret Kelly disembarked in Cobh on 9 May 1771. Sr Augustine Coppinger, along with her cousin Sr Ursula Kavanagh, spent some days with her family, whilst the other three continued on to Cork. They were met there by Nano, who received them into her cottage because the new convent was not finished. They lodged in a small house in Douglas Street, which was a little distance from the cottage but within the enclosure of their new convent.[46]

On the 18 September the Ursulines took formal possession of their convent, and a deed of agreement was signed by Nano Nagle and Margaret Kelly on behalf of the Ursuline community.[47] Dr Butler appointed Mother Margaret Kelly as superior, Dr Moylan as ecclesiastical director and Fr Patrick Shortall as the community's first chaplain. The Ursuline Annals recorded the occasion, and noted that there was inviolable fidelity to the regular observances, rules and prescriptions of the mother house in Paris with two omissions: the wearing of the Ursuline habit and the grilles of religious enclosure.[48] Until 1773 the community comprised only one professed religious and seven novices. This changed when a *Papal Brief* from Pope Clement XIV, dated 13 January, dispensed the full term of the Ursuline noviceship and endowed the convent with the same privileges that were enjoyed by the mother house in Paris. By April 1776 there were ten professed Sisters with Mother Augustine Coppinger taking over as superior on the return of Mother Margaret Kelly to Dieppe at Easter 1775.[49] The arrival of the new foundation was a source of disquiet and unfavourable comment in Cork. A piece that questioned the objectives of the newly established 'nunnery' appeared in the *Freeman's Journal*, contributed by an anonymous Protestant of Cork, in February 1772. In addition, summary measures were proposed for the suppression of the convent at a meeting of the court of d'oyer hundred.[50] Swayed by the arguments of Francis Carleton, the group took no action on the matter. However, extreme caution was still necessary and for some years the Sisters wore French nightcaps and black gowns instead of the religious habit. They wore the Ursuline habit only at receptions and professions until November 1779, when they decided to wear it all the time – a decision with which Nano disagreed.[51]

A New Sisterhood

The Ursuline Sisters opened their boarding school in January 1772. The first twelve girls admitted were the daughters of merchants. With pupils coming from Dublin and other parts of Ireland as well as from Cork, the numbers increased sufficiently to require additional buildings to provide more space for schooling and accommodation. The first addition, begun towards the end of 1772, connected with the original convent building and was completed in 1775. Other extensions were added in 1779 and 1790. A steady increase in the numbers of religious and pupils led the Ursulines to move from this campus to Blackrock in October 1825.[52] As a filiation of the Ursulines of Paris, they kept faith with the Constitutions, under which they were bound to enclosure.[53]

The Ursuline Annalist recorded that as they '… were bound by their Constitutions to enclosure and to the education of the higher orders of society, consequently could not, as she wished, visit the poor and the sick abroad nor devote themselves solely to the instruction of the poor at home'.[54] This meant that of the three schools in Cove Lane, they could only work in the one that lay within the enclosure. The Sisters taught in this girls' school every day, supplementing Nano's programme with needlework. Although she was a regular visitor to the convent and spent time in the religious instruction of the boarders every Saturday, Nano did not become a member of the community. Instead, she remained in her cottage at the gates of the convent.[55] Nano gained little respite from her own work even with the arrival of the Ursulines. All but one of the schools that she established still required her constant supervision and the need to give them permanence remained. Her visitation of the sick poor continued apace. During the years 1772–1773, she realised that her requirements could not be fulfilled within the framework of the Ursuline Constitutions and in 1774 she told Dr Moylan of her intention to extend her work for poor children. In disclosing this information to Teresa Mulally in Dublin, Moylan was unaware that Nano intended to establish a society which devoted itself exclusively to the poor.[56] Unable to find someone who was willing to undertake this project, whilst at the same time considering herself to be '... so improper a person to undertake it ...' in 1775 Nano Nagle embarked upon the establishment of a new religious congregation.[57]

The New Foundation

Having established and maintained the poor schools from the mid-1750s to 1771, and overseen the successful Ursuline foundation (1767-73), this new venture marked the beginning of a third phase in her work. Much was against it, however. Her age, at fifty-seven years, was a concern, as was her indifferent health. Most of her money was now spent and her proposal drew opposition from the Ursulines. Their concern lay in the belief that, having been the sole beneficiaries of Nano's support until now, another religious congregation would necessarily reduce the level of support that she could give them. They were also worried that a second religious house so close to their own convent would provoke renewed resentment among the Protestant population.[58] Dr Moylan shared their view, and remonstrated forcibly with Nano. In a meeting with her on the site of the proposed new convent in early spring of 1775, he threatened to destroy what had already been built and ordered her to move her work to the other side of the city away from the Ursulines. She withstood his appeals and threats, and suggested that, were it necessary, she would move her new foundation to some other part of the country. At this suggestion Dr Moylan withdrew his opposition.[59]

On 24 December 1775 Nano, Mary Fouhy, Elizabeth Burke and Mary Ann Collins began their novitiate in Nano's cottage. On the 24 June 1776 all four received the religious habit and took the names Sister St John of God, Sister Joseph, Sister Augustine and Sister Angela respectively. Taking simple vows, the Sisters were professed in the presence of the Bishop, Dr Butler, on 24 June 1777 and on the same day Nano was confirmed as superior by the bishop.[60] In her letter to Teresa Mulally, Nano wrote that the society was called '... The Sisters of the Charitable Instruction of the Sacred Heart of Jesus ...' and expressed the wish '... that we may unite in this Society.'[61]

The little cottage was too small to accommodate the number of people it now housed and was unsuited to the purpose of a religious congregation. Nano obtained a lease on a plot of land about one hundred metres from the cottage and construction on the new building started in the spring of 1775. After some delays, the convent was completed in 1777 and on Christmas day it was given a symbolic blessing when fifty beggars were invited to dinner. The community did not transfer to their new home until July 1780. During the intervening years classes were held for children in the new house.[62] The transfer from the cottage took place on 15 July and was described by Nano thus:

> ... So [I] waited till the times seemed quite peaceful, yet notwithstanding we stole like thieves. I got up before three in the morning [and] had all our beds taken down and sent to the house, before any was up in the street. [I] begged of the Ladies not to say a word about it to anyone of their company that would come to see them. Nor did [I] not let any person know of it in the town of my friends, as I was sure [that by] acting in this manner the good work would be carried on much better than in making any noise about it ...[63]

Little is recorded of the day-to-day life of the members of the new congregation. Nano's intention was that they become the servants of the poor, free to find them in their 'hovels of misery'. She exacted from the members of her congregation the same practices of self-denial that she imposed upon herself. Their meals were mean and frugal and she resolved to make it a rule that they would '... never dine abroad or visit or go abroad only to the chapel, the schools or business'.[64]

Their habit consisted of a plain black gown over which was worn a black handkerchief that was crossed in the front. They wore a plain round cap which was fitted close to the head and a broad black ribbon that was tied tightly. When they went out they wore long mode cloaks whose hoods were thrown over the small black bonnets that they donned when out.[65] Finding fault with those who lived far away from her, and unable to supervise the schools they took care of every day, Nano discharged all but one of the mistresses she had employed. In their place the Sisters took charge of the schools and, according to Nano, tended them better than they had been before in every respect.[66]

Duties of the Foundress: Nano Nagle Prepares for the Future

Between 1778 and her death in 1784, one of the main preoccupations for Nano was the selection of a French religious congregation whose rules and constitutions would meet Irish religious and social conditions. She already had some clear views on this, specifically, that foreign religious discipline was not suited to Ireland; that rules needed to be balanced between prayer and action; and that priority must be given for the work of the schools over every other activity.[67] In her September 1776 letter to Teresa Mulally, Nano described her foundation as the Sisters of the Charitable Instruction of the Sacred Heart of Jesus. She added to this in October 1779 by explaining that the religious rule being observed by them in Cork was drawn up by the Curé of St Sulpice.[68] With the help of her sister Elizabeth and Dr Moylan, whose view of and attitude towards the new congregation had changed completely by September 1776, she obtained information about the rules and constitutions of three French societies.[69]

Considering the rule of the Grey Sisters to be unsuitable, the Hospitallers of St Thomas seemed most in accordance with her ideals. Nano had difficulty in obtaining more precise details on the order as they did not wish their rules and constitutions made public. However, from the information sent by the Superior of the order, she considered that their obligations were largely similar to those of her new foundation, the differences being that the emphasis of the Cork foundation had to be on the schools and that they did not make vows for life. Nano's final reference to the matter was to request the opinion of Teresa Mulally and her spiritual director on the subject.[70]

Among her duties as foundress of the congregation, Nano was also concerned with the selection of candidates for the sisterhood. Whilst a number presented themselves as aspirants, not all were suited to the religious life. By 1782, four had joined the novitiate. Miss Hodnett and Miss Oliffe entered the novitiate during 1782. They were joined a little later by a young cousin of Nano's, Miss Johanna Connell and Miss Anastasia Tobin from Thurles.[71] Although she hoped to extend the Society with foundations in Killarney and Dublin, this proved beyond her resources both in terms of finances and personnel. Establishing the Ursuline foundation had cost her between £4,000 and £5,000 and they had continued to look to her for financial support for their schools. Undertaking the construction of the new convent for her second congregation proved more than she could afford at the time and sourcing the finance to complete the project had caused her great concern. Later she had to rely on public donations to build the home for old women.[72] Nano had clearly reconciled herself to this, as in the last existing letter to Teresa Mulally she attempted to console her by writing:

> ... The best works meet with the greatest crosses. I don't approve your desponding so much as I perceived in your last letter. Though [neither] you nor I should not [*sic*] live to see it prosper in our time, yet I hope it may [prosper] hereafter and be of universal service to the Kingdom. I comfort myself with this thought, when I am most dejected at the many disappointments I have met with.[73]

With the Sisters of her community assembled around her, Nano Nagle died on 26 April 1784 aged sixty-five years. With her strength in decline over the previous twelve months, her long indifference to her own health finally took its toll during the winter of 1783–1784. By the beginning of April the poor state of her health was a cause of alarm among the sisters.

Although she eventually agreed to be seen by a doctor four days before she died, it was to no avail. Some time before she died Nano had decided that she and her Sisters should be buried in the public cemetery St John's, sharing the common lot of the poor. Sister Augustine Burke, who had died the year previously, was interred there. However, the Ursulines opposed this, and proposed that Nano and her community should have a common burial place with them in their cemetery. The Sisters of the Charitable Instruction agreed and, without seeking the required permission from the Protestant bishop, Nano was laid to rest in a tomb which stood against the wall between the two convents.

In 1877 the remains were enclosed in a lead coffin encased in oak, and placed in a central position of the cemetery.[74] In recording her death, the *Hibernian Chronicle* noted '... the extreme of universal lamentation for the departure of a lady possessed of all that merit which for many years rendered her the object of unexampled admiration and acquired her the most unlimited esteem of all ranks of people'.[75]

Endnotes

1. See for example Carmen Mangion, '"Good teacher" or "good religious"? the professional identity of Catholic women religious in nineteenth century England and Wales', *Women's History Review*, 14:2 (2005), 223–42; Margaret Susan Thompson, 'Adaptation and professionalisation: challenges for teaching sisters in a pluralistic nineteenth-century America', *Paedagogica Historica*, 49:4 (2013) 454–70.
2. Rosemary Raughter (ed.), *Religious Women and Their History: Breaking the Silence* (Dublin: Irish Academic Press, 2005); Louise O'Reilly, 'Great changes, increased demands: education, teacher training and the Irish Presentation Sisters', in Deirdre Raftery and Elizabeth Smyth (eds), *Education, Identity and Women Religious: Convents, Classrooms and Colleges* (UK: Routledge, 2015).
3. Existing comprehensive examinations of Nano Nagle and the Presentation Sisters include William Hutch, *Nano Nagle: Her Life, Her Labours and Their Fruits* (Dublin: McGlashan and Gill, 1875) and T. J. Walsh, *Nano Nagle and the Presentation Sisters* (Dublin: M. H. Gill and Son, 1959). See also M. Raphael Consedine, *Listening Journey: A Study of the Spirit and Ideals of Nano Nagle and the Presentation Sisters* (Victoria, The Congregation of the Presentation of the Blessed Virgin Mary, 1983); Mary Pius O'Farrell, *Nano Nagle: Woman of the Gospel* (Cork: Cork Publishing, 1996); idem, *Breaking of Morn Nano Nagle* (1718-1784), *Francis Moylan* (1735-1815) *A Book of Documents* (Cork: Cork Publishing, 2001) for studies of the history of the Congregation from within its membership.
4. Walsh, 23–34; O'Farrell, *Woman of the Gospel*, 30–52.
5. *Act to Restrain Foreign Education*, 1695, 7 Wm. III. c. 4; 1703. II Anne, c. 6; Consedine, Listening Journey, 12–13; O'Farrell, Woman of the Gospel, 56.
6. Walsh, *Nano Nagle*, 38–42; O'Farrell, *Woman of the Gospel*, 57–62.
7. Mother Clare Callaghan to Bishop Coppinger, Autograph Letter, n.d. (1800–1804?), in Walsh, *Nano Nagle*, 381–3.
8. Mother Clare Callaghan to Bishop Coppinger, AL n.d., in Walsh, *Nano Nagle*, 382.
9. Walsh, *Nano Nagle*, 43; Consedine, *Listening Journey*, 27.
10. Nano Nagle to Miss Fitzsimons, AL 17 July 1769, in Walsh, *Nano Nagle*, 344–7. The sixteen complete letters are reproduced in the Appendices of Walsh, *Nano Nagle*, 344–67.
11. Walsh, *Nano Nagle*, 17–19.
12. J. Bush, *Hibernia Curiosa*, (Dublin: 1766) quoted in Consedine, *Listening Journey*, 39.
13. Walsh, *Nano Nagle*, 17–19: Bush, Hibernia Curiosa, quoted in Consedine, *Listening Journey*, 39.
14. Joseph Nagle died 24 April 1757. He lived in Blackrock, Cork and was a Counsellor-at-Law and acted as Nano's guide in her business.
15. Walsh, *Nano Nagle*, 44. It is possible that Nano opened her first school as early as 1749–50.
16. Nano Nagle to Miss Fitzsimons, AL 17 July 1769, in Walsh, *Nano Nagle*, 345.
17. ibid.
18. ibid.
19. ibid.
20. The *petites écoles* were the ordinary means of education for poor children in the towns of France and dated back to 1357. See Walsh, *Nano Nagle*, 47–8; O'Farrell, *Woman of the Gospel*, 77–8.
21. Nano Nagle to Miss Fitzsimons, AL '17 July 1769, in Walsh, *Nano Nagle*, 346.

22. ibid.
23. Coppinger, 'The Life of Miss Nano Nagle,' in Walsh, *Nano Nagle*, 387–8.
24. Walsh, *Nano Nagle*, 50; Consedine, *Listening Journey*, 51; O'Farrell, *Woman of the Gospel*, 93–4.
25. Coppinger, 'The Life of Miss Nano Nagle,' in Walsh, *Nano Nagle*, 389–91.
26. Consedine, *Listening Journey*, 52; O'Farrell, *Woman of the Gospel*, 95; 'The Constitutions of the Sisters of the Charitable Instruction, 27 March 1790', in O'Farrell, *Breaking of Morn*, 132–52.
27. Consedine, *Listening Journey*, 49; Walsh, *Nano Nagle*, 51–2.
28. Coppinger, 'The Life of Miss Nano Nagle,' in Walsh, *Nano Nagle*, 393; Walsh, *Nano Nagle*, 52–3; O'Farrell, *Woman of the Gospel*, 97–8.
29. Consedine, *Listening Journey*, 48–51; O'Farrell, *Woman of the Gospel*, 85–7.
30. Francis Moylan was born in Cork in 1735. He was sent to school in France in preparation for a mercantile career, but entered the religious life instead. In 1761 he was ordained as a priest for the diocese of Cork at the Irish College of Toulouse. He returned to Cork in 1763 and became an important figure in the revival of Catholic education. He was appointed Bishop of Kerry in 1775 and Bishop of Cork in 1787 a position he held until his death in 1815. (Walsh, *Nano Nagle*, 55–6, 83, 132).
31. Walsh, *Nano Nagle*, 54.
32. O'Farrell, *Woman of the Gospel*, 103.
33. Dr Moylan, Bishop of Cork, to Dr Troy, Archbishop of Dublin, AL 7 November 1788, in Walsh, *Nano Nagle*, 372.
34. Walsh, *Nano Nagle*, 56; Consedine, *Listening Journey*, 55 & 56; O'Farrell, *Woman of the Gospel*, 104–5.
35. Walsh, *Nano Nagle*, 57.
36. Nano Nagle to Miss Fitzsimons, AL 17 July 1769, in Walsh, *Nano Nagle*, 346; O'Farrell, *Woman of the Gospel*, 104.
37. 'Margaret Butler', in O'Farrell, *Breaking of Morn*, 45 & 46; Consedine, *Listening Journey*, 55 & 56; O'Farrell, *Woman of the Gospel*, 104 & 105.
38. Walsh, *Nano Nagle*, 61 & 62; O'Farrell, *Woman of the Gospel*, 105 & 106.
39. Walsh, *Nano Nagle*, 62; O'Farrell, *Woman of the Gospel*, 106 & 107.
40. Consedine, *Listening Journey*, 56; O'Farrell, *Woman of the Gospel*, 107.
41. Walsh, *Nano Nagle*, 62 & 63; O'Farrell, *Woman of the Gospel*, 107 & 108.
42. Nano Nagle to Miss Fitzsimons, AL 20 July 1770, in Walsh, *Nano Nagle*, 353.
43. Walsh, Nano Nagle, 64–5; O'Farrell, *Woman of the Gospel*, 112; Nano Nagle to Miss Fitzsimons, AL 17 July 1769, in Walsh, *Nano Nagle*, 347; 'A "Lease of Land" in 1768', in O'Farrell, *Breaking of Morn*, 56.
44. Nano Nagle to Miss Fitzsimons, 1770, in Walsh, *Nano Nagle*, 347 & 348; Nano Nagle to Miss Fitzsimons, AL 29 April 1770, in Walsh, *Nano Nagle*, 348–50; Walsh, *Nano Nagle*, 73, 78 & 79; Consedine, *Listening Journey*, 56.
45. Walsh, *Nano Nagle*, 79; O'Farrell, *Woman of the Gospel*, 131 & 132.
46. ibid., 79–81; ibid., 132 & 133.
47. Walsh, *Nano Nagle*, 81; O'Farrell, *Woman of the Gospel*, 133.
48. Walsh, *Nano Nagle*, 81 & 82.
49. Walsh, *Nano Nagle*, 73–82; 'The Apostolic Brief for the Ursulines in Cork, 13 January 1773', in O'Farrell, *Breaking of Morn*, 65 & 66.
50. Walsh, *Nano Nagle*, 84.
51. Walsh, *Nano Nagle*, 83–5; O'Farrell, *Woman of the Gospel*, 137 & 138.
52. Walsh, *Nano Nagle*, 85; see Sr Rosario Allen, *A Story of Love and Faith* (Cork: South Presentation Convent, 1979).

53. A filiation was a daughter house of a founding convent.
54. O'Farrell, *Woman of the Gospel*, 137 & 145.
55. Walsh, *Nano Nagle*, 86.
56. Nano Nagle to Miss Mulally, AL 29 September 1776, in Walsh, *Nano Nagle*, 357; Walsh, *Nano Nagle*, 86–93.
57. Nano Nagle to Miss Mulally, AL 29 September 1776, in Walsh, *Nano Nagle*, 357.
58. Walsh, Nano Nagle, 87–95; O'Farrell, Woman of the Gospel, 144; Consedine, Listening Journey, 66 & 67.
59. Walsh, *Nano Nagle*, 94–6; Consedine, *Listening Journey*, 67 & 68; O'Farrell, *Woman of the Gospel*, 146 & 147.
60. Walsh, *Nano Nagle*, 98–100; O'Farrell, *Woman of the Gospel*, 148–50; South Presentation Convent Cork Archives (hereafter SPC), MS First Profession Register, n.d. Sheet.
61. Nano Nagle to Miss Mulally, AL 29 September 1776, in Walsh, *Nano Nagle*, 357.
62. Walsh, *Nano Nagle*, 95, 111 & 112; O'Farrell, *Woman of the Gospel*, 146–63.
63. Nano Nagle to Miss Mulally, AL 29 July 1780, in Walsh, *Nano Nagle*, 364.
64. SPC Annals, quoted in Consedine, *Listening Journey*, 73; Nano Nagle to Miss Mulally, AL 24 August 1778, in Walsh, *Nano Nagle*, 359.
65. Walsh, *Nano Nagle*, 114 & 115.
66. Nano Nagle to Miss Mulally, AL 24 August 1778, in Walsh, *Nano Nagle*, 359.
67. Walsh, *Nano Nagle*, 101; O'Farrell, *Woman of the Gospel*, 158.
68. Nano Nagle to Miss Mulally, AL 30 October 1779, in Walsh, *Nano Nagle*, 364.
69. Walsh, *Nano Nagle*, 103–6.
70. ibid.
71. Nano Nagle's letters to Teresa Mulally, in Walsh *Nano Nagle*, 357–67; Walsh, *Nano Nagle*, 110, 111.
72. Nano Nagle to Miss Mulally, AL 24 August 1778, in Walsh, *Nano Nagle*, 358–9; Nano Nagle to Miss Mulally, AL 31 January 1783, in Walsh, *Nano Nagle*, 366–7.
73. Nano Nagle to Miss Mulally, AL 31 January 1783, in Walsh, *Nano Nagle*, 366.
74. Sr Angela Fitzsimons to Miss Mulally, AL 21 May 1784, in Walsh, *Nano Nagle*, 367–9; Walsh, *Nano Nagle*, 114–18; O'Farrell, *Woman of the Gospel*, 171–3.
75. The *Hibernian Chronicle*, Monday 26 April, quoted in Consedine, *Listening Journey*, 75.

Part Two

Sources of Inspiration for Nano Nagle

'Zeal' in the Writings and Life of St Paul and of Nano Nagle

Mary T. O'Brien PBVM

Today one does not talk much about 'zeal' in everyday conversation or even in theological circles. The word 'zeal' may seem rather archaic and outdated, although I do know of one Congregation of Sisters who, up to recent times, took a vow of zeal at their Final Profession. If one were to take such a vow, to what would one be committed? That question may be worth a thought. However, our current interest in 'zeal' comes from the fact that it figures hugely in the life and letters of St Paul and also in the life and letters of Nano Nagle. Because 'zeal' was so important to both, as we shall see, we have good reason to explore something of its relevance for us in the twenty-first century.

Zeal – What is it?

A dictionary definition of zeal may offer a few clues: Zeal is defined as 'eager and ardent interest in the pursuit of something; fervour; enthusiasm; ardour'. We note that these cognates all have fire in them. 'Ardour' implies burning; 'fervour' is linked at root with 'fervid' – intensely hot or heated; and 'enthusiasm' comes from two Greek words *en theos* meaning to be filled with God. So, it is obvious that zeal is the very antithesis of lukewarmness. There is fire in it, and passion and divine burning power. If we look to the Greek roots of zeal (*parazelos*) we find that it is closely linked with jealous loving, even with God's jealous love of Israel (Deut 32; Is 6). In ancient Graeco-Roman literature, it carries the notion of single-minded concern for the good of the other, as well as the constant call to something better, something more beneficial, something perhaps hitherto untried. In classical literature, it is linked to courage, to emulation, to pioneering and to crossing frontiers.

The Roots of Pauline Zeal

Looking at sample texts, we can get some insights into how zeal was understood and valued by St Paul. As a Pharisee he would have been an expert in interpreting the sacred texts of Israel. He would have understood a zealous person to be courageous, relentless in pursuit of a goal and uncompromising around certain issues regarded as essential. He would be aware that 'zealous love' is ascribed to YHWH, as for example in 2 Kings 19:31: 'Out of Jerusalem I will procure a Remnant ... The zeal of the Lord God will accomplish this.'

Acquainted with the prophets, he would have been familiar with Isaiah's poetic description of the prophet, 'wrapped in zeal as in a cloak' (Is 59:17), and with Jeremiah describing his predicament when called to speak the unpopular word: 'There seemed to be a fire burning in my heart, imprisoned in my bones.' (Jer 20:9)

From the Wisdom literature Paul would have learned, 'Be zealous for the fear of the Lord.' (Prov 23:17). He quotes many psalm texts in his Letters, such as Psalm 69, cited twice in Romans[1] 'Zeal for your house has consumed me, since my oppressors forget your word.' (Psalm 69:9; also Psalm 119:139).

Zeal in the Life and Letters of St Paul

For evidence of Paul's zeal we look primarily to the thirteen Letters ascribed to him and to the Acts of the Apostles.[2] The zeal of Saul of Tarsus, a committed Pharisee, set him on a path of destruction, persecuting any followers of the Christian way, including the very extreme measure of imprisoning women and children (Acts 8:59; 9:1–2; 22:4–5). His encounter with the Risen Lord on the Damascus Road (Acts 9:3–9; 22:6–11; 26:12–18) transformed him into an apostle of Jesus Christ. It transformed and redirected his zeal as well. For the rest of his life he would preach the Good News of Jesus, day in day out, irrespective of the cost. Because Paul exemplified zeal in his new, transformed existence, he could exhort others to imitate him. With his Roman converts he could plead, 'Never be lacking in zeal.' (Rom 12:11). To the church in Corinth he could write, speaking of the spread of the Gospel, 'Your zeal has been a spur to many others.' (2 Cor 9:3) Such examples could be multiplied. One of the most convincing texts illustrating the transforming power of zeal occurs in Paul's Letter to Christians at Philippi:

I was born of the race of Israel, and of the tribe of Benjamin, a Hebrew born of Hebrew parents ... As for the law I was a Pharisee; as for working for religion, I was a persecutor of the Church; as far as the Law can make you perfect, I was faultless. But, because of Christ, I have come to consider all these advantages that I had as disadvantages. Not only that, but I believe nothing can happen that will outweigh the supreme advantage of knowing Christ Jesus, my Lord. For him I have accepted the loss of everything, and I look on everything as so much rubbish, if only I can have Christ and be given a place in him ... (Phil 3:5-8)

So much for the zeal of Paul! It propelled his missionary work in the Mediterranean region – his teaching, preaching and nurturing of Christian communities. Rightly we salute him as the greatest missionary of all time, as Apostle to the Gentiles.

Zeal Enkindled – Nano's Damascus Road Experience
We do not know exactly what factors, or combination of factors, led Nano to forsake that life of high society among her *émigré* cousins in Paris. The death of her father, Garret Nagle, in 1746 and her mother's consequent move to Dublin must have provided an incentive. It is also probable that the writings (and perhaps direct influence) of scholars like Fr Andrew Donleavy of the Irish College in Paris, with whom the Nagle family had many connections, were contributing factors. This priest had published details of the plight of neglected Irish youth[3] as well as a catechism in 1742, while Nano was still enjoying the bright lights of Paris. And, doubtless, the recorded incident where Nano and her sister Ann, returning from a ball in the early hours of the morning, were struck by the example of a small group of people waiting outside a church door for morning Mass, concerned about 'the one thing necessary' – this, too, played its part. She does not speak of a blinding light such as Paul experienced on the road to Damascus. But, one way or another, under God, a spark of that zeal which would consume her for the rest of her life was set alight, and she responded with immense courage and trust.

Back in Dublin with her sister Ann and their widowed mother, Nano encountered at first hand the poverty and degradation of Ireland's youth. Another phase of her Damascus Road experience occurred when her sister Ann confided to her that a roll of silk, which

Nano had purchased in Paris to make a dress, had been donated by Ann to a starving family. This incident, outwardly bearing little resemblance to that of Paul on the Damascus Road, nevertheless became a turning point in her life. We read in the Annals:

> This circumstance, together with the death of this sister soon after, wrought so powerfully on the heart of Miss Nagle as perfectly to disengage it from the fashionable world, which she had tasted so much of, and enjoyed until then. She often said to her sisters in religion that it was this trifling circumstance which fired her determination to devote the remainder of her life to God in the service of the poor.[4]

From Dublin to France and from France back to Ballygriffin, Nano searched for a way forward. Doctor Coppinger notes, in relation to Nano's experience of the ignorance and poverty of her neighbours in Ballygriffin,

> Had she thousands at her disposal, she would gladly have expended them in remedying the miseries she beheld.[5]

Even at this early stage, her zeal was taking on the face of compassion.

Zeal in the Letters of Nano Nagle

The Letters of Nano Nagle carry a notable number of references to zeal. In writing to Eleanor Fitzsimons, the Ursuline novice in Paris, she speaks about her own brother and his wife as being 'very zealous', but expresses puzzlement that they got quite annoyed when they heard that she has defied the Penal System by setting up a school for poor children.[6] In other words, she expected a zealous person to be readily in tune with her gospel project. On hearing of a candidate for the Ursuline foundation who is wavering about the prospect of becoming a novice in Ireland and considering taking the safer option of joining the Ursulines in France, she writes with some irony,

> If she has so much zeal, she will never have such an opportunity of exercising it as here.[7]

For Nano, it seems that Penal Ireland is the best possible ground for exercising zeal. Again, writing about another unnamed candidate, of whom she approves, she says, 'her zeal is great … she may be compared to the mustard seed in the gospel ...' whose growth is quite phenomenal.[8]

Nano registers her gratitude to the Novice-mistress of Eleanor Fitzsimons who is willing to leave her native country of France and come to Penal Ireland, with all the risks and dangers involved. She writes, 'We all admire that amiable lady's zeal and fortitude to leave her own country ...' and she goes on to mention the fruits of this as 'universal good'.[9] In similar vein, she links the virtue of zeal with mission, and with the willingness to leave the safety of home and family for the sake of the Gospel. Of Dr Moylan, who had been very supportive of her project, despite multiple problems, she writes: 'I always admired his zeal'.[10]

At a later date, Nano writes to Teresa Mulally in Dublin, confiding in her the fact that she (Nano) has dismissed a certain candidate because of lack of zeal, and that not everybody agreed with her decision. This lack of zeal had become evident, according to Nano, to those who lived under the same roof as the said candidate.[11] From this incident at least two things can be deduced: firstly, that zeal, or the lack of it, became easily apparent in community living and secondly, that Nano did not want among her early companions anyone lacking in zeal.

The references just mentioned provide some convincing samples of how Nano values this quality of zeal in her family members, in formation personnel and in prospective candidates for religious life, whether Ursuline or Presentation. She goes beyond this in a letter to Teresa Mulally, dated 24 August 1778, where she specifies that the teachers employed in 'this establishment' shall be characterised by zeal. Hinting that there were some who were teaching 'only for bread' she is determined that 'It must be those that have true zeal'.[12] So it seems that if a young man or woman wished to be employed in one of Nano's schools, he or she would have to present some evidence of possessing this quality called zeal. Nano, as employer, was looking for something quite specific in prospective collaborators in her project: only the zealous need apply.

Zeal is what drives her to introduce the Ursuline Sisters to Ireland. To Eleanor Fitzsimons, in a letter dated 29 April 1770, she writes:

> I can't admire too much your zeal and trust in Divine Providence, which I always looked on as the most settled beginning any foundation of this kind could have.[13]

This is another way of saying that for Nano Nagle, a combination of zeal and trust in Divine Providence was not just desirable, but absolutely fundamental for those who would collaborate with her in her pioneering mission. In one of her last letters to Teresa Mulally, concerning the establishment of schools in Dublin, she speaks of 'the spirit of zeal (on) which the Almighty has given such blessing and success'.[14]

For Nano Nagle, then, and for those associated with her in her earliest endeavours, zeal was an absolute essential. Little wonder that the late Sr Mary Pius O'Farrell, to whom we owe so much, can summarise the situation as follows: 'If Nano's letters are taken *en bloc*, it is evident that she was forever looking for this virtue.' [zeal][15]

Nano and St Paul – Driven by Zeal for the Reign of God

There are obvious parallels to be drawn between the zeal so cherished by Nano and the zeal of St Paul. Both were zealous in their earlier years for what they later repudiated – Paul, as a devout Pharisee, zealous for Israel's Law and all that it prescribed; and Nano for high society life in the Parisian court. Both had come to see former advantages as disadvantages. Paul could write:

> Because of Christ, I have come to consider all these advantages that I had as disadvantages. (Phil 3:6)

The Annals of South Presentation, as well as Dr Coppinger's *Life of Miss Nano Nagle*, record that she was 'so delighted … with the gaieties of Paris that she began to think it impossible that she could live happily elsewhere.'[16] Dr Coppinger describes her as follows:

> Being gifted with superior talents, she fulfilled in every particular the expectations of her friends – uniting with an agreeable personality the most engaging manners and the most lasting attractions of a cultivated mind.[17]

One gets the impression that Nano had been quite enthusiastic about courtly life and that she had an extraordinary capacity for enjoying it. However, in a letter to Eleanor Fitzsimons in 1769, she indicates that her enjoyment is elsewhere, namely in her schools:

> I only take delight and pleasure in them.[18]

Both Paul and Nano had their value systems revised, if not totally reversed. Both were gifted with abundant natural talent. Both experienced a call and conversion which set them on a course they had not envisioned. That course, in both cases, was fired by zeal.

Paying the Price

For both Paul and Nano, zeal for the Reign of God demanded their all. Paul could write to his Corinthian converts who doubted his credentials:

> Five times I had the thirty-nine lashes from the Jews; three times I have been beaten with sticks; once I was stoned; three times I have been shipwrecked and once adrift in the open sea for a night and a day. Constantly travelling, I have been in danger from rivers and from brigands; in danger in towns, in danger in the open country; danger at sea and danger from so-called brothers. I have toiled and laboured, often without sleep; I have been hungry and thirsty and often starving; I have been in the cold and without clothes ... If I am to boast, let me boast of my weakness. (2 Cor 11:24–28)

Nano, too, could boast of her weakness:

> The Almighty makes use of the weakest means to bring about his works.[19]

An excerpt from the Annals of South Presentation, written shortly after her death, provides a parallel to the story of Paul in 2 Cor 11: 24–28:

> ... by nature, she was timid and retiring ... and fully aware of the almost insurmountable obstacles then raised by the penal laws to every laudable design ... She had therefore to encounter the censure of her friends – the shafts of worldly prudence. She had to apprehend the sneers of ill-nature, and all that was disgusting in the probable failure of her design. She had, together with all this, to bear up against the weakness of her frame, unequal, as it seemed to be, to her intended painful undertaking. 'She hath considered a field, and bought it.' – She was deeply wounded at the sight of so many that were delivered up a prey to the miseries of ignorance – She saw the churches deserted, and the voices silent which should have thundered aloud with all their energy – she was shocked

to see the Word of God chained down by injustice – with such incentives nothing could deter her.[20]

From this precious excerpt we obtain a list of difficulties encountered by Nano, not mentioned elsewhere:

› The insurmountable obstacles placed in her path by the Penal Laws
› The reproaches of her friends
› The 'shafts of worldly wisdom' advising her to play safe
› The sneers of those who disagreed with her
› The grim forecasts of those who assured her that her plans would fail
› Detailed descriptions of the punishment she would incur
› Her own frail health, seemingly unequal to the task in hand.

Displaying a single-minded sense of purpose in pursuit of their aims, both Paul and Nano were driven by the inner fire of zeal. Nano describes herself as 'a woman in a hurry'.[21] Paul could say, 'The charity of Christ urges us on.' (2 Cor 5:14) Both devoted all of their energy to the task in hand. Paul came near to death many times, and Nano risked her life and that of her family as she flouted unjust laws. She gave all of her wealth and inherited funds to her projects, and ended up begging from Cork merchants and later from the public on the streets of Cork.

Reduced to extreme deprivation for the sake of the Gospel, Nano and Paul faced opposition, misunderstanding, and downright hostility from those who knew them. Paul was accused of blasphemy and died a martyr's death. Nano was accused of encouraging prostitution on the streets of Cork and of befriending 'beggars' brats'. Both were relentless in the pursuit of their aims, trying first by one method, then by another. Paul tried preaching firstly in the Jewish synagogues, then from his workshops on the street, sometimes in the marketplace in big cities and even from his prison cell in Ephesus. Nano, for her part, after much disappointment and hardship, introduced the Ursuline Sisters to Ireland, built them a residence and schools, only to discover that their rule forbade them to visit the poor in their hovels or the sick who needed medical attention. Then she started all over again, all the while learning to discern the will of the Almighty through trials and apparent failure. Both Nano and Paul were conscious of God working through them: Paul could use a metaphor from the world of gardening to say to his Corinthian converts:

> Neither the planter nor the waterer matters; only God, who makes things grow. (1 Cor 3:7)

Nano could write to Eleanor Fitzsimons:

> I began in a poor, humble manner; and, though it pleased the divine Will to give me severe trials in this foundation, yet it is to show that it is His work, and has not been effected by human means.[22]

Both relied, not on their own strength, but on the power of God. Paul could proclaim the message received from the Lord: 'My grace is sufficient for you because power is made perfect in weakness.' (2 Cor 12:9). Nano could write: 'The Almighty is all-sufficient'.[23] Both accomplished tasks greater than could have been forecast by themselves or their contemporaries. Both poured out their lives in service of the Gospel and of their fellow human beings. Both left a living and lasting heritage born of zeal.

Unchaining the Good News

An entry in the Annals of South Presentation Convent, Cork is noteworthy:

> She [Nano] was shocked to see the Word of God chained down by injustice.

This is a powerful image of how Nano interprets the oppressive social milieu of her day. The corollary, of course, is that she sees her own evangelical task as that of 'unchaining the Gospel.' By a serendipitous coincidence, Raymond E. Brown could speak of the apostle Paul as 'the apostle whose preaching unchained the Gospel' for the entire world.[24]

Impelled by the Fire Within

Today we give God thanks for the zeal of Paul and for the zeal of Nano Nagle. The fire of zeal within them was contagious. In Paul's case it unchained the Gospel for the Gentile world. In Nano's case it unchained that same Gospel in Ireland's darkest hour. Once unleashed, it spread to all five continents. Considering their heroic achievements and the many obstacles overcome during their lifetimes it would be tempting to think of the zeal of these heroic persons as sheer will-power and determination. A glance at their letters offers a sure corrective. She speaks of her engagement with 'a work of God', and she relies on 'the power of the Amighty'. She speaks of the Almighty as 'all-sufficient'.[25] Paul can say, 'It is all God's work' (2 Cor 5:17) and as advice to the church at Philippi, 'It is God who is at work in you, both to will and to accomplish' (Phil 2:13). From these and other texts it is clear that both drew their strength from the divine fire within. Their zeal was a participation in the very life of God, a spark from the divine furnace. St Paul could say, 'For me, to live is Christ ...' (Phil 1:21). Nano's zeal was nurtured by hours of prayer in St Finbarr's Church each morning and by further time each evening in her simple cabin in Douglas Street, known then as Cove Lane. She was, in the words of the late Sr Mary Pius O'Farrell, first and foremost a Woman of the Gospel. She walked in faith and lived by faith. She saw no limit to the horizons where God could work through her: 'If I could be of any service ... in any part of the world I would willingly do all in my power.'[26]

The South Presentation Annalist says of Nano that 'nothing could deter her'. When her plans were thwarted she prayed for guidance and she took inspired action. That action included considering alternatives, changing course and, at the end, when funds ran out, begging for alms on the streets of Cork city. Paul can boast, not of his achievements but of his weakness, and of what God has done through him:

Let the one who boasts boast in the Lord. (2 Cor 10:17)

I have fought the good fight. I have finished the course. I have kept the faith ... (2 Tim 4:7)

From persecutor of the church to apostle of Christ Jesus, from zealous Pharisee to Christian martyr, Paul's journey is truly remarkable. From her comfortable home in the Blackwater Valley and the luxury of the Parisian court to begging on the streets of Cork – from riches to rags – that is Nano Nagle's upside-down fairy story. Two saintly lives fuelled by zeal – this is our astonishing heritage. It is good for us to consciously touch into that burning fire at the root of our apostolic calling, as we seek to follow Jesus in the way of Saint Paul and of Nano Nagle.

Endnotes

1. Rom 11:9–10; 15:3.
2. An important reference also occurs in John's gospel (Jn 2:17). When Jesus is dealing with the money-changers in the Temple, 'His disciples remembered that it is written, "Zeal for your House has consumed me"' – a reference to Psalm 69:9 which was understood in a Christological sense in the early Christian era.
3. T. J. Walsh, *Nano Nagle and the Presentation Sisters* (Dublin: Gill & Son, 1959), 40–1. Fr Donleavy had published in Paris in 1742 an Irish-English Catechism for the use of Irish people, 'whose children were often educated in vanity and the love of earthly goods … partly for the want of virtuous and well-instructed schoolmasters or catechists who would zealously employ their time and labour in making youth understand the science of salvation.'
4. cited in Walsh, *Nano Nagle*, 42.
5. ibid.
6. Nano Nagle to Miss Fitzsimons AL 17 July 1769, par 4, in Walsh, *Nano Nagle*, 345.
7. Nano Nagle to Miss Fitzsimons AL 17 July 1769, par 10, in Walsh, *Nano Nagle*, 346.
8. Nano Nagle to Miss Fitzsimons AL early in 1770, par 1, in Walsh, *Nano Nagle*, 347.
9. Nano Nagle to Miss Fitzsimons AL 29 April 1770, par 4, in Walsh, *Nano Nagle*, 349.
10. Nano Nagle to Miss Fitzsimons AL 20 July 1770, par 1, in Walsh, *Nano Nagle*, 353.
11. Nano Nagle to Miss Mulally AL 29 July 1780, par 3, in Walsh, *Nano Nagle*, 365.
12. Nano Nagle to Miss Mulally AL 24 August 1778, par 3, in Walsh, *Nano Nagle*, 359.
13. Nano Nagle to Miss Fitzsimons AL 29 April 1770, par 2, in Walsh, *Nano Nagle*, 349.
14. Nano Nagle to Miss Mulally AL 21 August 1777, par 1, in Walsh, *Nano Nagle*, 357.
15. Sr Mary Pius O'Farrell, Nano Nagle. *Woman of the Gospel* (Monasterevin: Presentation Generalate, 1996), 114.
16. Dr Coppinger: *Life of Miss Nano Nagle* (Cork: Haly, 1794). 1st edition. Cited in the Annals of South Presentation Convent, Cork.
17. Dr Coppinger: *Life of Miss Nano Nagle*, 12.
18. Nano Nagle to Miss Fitzsimons AL 17 July 1769, par 8, in Walsh, *Nano Nagle*, 346.
19. Nano Nagle to Miss Mulally AL 29 September 1776, par 1, in Walsh, *Nano Nagle*, 357.
20. Annals of South Presentation Convent, Cork.
21. Nano Nagle to Miss Mulally AL 31 October 1778, par 1, in Walsh, *Nano Nagle*, 360.
22. Nano Nagle to Miss Fitzsimons AL 17 July 1769, par 9, in Walsh, *Nano Nagle*, 346.
23. Nano Nagle to Miss Fitzsimons AL 17 July 1769, par 12, in Walsh, *Nano Nagle*, 347.
24. Raymond E. Brown, *An Introduction to the New Testament* (New York: Doubleday, 1996), 455.

25. Nano Nagle to Miss Fitzsimons AL 17 July 1769, par 12, in Walsh, *Nano Nagle*, 347.
26. Nano Nagle to Miss Fitzsimons AL 17 July 1769, par 11, in Walsh, *Nano Nagle*, 347.

Nano Nagle and St John of God: Parallel Lives

Anne M. O'Leary PBVM

In recent years this author has become fascinated by the fact that the charism of Nano Nagle manifested itself in North Dakota and South Dakota to a very great degree in the area of health care.[1] To some, including Susan Carol Peterson and Courtney Ann Vaughn-Roberson, authors of *Women with Vision: The Presentation Sisters of South Dakota 1880–1985*, it would appear that the pursuit of Presentation health care 'had diverted the attention of the Sisters from the order's original focus'.[2] But, clearly, the Sisters were responding to the needs of the time, a valid and sufficiently Gospel-inspired reason for the change of direction in the apostolate of the Sisters from education to health care. Therefore, in the embracing of the ministry of health care, were the Sisters of the Dakotas moving away from the founding charism or were they being drawn more deeply into it? Were the Sisters, in fact, recovering an authentic dimension of the charism of Nano Nagle or were they complementing it?

Returning to the Source
Reviewing the *Rule and Constitutions* of the Order of St Thomas de Villeneuve in order to craft one for her own Order, Nano Nagle notes that in various houses of this religious congregation, the members take care of the sick and the aged, instruct orphans, receive boarders, house penitents, serve prisoners and conduct schools for poor girls. She adds further that, 'As to their obligations in other things, it's just the same [as] we have in their constitutions. And we are obliged to most of these charities, only we must prefer the schools to all others …'[3] While we note the primacy that Nano gives to the ministry of schooling, understandably given the Penal Laws of her time, in this chapter, we wish to draw particular attention to some of 'these other charities' that formed part of the cloak of her charism.

The 1790 draft Rule and Constitutions for Nano's Order sent for approval to Rome included a chapter 'On the Care of the Sick' (chapter thirteen) and a chapter 'On Visiting the Hospitals of the Old and on the Medical Care of the Poor' (chapter sixteen).[4] Based on the recommendation of the Congregation in Rome and its then requirement of the practice of enclosure if the Order was to receive the status of a religious congregation, these chapters were omitted in the first Rule and Constitutions for the Presentation Sisters that received Papal approval in 1805. However, the 1790 draft makes clear what some of 'these other charities' that the early Sisters inherited consisted of – care of the sick, visiting hospitals of the old, and medical care for the poor among other things.

What's in a Name? Mother Mary St John of God

Upon receiving the habit on 24 June 1776, Nano Nagle chose to be named in religion, Mother Mary St John of God. What's in a religious name, one might ask? Everything, we would suggest. At least, everything that is core to one's identity in Christ.

We have no known record that would enlighten us as to the reason for Nano's choice of name. Yet, the name itself provides us with a very valuable insight into how she understood her vocation and her mission. What was it about this Portuguese saint, John of God, that might have inspired her? What was it about him that she was drawn to imitate in order to imitate Christ? A parallel study of the lives of Nano and St John of God provides further insights into not only the charities other than schooling that Nano engaged in, but the spirit in which she did so.

John of God (Juan Ciudad) was born at Montemor-O-Novo, Portugal, in 1495. After a checkered childhood, he spent his early adulthood, first, as a shepherd (1503–1522), and, then, as an army officer. He fought in the war waged by Charles V, Emperor of Spain, against the French (1523–1524).[5]

At the age of forty-two, something stirred this prodigal son to begin a mission to care for the poorest and most neglected in Granada, Spain – a mission that was to last until his death, thirteen years later on 8 March 1550. Other men were attracted to his charism for the poor. With a small group of companions, he founded the Order of the Brothers Hospitallers. The Brothers received the rule of St Augustine – the same rule that would later be assigned by Rome to the Presentation Congregation. John of God was canonized by Pope Alexander VIII in 1690. By the 1740s, during the time when Nano would have been in Paris as a young lady, and later as a novice, the Order of Hospitallers grew to having forty hospitals in the city with, according to one source, over four thousand patients.[6] It would not be credible that the status of John of God as exemplar missionary of the Gospel, and the extent of the mission of his Brothers in Paris, would have escaped Nano during her sojourn there, given that 'the problems in Paris and Cork in the years between 1642 and 1775 were very similar. The sick, the aged, and the illiterate swarmed the left bank of the Seine,' as they did the banks of the river Lee.[7]

Nano Nagle and St John of God: Parallel Lives

While we cannot know exactly what it was about St John of God that inspired Nano Nagle, we can be sure of how her spirituality and Gospel-inspired charism came to parallel his in so many respects. One might say that we recognize her prototype in the great and humble servant, St John of God.

What are some of the signs of an ever-deepening union with Christ that happened for John of God, and are evidenced later in Nano's life? Here, we will outline five such signs: first, both John of God and Nano battled with what St Ignatius of Loyola (1491–1556) might call the 'testing of spirits' (Lk 4:1–30); second, both came to extend unlimited hospitality to those in need (Jn 6:1–15); third, both practised a hands-on type of hospitality (Mk 7:31–35); fourth, both were free enough to become as fools for Christ's sake (Mk 3:20–22); finally, they both became people of vision: they had the ability to see with eyes of faith what lay beyond the horizon of the visible (Lk 24:36–53).

The Testing of Spirits

After a number of years as an itinerant worker, John took to book-peddling as an occupation to support himself on the streets of Gibraltar and later at the Elvira Gate of Granada (1538–1539). During this time, he experienced a stirring of religious sensibilities. This became manifest when he began to buy supplies of books, religious as well as secular. When anyone approached him to purchase a non-religious book, he tried to talk them into buying a devotional one instead. His first biographer, Francisco De Castro notes how, 'He used temporal merchandise in order to sell a spiritual one.'[8]

A great leap in the awakening of his spiritual consciousness happened for him during a sermon he heard preached by a charismatic and illustrious preacher and priest, Master John Avila (BC 1499). Avila's words 'struck him [John of God] to the very depths of his soul.'[9] His message of the tremendous love that the Lord had for each one left John feeling contrite and repentant of his faults. As a way of making atonement for his sins, John chose to increase his sufferings by acting in such a deranged manner that the people of Granada poked fun at him and derided him, thinking he was *loco* or out of his mind. During this phase of his life on the streets, John became only too aware that 'there existed, in fact, two Granadas: the marvellous city of the wealthy, and the shadowed city of the miserable … [where] the poor teem like miserable rats in the sewers of the city'.[10]

John later asked Master Avila to be his spiritual director. In dialogue with him, John traced the first impulses he had to serve the poor, especially those ill in body and mind that he encountered on the streets. In a type of holy conspiracy with his spiritual mentor, John of God's (feigned)[11] deranged behaviour caused him to be admitted to the Royal Hospital of Granada where the insane of the city were treated.[12] His desire was to experience the lot of people sick in body or mind. Only the grace of God and the fire of God's love being kindled in his soul for his brothers and sisters there helped him to endure the experience. It was truly a testing of spirits from God out of which a clarity and resolve came for John of God. De Castro expresses it thus: 'May Jesus Christ eventually give me the grace to run a hospital where the abandoned poor and those who suffer mental disorders might have refuge and that I may be able to serve them as I wish.'[13]

In reviewing the life of Nano Nagle, many trace the first stirrings of what would later blossom in her response to a special call of God to serve the poor and needy in Cork to an experience she had in Paris. Upon returning from a ball in the early hours of the morning in the French capital, she saw a little group of poor people gathered at the yet unopened doors of a church, awaiting Mass. Decades later, one of the early Presentation Sisters, Mother Clare Callaghan, writes about it thus: 'The early morning scene did not precipitate a crisis in Nano Nagle's life … That upheaval came later for different reasons'.[14] However, we do have in this account evidence of Nano's growing sensibilities in relation to God and the poor.

We might say that the great leap in the awakening of her spiritual consciousness happened for Nano after her return from Paris to Dublin to live with her mother, Ann, and her sister of the same name, after the death of her father, Garret (c. 1746). Desiring a new gown to be made up, the experience of finding that her sister, Ann, had surreptitiously sold the silk material in order to get money to relieve the distress of a poor family 'fired her [Nano's] determination to devote the remainder of her life to God in the service of the poor'.[15] To this end, Nano resolved to return to Paris and entered a convent there where she planned to spend the rest of her days.

Her time in the French convent turned out to be a time 'of spiritual ferment.'[16] The account of this period by her first biographer, Dr Coppinger, Bishop of Cloyne, is telling: 'She wept – she prayed – she consulted … she sought advice … she laid open the agitation of her mind … her feeling for the poor of her own country'.[17] In an agony of indecision she opened her soul to her director, a Jesuit priest, whose name is not recorded. According to Walsh, 'To him and to her friends she [Nano] protested her unfitness, lack of means, lack of health, lack of perseverance, lack of everything that was necessary'.[18]

Only the grace of God and the fire of God's love being kindled in her soul for her brothers and sisters in Ireland could have freed Nano to make the momentous decision to return to Cork's poor. It was truly a testing of spirits from God out of which a clarity and resolve came for her. Nano writes: 'Nothing would have made me come home but the decision of the clergyman that I should run the great risk of salvation if I did not follow the inspiration.'[19]

Unlimited Hospitality

A second great sign of the ever-deepening union with Christ that happened for John of God, and is evidenced later in Nano's life, is that of offering unlimited indiscriminate hospitality (Heb 13:2).[20]

Before entering the asylum, John of God had begun to invite beggars or anyone in need of shelter to share the porch of the Venegas palace, Granada, that he inhabited as payment for his work as a shepherd.[21] After leaving the asylum he rented a house and 'not content with gathering up the beggars off the streets; he went and searched them out in the hovels in which they lived.'[22] It did not matter who the homeless were – tramps or 'vagabonds, cripples begging at church doors, the poor in the streets … prisoners let out of gaol.'[23] As many as could fit were offered hospitality and given a space where they could be healed and made whole. And all were treated with dignity.

Nano's zeal to seek out as many of the poor as she could find, like St John of God, is recorded in the Annals of South Presentation

Convent, Cork (1777): 'It was said of her that there was not a garret in Cork that she had not visited. She built on love.' Moreover, her zeal was contagious. On this, Walsh writes: 'Charitable instruction of children and charitable visitation of the sick and destitute were the special manifestation of the love of Christ that won Elizabeth Burke, Mary Fouhy, and Mary Ann Collins to her side'.[24] Below the radar of those in power in her day, and with characteristic simplicity, Nano, along with these three women, founded her new Congregation on Christmas Eve, 1775, at her cottage at Cove Lane, Cork.

The gift of unlimited hospitality remained with Nano all her life. Just one year before she died, she opened a home (called then, an asylum) for women who were 'of such age as to be incapable of procuring their livelihood by labour.'[25] The degree of Nano's deep care for these poor women can be glimpsed from an early document which records the 'Regulations For the Home for Old Women':

> Special care is at all times to be freely given to the sick by those who may have been selected by the Religious for that object, especially with regard to cleanliness, kindly attention, and food. It is to be always understood that the best food the house can afford will be provided for the invalids, if any ... It is important that spiritual assistance be made paramount. Mass prayers are to be read for those who are unable.[26]

Clearly, for Nano, as for St John of God, Christ continued to appear in multiple guises, not least in the faces of the poor and needy. They took to heart the divine imperative: 'As long as you did it to the least of these my brothers and sisters, you did it to me.' (Mt 25:40)

Hands-on Hospitality and Care of the Sick

A third sign of John of God's ever-deepening union with Christ is reflected in the fact that when he opened his house of hospitality he did practically all the work himself. He had, at first, no helpers and no nursing assistants. He set to work with the little he knew: 'He could wash his guests' feet and dress their sores; he could kiss their feet and let them know that somebody cared; he could sit by their side and be merry with them, and then could induce them to go to confession and pray.'[27] He could set the table and prepare what seemed to them a banquet before them (Psalm 23). At first his neighbours resented his work, but before long they saw the benefits and blessings of his service to his neighbour (Gk, *diakonia*).

We find this hands-on type of approach to hospitality reflected in the life of Nano also. It is recorded in the earliest extant Annals of the religious congregation that Nano founded that:

> [The first convent] was opened on the solemn and appropriate Festival of Christmas day, in honour of the Infant God, with a most uncommon act of hospitality ... she invited fifty beggars to dinner. She waited on them at table with great joy and singular charity; she helped them as their menial servant, faith strongly representing to her the Great Patron of the Poor who on that day made His first appearance among men and who came not to be ministered to but to minister.[28]

We can be confident also that she ministered to the poor that she visited, the people in the garrets of Cork as their servant, with equally 'great joy and singular charity'.

The earliest extant draft Rule and Constitutions of Nano's Order (1790) gives us further insight into the incarnational aspect of her spirituality. We read in chapter thirteen of this document that: 'The sisters should devote special care to those who are sick, and should themselves provide whatever treatment is suitable, according to the prescription of the doctor.'[29] And in chapter sixteen of the same document, we read: 'When sick women, or women who are afflicted with ulcers, come to them, the sisters shall receive them with the greatest humanity ... they shall apply poultices to them tenderly, they shall teach them to aspire to the heavenly kingdom ... so that the loss of their health may be for the benefit of their souls.'[30] The compassionate manner with which the Sisters are to care of the sick is striking, as well as the holistic approach, namely, caring for the health of each person's soul as well as their mind and body.

Being Taken for a Fool for Christ's Sake

A fourth sign of John of God's ever-deepening union with Christ was his trust in Divine Providence. He began begging the charity of others for the support of his house of hospitality.[31] Inevitably, his begging provoked opposition. Some scolded him for encouraging vagabonds and idlers in their evil ways; others accused him of embezzlement; some never let him forget that he had once been an inmate of a lunatic asylum and treated him accordingly. Even some of his guests abused him – including the prostitutes who looked on themselves as superior to their beggar host. John never took offence at these abusers. It appeared that these outside trials troubled him very little – a clear indication that he had gained an inner spiritual freedom in his soul and had come to empty himself (Gk, *kenosis*) so that he might be filled with the love of Christ.

A small number who gave John alms followed him to see what he did with them. These benefactors found that 'their eyes were opened' (Lk 24:31) when they came to know that John would wear the suit of clothes he had taken from a beggar in exchange for his own.[32] He grew in kenotic love in imitation of Christ Jesus who 'emptied himself, taking the form of a slave' (Phil 2:6–11). They were astonished at what this man of faith would do to transform the lives of so many.

When Nano's own financial resources ran out, mirroring the life of St John of God, she, too, trusting Divine Providence, began begging to support her schools, ministry of healing, hospitality and almsgiving. The South Presentation Annalist records this story about Nano's habit of begging:

> She went from door to door begging a support for these schools, which her own exhausted finances could not administer. In making this charitable sacrifice of her own feelings, she exposed herself to the rude refusals of some, and to the malignant sarcasms of many more; satisfied, if even at this expense, so painful to nature, she could succeed in obtaining the aid of some humble benefactors.

However, we get a more complete account of how she was willing to be taken as a fool for Christ's sake from her first biographer, Bishop Coppinger. His record is, uncannily, a mirror reflection of what had been endured by her favourite saint, St John of God. Coppinger writes:

> She [Nano] has been bitterly cursed in our streets as a mere impostor; she has been charged with having squandered her money upon the building of houses for the sole purpose of getting a name, and with deceiving the world by her throngs of beggars' brats. Has it not been even said that her schools were a seminary of prostitution? He added that Nano would not have revealed these insults but for the need to prepare her sisters in religion for what might befall. On her own part, there was a humble acceptance of the reviling.[33]

Accepting that her exertions were for the sake of the mission, the South Presentation Annalist makes a disconcerting disclosure about Nano:

> One circumstance, which was only discovered after her death will throw new light upon [her] ... Such prominent and such angry excrescences were then observed upon the soles of her feet, as to make it a matter of surprise how she could by any possible exertion even stand upon them, much less walk as she did so much and so constantly during the last three years of her life.

While Nano's absence of references to such wounding experiences would suggest a that outside trials troubled her very little, it also reflects a shadow side to her personality, namely, the excessive degree to which she was willing to punish her body and withhold information regarding the true state of her health from her Sisters. However, it is clear that those who gave Nano alms – family members, shopkeepers, and merchants – saw in her a reflection of the Suffering Servant she sought to imitate (Is 53:3–4; cf Jn 13:1–35). These benefactors were astonished at what a woman of faith would do to transform the lives of so many.

The Ability to See What Lies Beyond the Horizon

During the final years of his earthly life, St John of God gave away so much that he had nothing for himself. Moreover, 'when he was ill, which was often, he took no notice of his illness that he might serve others who were worse'. It was as if he could see with eyes of faith a treasure far greater in ministering to those in need than in taking care of his health. His final illness came about as a result of his attempt to save a man from drowning in a river. After this event, he was obliged to lie down in his own house of hospitality and be ministered to by his ragged guests who became for him in every sense God's wounded healers. John lived his motto to the fullest: 'Labour without stopping. Do all the good works while you still have time.'

The tradition associated with his death is later recorded by Alban Goodier thus: 'He requested those round his bed to leave him alone for a few minutes. When they were gone he rose from his bed and knelt before a crucifix. The nurses entered shortly and found him still kneeling there, his face resting on the feet of the Savior, but he was quite dead.'[34] Allowing for a degree of hagiography in this account, one might say of John, that, as in life, so in death – his devotion to the Passion is paramount. He was fifty-five years of age.

Not dissimilarly, in her final years, Nano spent herself utterly. Her dear friend, Eleanor Fitzsimons (alias Sr Angela, whom Nano had supported to become one of the founding member of the Ursuline Sisters in Ireland) paints a vivid picture: 'N[ano] Nagle, whose strength has been visibly declining these twelve months, particularly this last and severe winter. Her limbs were so feeble that she was obliged to use a stick in walking, and has been seen to stop frequently in the streets to get a little strength to proceed in her long and painful walks ... There were, indeed, so many steps on the road to eternal life'.[35] Clearly, Nano, too, beheld a treasure far greater in ministering to those in need than in taking care of her own physical wellbeing. She loved to the utmost with an agamic love and lived the Nagle motto to the fullest: 'Not words, but deeds'.

Her final days on earth coincided with Holy Week and Easter. Only after her death did her companions realize the extent of her devotion to the suffering Christ. Coppinger records it thus: 'In paying the last attention to her dead body, they found that her knees had long been in a state of ulceration ... what anguish must she not have felt when from five o'clock in the morning until nine, the excoriated joints were daily applied to the ground.'[36] Clearly, Nano's whole life was a pilgrim journey 'towards union with Christ'.[37] She was sixty-five years of age.

Conclusion

Both humble servants of God, Nano Nagle, founder of the Presentation Sisters, and St John of God, founder of the Order of Hospitallers, sought to actualize love – love of God and love of neighbour. Moreover, the pattern of discipleship traceable in the lives of both – namely, the testing of spirits, the call to practice unlimited hospitality, a hands-on type of hospitality and care of the sick, the freedom to be taken as a fool for Christ's sake, and the ability to see beyond the horizon of the visible – is one that those who choose to walk in their footsteps will see mirrored in their own lives.

We may be confident that what was lost in words – or omitted from the early draft Rule and Constitution (1790), or the further inspiration that would have been generated if circumstances allowed Nano to be called more often by her religious name, Mother Mary St John of God – was not lost in terms of deeds. In many parts of the globe, many Presentation Sisters in partnership with others have, through the years, spent themselves wholly in relation to 'these other [than schooling] charities' that were dear to Nano's heart. Those involved in health care and related ministries, or in ministries such as hospitality, visitation, care of the sick and medical assistance for the poor wear the mantle of Nano's founding charism, along with those involved in the ministry of schooling.

It is hoped that this chapter might serve as a timely reminder of the value of delving more deeply into the pockets of the cloak of Nano's charism to find the lesser known treasures that they hold, and of drawing upon the Divine Source of her store of healing love, a store replenished through daily prayer and contemplation. Concomitantly, we can say with confidence that Jesus' mission of healing, when charged with the Spirit of God and the spirit of Nano Nagle, is authentically Presentation.

Endnotes

1. The inspiration and impetus for this chapter came when I was invited to co-facilitate a Presentation Spirituality and Charism retreat, along with Mary O'Brien, in July 2010 by the Presentation Sisters, Aberdeen, SD, who for decades have embodied the charism of Nano Nagle through the mission of healing and health care. The Benedictine and Presentation Sisters brought their health ministries together in 2000 under the name Avera – a name derived from a Latin word meaning 'to be well.' With more than 13,000 employees and physicians, Avera is South Dakota's largest private employer. See Chapter 15 below and http://www.avera.org.
2. Susan Carol Peterson and Courtney Ann Vaughn-Roberson, *Women with Vision: The Presentation Sisters of South Dakota, 1880–1985* (SD: University of Illinois Press, 1988), 165.
3. Nano Nagle to Teresa Mulally, AL 30 October 1779, par 4, in T. J. Walsh, *Nano Nagle and the Presentation Sisters* (Dublin: M. H. Gill and Son, 1959), 364.
4. This document is extant. See Mary Pius O'Farrell, *Breaking of Morn: Nano Nagle (1718–1784) and Francis Moylan (1735–1815). A Book of Documents* (Cork Publishing Limited, 2001), 132–52. The later draft of the 'Rules and Constitutions of the Sisters of the Congregation of the Charitable Instruction' of 1793, continues to include guidelines in relation to ministry to the sick: 'On the Care of the Sick, and the Suffrages of the Dead' (Chapter 18); and 'Alms Houses and Sick Externs' (Chapter 19). For a copy of this Rules and Constitutions, see Raphael Consedine, *Listening Journey: A Study in the Spirit and Ideals of Nano Nagle and the Presentation Sisters* (Victoria: Congregation of the Presentation of the Blessed Virgin Mary, 1983), 406–26. See ibid, 416.
5. J. M. Javierre, *John of God: Loco in Granada* (Seville: 2000). Translated by Benedict O'Grady (Sydney: John of God Brothers, 2000), 157.
6. 'Brothers Hospitallers of St John of God'. New Advent Encyclopedia. http://www.newadvent.org/cathen/02802b.htm
7. Mary Pius O'Farrell, *Nano Nagle: Woman of the Gospel* (Cork: Cork Publishing Ltd., 1996), 197.
8. In *The First Biography of St John of God* (Published in Granada, 1585; trans. from the original Spanish with commentary notes by Benedict O'Grady (Dublin: John of God Brothers, 1986), 40.
9. Javierre, *John of God*, 269.
10. Javierre, *John of God*, 369, 441.
11. Scholars differ as to the true nature of John's deranged behaviour. The earliest biographer, De Castro, 'likens John's emotional breakdown to the dying grain, a metamorphosis in a rebirth yielding an abundance of fruit – charity.' See De Castro, *First Biography*, 61, n. 4; Javierre, *John of God*, 309.
12. De Castro, *First Biography*, 48–9.
13. De Castro, *First Biography*, 52; Javierre, *John of God*, 308.
14. Walsh, *Nano Nagle*, 41.
15. South Presentation Annals, cited in Walsh, *Nano Nagle*, 41–2.
16. Walsh, *Nano Nagle*, 43.
17. Cited in Walsh, *Nano Nagle*, 386.
18. Walsh, *Nano Nagle*, 43.
19. Nano Nagle to Miss Fitzsimons AL 17 July 1769, par 3, in Walsh, *Nano Nagle*, 345.
20. Javierre, *John of God*, 24.
21. Javierre, *John of God*, 368, 494.

22. Alban Goodier, *Saints for Sinners: Nine Desolate Souls Made Strong by God* (Manchester, NH: Sophia Institute Press, 2007), originally published (Garden City NY: Image Books, 1959), 49.
23. ibid.
24. Walsh, *Nano Nagle*, 121.
25. O'Farrell, *Nano Nagle*, 99.
26. O'Farrell, *Nano Nagle*, 101.
27. Goodier, *Saints for Sinners*, 48.
28. South Presentation Annals, Cork, 1777.
29. O'Farrell, *Breaking Morn*, 142.
30. O'Farrell, *Breaking Morn*, 143.
31. De Castro, *First Biography*, 63, 66.
32. De Castro, *First Biography*, 92.
33. Walsh, *Nano Nagle*, 392.
34. Goodier, *Saints for Sinners*, 54.
35. Sr Angela Fitzsimons to Miss Mulally AL 21 May 1784, in Walsh, *Nano Nagle*, 367.
36. Cited in Walsh, *Nano Nagle*, 125, 393.
37. Walsh, *Nano Nagle*, 120.

'For the Greater Glory of God':
A Reflection on the Jesuit Influence on Nano Nagle

Mary T. O'Brien PBVM

Even a superficial glance at the writings of Nano Nagle will invite questions about the Jesuit influence on her spirituality. Constantly searching for 'the Divine will', discerning it in the daily happenings of life and respecting it by the decisions taken – this is the underlying stratum in each one of those sixteen letters of hers that have come down to us. Her efforts, as she repeatedly says, are directed, towards 'the greater glory of God'. She is alert to God at work through her and in her experience. Devotion to the Sacred Heart of Jesus, promoted by French Jesuits, is important to her. She names her fledgling community 'Sisters of Charitable Instruction of the Sacred Heart of Jesus' and her first residence in Cork was known as 'The House of the Sacred Heart'. She is anti-Jansenist, as the Jesuits of her time were known to be, and she expresses concern lest one of the Ursuline novices in Paris be tainted with Jansenism. Even though she does not explicitly mention St Ignatius, the Society of Jesus or the Spiritual Exercises in her writings, she does mention individual Jesuits many times. I believe that Jesuit influence features strongly in her spirituality, and that it can be traced in her letters and in some of the biographical data available to us. Drawing from this unexplored well may have some implications for us and for Presentation today.

This chapter is in two parts. Part One will focus on two things: firstly, that Nano could not have escaped Jesuit influence because of the many established connections between her journey and that of Jesuit priests; secondly, that the Jesuit influence on her spirituality was quite pervasive and ultimately determinative of the major steps taken by her. Part Two will trace some of the key elements in her letters as echoes of The Spiritual Exercises of St Ignatius or derivative of Jesuit spirituality.

Part One: Jesuit Influence on Nano Nagle

Childhood and Early Years

Beginning with Nano's childhood in Ballygriffin, in the lovely Blackwater Valley in Cork, in early eighteenth-century Ireland when legislative restrictions on Catholics within Ireland and Britain were quite stringently enforced,[1] we know that the Nagle family had many relatives in mainland Europe who were Jesuit priests. Many had been expelled from Ireland during the persecutions in 1698. According to Tuckey's *Cork Remembrancer*, seventy-five clergy, including Jesuits and Friars, were shipped from Cork in that year, their passage being paid for by Act of Parliament.[2] Among them was the Catholic Bishop of Cork, Dr John Sleyne, who was first imprisoned for five years, before being sent to Lisbon where he died in 1712, just six years before Nano was born. We can only surmise that such events were part of table-talk in Nano's home in the years which followed, and that the Nagle family members were deeply concerned about the future and whereabouts of their exiled Jesuit cousins. We know that some of these did not even reach the Continent, but opted to stay as pastors working in disguise in Dublin.[3] It is reasonable to assume that there would have been contact between these banished Jesuits and Nano's parents, Garret and Ann Nagle, through correspondence at least, and perhaps also through Garret Nagle's regular travels in Belgium and France.[4]

Because of the legal restrictions on Catholic schooling in the early eighteenth century (restrictions that were relaxed considerably over the following decades) Nano's early education took place at home in Ballygriffin and at a hedge-school in the nearby ancestral home at Monanimy Castle. This hedge-school was run by a Mr O'Halloran, a travelling teacher, about whom little is known, and the hedge-school had the honour of also educating Nano's cousin, the renowned Edmund Burke.

Jesuits and Jansenism

Cornelius Jansen (1585–1638), Professor at the Catholic University of Leuven, before becoming Bishop of Ypres, where Nano was later a boarder, taught some controversial versions of St Augustine's teachings on grace and predestination. Even though he died professing full allegiance to the Catholic faith and to the teaching authority of Rome, his teachings were strongly refuted by the Jesuits (he had once applied for admission to the Jesuits and was refused), and were later condemned by the Church as heretical. Jansen and his supporters held that human nature was intrinsically corrupt, and they professed an extremely austere manner of living the Christian life, and a joyless spirituality. The Jesuits did not agree. Neither did Nano.

Because Jansen had been Bishop of Ypres (from 1636 to his death in 1638),[5] where Nano spent six of the most impressionable years of her life, and because of the long-standing theological battle between Jansenists and Jesuits which still raged during her time at Ypres, she cannot have been unaffected by that battle. We know from her letters and from other sources that she was anti-Jansenist.

Boarding School in Mainland Europe

When Nano was about ten years old, she was sent abroad to continue her education, as was the custom among well-to-do Catholic families in Ireland at the time. But where did she go? Up to 1969, it was generally thought that she was educated either in the Benedictine Convent at Fontevraud near Saumur, in western France, where she had two Kearney cousins, or else in the prestigious Convent of St Cyr in Paris, run by Les Dames de Saint Louis. The jury was out on the issue for many years, until an important piece of correspondence was discovered in 1969.

Now, it is generally recognised that she was not educated in either of those places, but in the Benedictine Convent at Ypres, about fifty kilometres west of Brussels. So many Irish women belonged to the community at Ypres, that it was known as the Royal Irish Abbey at Ypres, and it merited a worthy and extensive history by Patrick Nolan OSB, entitled *The Irish Dames of Ypres*.[6] The strongest evidence that Nano was a boarder there, comes from a letter written in 1969 by Maureen Stewart (later Sr Bernard OSB) to Sister Camillus Galvin of Presentation Convent, Fargo, ND.[7] In that letter, Sr Bernard, who was a boarder in Ypres from 1908 to 1912 before joining the community there, states that she was told by the Abbess, Dame Josephine Fletcher, in 1908, that Nano Nagle, foundress of the Presentation Sisters, was educated at that school. I quote a relevant extract from that letter, because it tells us quite a few things about factors which influenced Nano's spirituality:

> When I went to school at Ypres in October 1908 Dame Josephine Fletcher told me that Nano Nagle, the foundress of the Presentation nuns, was educated here … In 1730 (altered later to 1728) she was sent to school at Ypres. She was twelve

> (later altered to ten) years old when she came, and according to the Constitution, she left at the age of sixteen ... Dame Ignatia Goulde was Mistress of Pensioners (sic Boarders). She was related to the Nagles, as were several of the community .... There is also a tradition that Nano entered but remained only a short time, as a Jesuit Confessor advised her to return to Ireland and give herself to work for the poor of that nation. From Ypres she went to Paris, where she had many relatives ... In 1704 Devotion to the Sacred Heart had been officially established (at the school) and the pupils were enrolled ...[8]

During the time when Nano was a boarder at Ypres (1728–1734) the Abbess happened to be Dame Xaveria Arthur (Abbess 1723–1743), whose family of origin was Norman-Irish from County Clare. Her sister was married to James Creagh, nephew of the Archbishop of Dublin.[9] Of Dame Arthur we are told that before coming to Ypres she had 'with remarkable fervour, performed the Spiritual Exercises of St Ignatius in a Convent of Ursulines at St Germain ...'[10] Furthermore, in 1727, a year before Nano arrived in Ypres, we learn of the efforts of a certain Rev Stephen Amiot SJ to exempt the Irish Benedictine Nuns from taxes, because of their exiled situation.[11] Of another Jesuit priest, Fr Dalas, some decades later, we are told that he was 'director of the Convent and of the boarders' and that he founded a Confraternity in honour of the Sacred Heart of Jesus with authorisation from the Bishop of Ypres in 1780. Of course Nano was back in Ireland then, but the letter of Dame Bernard Stewart already cited states that 'Nano established the devotion in Cork', even before that devotion got official recognition by Pope Clement XIII in 1765.

An article submitted to the website of the Union of Presentation Sisters by Sr Rosario Allen provides a vital clue to the Jesuit involvement in the establishment of devotion to the Sacred Heart of Jesus at Ypres:

> In 1704, during the Octave of Corpus Christi, a retreat was preached to the Ypres community by Fr Louis Sabran SJ. He had been a companion of Blessed Claude de la Colombiere at the court of St. James, and was then stationed at Paray le Monial. He preached on devotion to the Sacred Heart as revealed by Our Lord to St Margaret Mary. At the end of the retreat, the community made a solemn Act of Consecration to the Sacred Heart and thus the devotion was established. In 1720 the entire community, with the chaplain, Mr Jeremy

O'Donnell, joined a confraternity established with Episcopal approval, by the Jesuits at Bruges. Finally, in 1732, when the Archconfraternity was established in Rome, the community and their pupils were enrolled, and a private association was established in the school to promote the devotion among the pupils, one of whom was Nano Nagle (1728–1734) ... It was not till 1765 that the Feast of the Sacred Heart was authorised by Pope Clement XIII ...[12]

According to Nolan, 'The Irish Dames were one of the first communities outside France to introduce devotion to the Sacred Heart after its establishment at Paray-le-Monial ...'[13]

Sr Rosario's historical note continues:

As mentioned above, Nano Nagle was at the Abbey school when the first Association was established among the pupils. She gave the devotion to the Presentation Sisters and to the Ursulines, both of whom carried it wherever foundations were made. Another pupil, Judith Browne (1767–1774), was Foundress of the Brigidine Sisters in the Diocese of Kildare. From her the Sisters received the devotion and their Mother House was the first to have granted the Mass (*Egredimini*) in Ireland. Soon there were branches of the Confraternity in all the parishes of the Diocese of Kildare ...

Nano in Paris

There is little direct evidence available about Jesuit influence on Nano during her years in Paris before the death of her father in 1746. Soon after that date she and her sister Ann returned to Ireland to live with their mother in a house in Dublin on Bachelor's Quay. We learn that she greatly missed the attractions of Parisian life. We are told that 'she enjoyed its amusements and, when obliged to return from Paris to Ireland, regretting its various enjoyments, she felt as if deprived of everything pleasant or desirable ...'.[14] The incident where her sister Ann had given away a precious roll of silk to a needy family, followed by the deaths of both Ann and her mother soon afterwards, became significant landmarks on Nano's journey. These she read as important directives for her future. Was she helped in this by some Jesuit? We cannot be sure. The poverty she witnessed in Dublin and the lack of familiarity among some of her neighbours in Ballygriffin with the official teachings of the Church strengthened her resolve to do something, but she could not see a way. Soon she was back in mainland Europe (Ypres or Paris?) seeking out the peace of cloistered life. Bishop Florence McCarthy, in his anniversary sermon, reports that:

> Her spiritual director was actuated to discourage and oppose her intention of remaining. He dissuaded Miss Nagle from indulging her inclination for a cloistered life in France.[15]

Who was this spiritual director? From Canon William Hutch, we get some clues. His biography of Nano Nagle was published in 1875. He writes:

> Severe mental trials affected her health ... She determined to seek relief in the counsel of a pious and enlightened spiritual director. With this intent she placed herself in the hands of a Jesuit father, remarkable for his prudence and skill in the direction of souls. His advice was that she should return to Ireland ...[16]

We do not have the name of this Jesuit priest, but we know that his influence, under God, on the course of Nano's life from that time onwards was immense.

Humble Beginnings in Cork

The name of Fr Patrick Doran SJ, uncle to Fr Francis Moylan (later Bishop Moylan), is entwined with all of Nano's attempts to bring the Ursulines to Ireland and with the establishment of the first Catholic schools in the city. He is the Mr Doran, frequently mentioned in her letters. He was a learned and wise counsellor, with experience as Professor in Toulouse and as pastor in Paris. He was well acquainted with the positive effects of *Les Petites Écoles* in France, and also with the deprivation and needs of Irish youth. He, with his nephew, Dr Moylan, may be considered as co-founders with Nano Nagle of the Ursuline and Presentation Congregations, according to Sr Ursula Clarke, author of *The Ursulines in Cork*.[17] Not everyone agrees with that. However, one cannot deny the significant role played by Fr Doran SJ in the guidance of Nano Nagle and in offering encouragement and support in her projects.

> It was Fr Doran who suggested a convent of the Ursuline Order as that best calculated to promote Nano's objective ...

> The Jesuit, Father Patrick Doran, was God's special instrument in the coming of the Ursulines to Cork.

It was Fr Doran who directed the vocation of Elizabeth Coppinger, one of the earliest novices. Nano trusted his judgement in the direction of two other unnamed aspirants. In 1770, when 'vexatious difficulties' were being experienced in Paris by the early candidates Eleanor Fitzsimons, Margaret Nagle and Elizabeth Coppinger (these 'difficulties' were not unrelated to the Jansenist-Jesuit battles), Nano consulted Fr Doran. He went to Paris to assess the situation and to iron out the problems. It would seem that Jesuits were very much involved in creating the climate in Penal Ireland where the Ursuline foundation would be received. I quote once again from Sr Mary Pius O'Farrell:

> We learn about the painful reality that Nano's planned Ursuline foundation earned mostly disapproval, so much so that Fr John Austin SJ in Dublin lost interest in the project until Fr O'Halloran SJ told him the real good news ...

And she adds: 'Over all the good work done in secret, Fr Doran SJ kept a watchful eye ...'[19]

Unfortunately, Fr Doran did not live to see the arrival of the Ursulines in Cork. He died in February 1771, just three months before they arrived. It is interesting to note that the Ignatian motto of *Soli Deo Gloria* is incorporated into the coat of arms of the Cork Ursulines. Did Fr Doran and/or other Jesuits have a hand in that? We can only guess.

The names of three Jesuits feature in the final decade of Nano's life, when her sights were set on the continuation of her 'work of God' through the Sisters of Charitable Instruction of the Sacred Heart. The first is Fr James O'Halloran SJ (1726–1800), already mentioned in connection with the Ursuline foundation. He maintained interest in all of Nano's work right up to the end. A native of Limerick, he joined the Jesuits in France and returned to Ireland during the suppression of the Jesuits there in 1763. He was appointed catechist in the Cathedral Parish, Cork, by Bishop Butler.[20] In that position, he was well placed to evaluate the contribution Nano's schools were making to Church and society in Cork. He kept regular contact with Fr John Austin SJ of St Michan's Parish in Dublin, who was advisor and friend to Teresa Mulally. Both Jesuits are frequently mentioned in the correspondence between Nano and Teresa. Fr John Austin SJ (1717–1784), almost an exact contemporary of Nano Nagle, was born in Dublin and educated in France, where he joined the Jesuits. When the Jesuits were suppressed he returned to Dublin, where he devoted his energies to Catholic education. He founded a school for boys in Saul's Court in St Michan's parish, and 'he was a staunch supporter of Teresa Mulally's poor schools.'[21] John Austin House in Cabra, Dublin, which still exists today, gets its name from this champion of Dublin's poor.

Lastly, mention must be made of Fr Nicholas Barron SJ, who presided at the first elections held for the new Institute of Charitable Instruction of the Sacred Heart. This took place on 8 September 1780. Nano was elected Superioress of the fledgling community consisting of three others, Elizabeth Burke (Sr Augustine), Mary Fouhy (Sr Joseph) and Mary Ann Collins (Sr Angela). Two years later in 1782 the same Fr Nicholas Barron preached a sermon at the Reception ceremony of Miss Oliffe. Nano refers to this as 'a very fine sermon' in her letter to Teresa Mulally afterwards. The full text of this sermon on 'The Qualities of a Sister of the Sacred Heart' is to be found in Sr Mary Pius O'Farrell's *The Breaking of Morn*.[22] The sermon begins with a reference to the office and duty of a Sister of the Sacred Heart:

> No office under heaven is, in the eyes of God, more honourable: It is nothing less than being co-partner with Christ in the completion of the redemption of the world ... Examine well your heart, and see whether it is impelled by the Spirit of God, having no other view than His greater honour and glory ...[23]

Conclusion

From the limited list of examples given, it becomes evident that sustained connections existed between Nano Nagle and many Jesuit priests in Dublin, Cork and mainland Europe. Because some, at least, of these Jesuits were also Nano's spiritual directors, the connections cannot be without significance for the development of her spirituality. Apart from this, their role as advisers and monitors of the steps she took in beginning what she calls 'a work of God' cannot be discounted.

Part Two: Tracing Jesuit Influence in the Letters of Nano Nagle

Because the number of possible references is so extensive, and beyond the scope of this chapter, I will concentrate on indicative samples, under the following headings:
> Discerning the Divine Will
> Seeking the honour and glory of God
> Devotion to the Sacred Heart/Antidote to Jansenism.

The list is not meant to be exhaustive. I hope it will invite further reflection on the topic.

Discerning the Divine Will

This presupposes a keen awareness of God at work in daily experience and in the surrounding environment. Ignatius would call this 'Discernment of Spirits.' He recognised as 'a divine gift' the discovery he made at Manresa in the sixteenth century that God communicates His will (today we would probably say 'God's desire' or 'God's dream') directly with the human person through feelings of joy or desolation. He re-discovered the ancient prophetic insight that it is possible, through personal and communal discernment, to seek out and discover God's direction for one's life, which both Ignatius and Nano call 'the Divine Will.' The art of discerning good and evil spirits is among the most notable divine gifts associated with Ignatius and his followers. Nano speaks of discernment (without using the word) several times in her letters. She is also an exemplary practitioner of it.

Writing to Eleanor Fitzsimons regarding a huge disappointment, when her project is delayed, she refers to God's design: 'It has pleased God to order things otherwise ...'.[24] She attributes her success to the divine purpose at work in her life. To the same person:

> You see, it has pleased the Almighty to make me succeed, when I had everything as you may say, to fight against.[25]

And again, in a telling manner, she recognises God's design in the trials that have come her way:

> It pleased the Divine Will to give me severe trials in this foundation, yet it is to show that it is His work, and has not been effected by human means.[26]

God is actively at work in her universe:

> Divine Providence has ordered everything for the best ...[27]
> ... My impatience made me not submit to His Divine Will as I ought ...[28]

Regarding divine approval of teaching in her poor school, she uses an Ignatian phrase: 'to take delight':

> It shows a particular call from the Great God to take delight in it.[29]

Referring to a ministry conducted by the Sisters of St Thomas of Villeneuve for penitents, she tells Teresa Mulally that a certain person 'was honoured in these employments, wherein she found most solid consolation ...'.[30] One can easily understand how this kind of discernment led Nano herself to set up a house for penitents in Cork in her later years.

Seeking the Honour and Glory of God

Ignatius in his earlier life as a soldier had sought military glory as a goal. After his conversion, the focus changed to seeking the Glory of God. The Ignatian motto of *Ad Majorem Dei Gloriam* – for the greater glory of God – is found in various guises in Nano's writings. To Teresa Mulally, actively engaged in seeking a stable foundation for her work among the poor of Dublin, Nano writes: '(I) am confident that the great God will direct you to what is most to His glory.'[31] Expressing concern for the health of her friend, and a concern that a Rule of Life be established for the Dublin group, she writes: 'I think none can tend more to His honour and glory in the world than it does.'[32] On hearing of a certain Miss Bellew willing to assist Teresa Mulally in her hour of need, Nano writes: 'I hope the Almighty will direct (to) what is most to His honour and glory.'[33]

In summary, it can be said that the focus of Nano's endeavours was 'the honour and glory of God'. This was the mystical dimension of her action on behalf of persons who were poor or sick or neglected or oppressed and of her dream for an extension of that work of liberation across the globe. Within that optic, the 'works' she accomplished found their meaning. This explains her preoccupation with 'the honour and glory of God'. The tradition was honoured by her followers. The first page of the Constitutions of 1801 begins with the Ignatian motto: *Ad Majorem Dei Gloriam.*

Devotion to the Sacred Heart/Anti-Jansenism

It has been noted that Nano was among the first (if not the very first) to introduce devotion to the Sacred Heart to Ireland. Influenced by her negative experience of Jansenism in mainland Europe, and by positive memories of Devotion to the Sacred Heart during her school days at Ypres, she named her fledgling Congregation, Sisters of Charitable Instruction of the Sacred Heart. The first residence of the Sisters was known as the House of the Sacred Heart.

There is one clear reference in Nano's letters to Jansenism, and another which offers a clue to Nano's attitude towards it. The first occurs in her letter to Eleanor Fitzsimons early in 1770, regarding the suffering endured by the novice, Margaret Nagle, in Paris at the Convent of St Joseph:

> Had I known that the Filles de Saint Joseph were Jansenist(s) I should never have sent her there.[34]

The other reference is less explicit, but it gives us a sense of where Nano stands in regard to the type of strict discipline typical of some French communities. She writes:

> I think religious discipline [sic of the sort mentioned] would be too strict for this country, and own I should not rejoice to see it kept up.[35]

Sr Mary Pius O'Farrell offers a fitting summary:

> Vital to any consideration of her spirituality is her aversion to Jansenism ... Nothing that could be written about Nano Nagle is of more importance than her deep and life-long trust in the Heart of Jesus.[36]

Nine years after Nano's death (1793), when refugees from French convents arrived in Cork, Fr Lawrence Callanan OFM respected the tradition by placing the Sisters under the protection of the Sacred Heart. He was also involved with the sisters in the drafting of the first Constitution. From T. J. Walsh's history we learn that

> Statute 157 of the final draft of the Constitutions ... was a reminder of the foundress's boundless love of the Passion and her reparation of love to the Sacred Heart in the Blessed Eucharist.[37]

The fact that direct references to the Sacred Heart do not occur in the preserved letters of Nano can be explained by the fact that the devotion was so novel at that time and still under suspicion in certain quarters. Even though the devotion had been officially recognised by Pope Clement XIII in 1765, it was not widespread. Nano's reticence in this matter is in keeping with her stated policy of 'not making a noise' about things.

An interesting note appears in the Annals of South Presentation (1793), written just nine years after the death of Nano. It concerns the difficulties experienced by the newly founded and impoverished community in Killarney. They were given 'several occasions of practising that poverty of which their Master had given them an example.' The Annalist continues:

> They felt, however, that in possessing God, they had found all things: 'Only give me Thy grace and Thy love; I am then sufficiently rich, and nothing more do I ask.' (Saint Ignatius).

To this convincing postscript one other may be added. It comes from the pen of Dr William Hutch, one of Nano's earliest biographers, establishing the connection between Nano and Ignatius:

> We need not hesitate to affirm that the Church has gained more largely by the life and labours of Nano Nagle than by the exertions of any one of her children since the days of Ignatius of Loyola.[38]

Conclusion

There are many important inferences to be drawn from this preliminary study. The Presentation charism, as it evolved in the founding years, was hugely influenced by Ignatian persons and perspectives. This has implications for Presentation spirituality today as it seeks to draw from original wellsprings. The Jesuit influence cannot be discounted in any consideration of the evolving charism.

Endnotes

1. I am indebted to Dr Maura Cronin of the History Department in Mary Immaculate College, University of Limerick, for introducing me to the complexity of the term 'Penal Laws' and the variety of ways in which restrictive laws on Catholic practice were applied in early eighteenth-century Ireland.
2. Sr Mary Pius O'Farrell, *Nano Nagle, Woman of the Gospel* (Cork: Cork Publishing, 1996), 7.
3. T. J. Walsh, *Nano Nagle and the Presentation Sisters* (Dublin: Gill & Sons, 1959), 24–6.
4. See Walsh, *Nano Nagle*, 30–2 on Garret Nagle's business interests in Flanders. For Irish connections among French military personnel, see Patrick Nolan, *The Irish Dames of Ypres* (New York: Benziger Brothers, 1908), 15–18.
5. Jansen's *Augustinus* was published posthumously in 1640.
6. Nolan, *The Irish Dames*, 29.
7. Author of *From Acorn to Oak. A Study of Presentation Foundations 1775–1968*.
8. Letter of Dame Bernard Stewart of Kylemore Abbey to Sr Camillus in Presentation Convent Fargo, 1969. Submitted to Union of Presentation Sisters website by Sr Una Burke (2012).
9. Nano makes several references to this Creagh family in her letters.
10. Nolan, *The Irish Dames*, 258. Also, a consideration of the Chronicles of the Benedictine Convent at Ypres, with lists of community members in the seventeenth and eighteenth centuries, reveals that several members had surnames Goulde, Nagle, and Butler. This suggests that Nano had many family connections with Ypres.
11. Nolan, *The Irish Dames*, 260. Also to be acknowledged is the information provided by Jesuit scholar and archivist, Fr Fergus O'Donoghue who reviewed this Paper and made helpful suggestions. The Jesuits were suppressed by Rome in 1773. Irish Jesuits accepted the Brief of Suppression when it reached Dublin in 1774. They became diocesan priests, dropping the initials SJ from their names. Very few Irish Jesuits were to be found in Cork during Penal times, while many ministered in Waterford and Dublin.
12. Union of Presentation Sisters website, *Devotion to the Sacred Heart in the Irish Benedictine Abbey of Ypres*, from the South Presentation Archives, submitted by Sr Rosario Allen.
13. Nolan, *The Irish Dames*, 351. However, through the Brigidine Sisters in Kildare, whose co-founder (the other being Bishop Delaney) was also a boarder in Ypres at the same time as Nano Nagle, devotion to the Sacred Heart was promoted in Kildare Diocese. Fr P. Kelly states that 'the devotion was brought to Ireland around 1752 (to Dungarvan).' See Presentation Sisters, *Reflecting with Nano* (Swords: Levins Print, 2009), 56, with Note.
14. Letter of M. Aloysius Moylan to M. Joseph McLoughlin, cited in Sr M. Pius O'Farrell, *Nano Nagle, Woman of the Gospel*, 60.
15. O'Farrell, *Nano Nagle, Woman of the Gospel*, 64.
16. William Hutch DD, *Nano Nagle. Her life, her Labours and their Fruits* (Dublin: McGlashin & Gill, 1875), Chapter 4.
17. Sister Ursula Clarke, *The Ursulines in Cork 1771–1996* (Cork: Tower Books, 1996), 2.
18. Clarke, *The Ursulines*, 4.
19. Sr Mary Pius O'Farrell, *In Praise of Nano Nagle's Spirituality* (Monasterevin: Union of Presentation Sisters, 2010), 1.
20. Walsh, *Nano Nagle*, 68, Footnote 10. But note also the possible influence

on Nano of another Fr O'Halloran. Fr Joseph Ignatius O'Halloran (1718–1800), also a native of Limerick, chair of theology at La Rochelle until the Suppression of the Society, after which he ministered in Cork (1763–1773). He later became curate in Dublin in Townsend Street. He died in Dublin in 1800. An entry in Presentation Union website, February 19 2014, mentions the likelihood that Nano consulted this Jesuit priest.

21. Walsh, *Nano Nagle*, 67, Footnote 9.
22. Sr Mary Pius O'Farrell, *The Breaking of Morn* (Cork: Cork Publishing Ltd., 2001), no 31, 92. The author of this sermon was discovered to be Fr Nicholas Barron by Sr Pius in 1992 by comparing the handwriting in the sermon with that of the signing of a Profession document at the Jesuit House of Studies.
23. O'Farrell, *The Breaking of Morn*, 96.
24. Nano Nagle to Miss Fitzsimons, AL 17 July 1769, par 1, in Walsh, *Nano Nagle*, 344.
25. Nano Nagle to Miss Fitzsimon, AL 17 July 1769, par 12, in Walsh, *Nano Nagle*, 347.
26. ibid.
27. Nano Nagle to Miss Fitzsimons, AL 13 May 1770, par 2, in Walsh, *Nano Nagle*, 351.
28. Nano Nagle to Miss Fitzsimons, AL 28 September 1770, par 2, in Walsh, *Nano Nagle*, 354.
29. Nano Nagle to Miss Fitzsimons, AL 17 December 1770, par 5, in Walsh, *Nano Nagle*, 356.
30. Nano Nagle to Miss Mulally, AL 30 October 1779, par 3, in Walsh, *Nano Nagle*, 363.
31. Nano Nagle to Miss Mulally, AL 29 September 1776, par 3, in Walsh, *Nano Nagle*, 357.
32. Nano Nagle to Miss Mulally, AL 24 August 1778, par 1, in Walsh, *Nano Nagle*, 358.
33. Nano Nagle to Miss Mulally, AL 30 October 1779, par 1, in Walsh, *Nano Nagle*, 363.
34. Nano Nagle to Miss Fitzsimons, AL early in 1770, par 3, in Walsh, *Nano Nagle*, 348.
35. Nano Nagle to Miss Fitzsimons, AL 17 July 1769, par 13, in Walsh, *Nano Nagle*, 347.
36. Sr M. Pius O'Farrell, *In Praise of Nano Nagle's Spirituality*, page 4.
37. Walsh, *Nano Nagle*, 164.
38. Hutch, *Nano Nagle*, vi.

'You Did it to Me' (Mt 25:40): The Religious Motivation of Catholic Philanthropy in Eighteenth and Nineteenth-Century Ireland

Frank Steele

The Christian Brothers at their General (Congregational) Chapter at Rome in 1910 decided to introduce the Cause for the Canonisation of Edmund Rice. Two years later, at the behest of the Congregation and in support of that decision, Brother Mark Hill commenced gathering recollections of the Founder extant among the people. Br Hill gave two years to this exercise and the results of his efforts were published some sixty years later.[1] Amongst the recollections gathered by Br Hill there is one relating to John Thomas (aka John Smith) a black boy, known in Waterford as Black Johnnie. The tradition as recounted to Br Hill was that 'Brother Rice saw him with the Captain of a vessel at Waterford Quay. He negotiated the poor boy from the Captain.'[2]

Commenting on this episode, Daire Keogh[3] outlines the scriptural and other spiritual texts which inspired and guided Edmund in good works such as this and, in so doing, adumbrates the specifically faith-based frame of reference which would have been familiar and compelling to Edmund Ignatius Rice, and, indeed, to the great originators of the various religious congregations founded in Ireland in the eighteenth and nineteenth centuries to serve the poor, the Venerable Nano Nagle at their head. Maria Luddy writes:

> Religion was a primary motivating factor in engaging in charitable work in the eighteenth century, as it was in the nineteenth century. Good works were a means toward spiritual salvation and were expected of members of all religious denominations.[4]

Though our focus here will be on Catholicism, this must not be taken to suggest that good deeds towards the afflicted and deprived are the exclusive prerogative of Catholics or, indeed, of Christians. To go no further than the other two Abrahamic faiths, Judaism and Islam, it is clear that, however defined, caring for others is a central constituent of religious faith and practice for their respective adherents.

It bears emphasis that the anti-slavery movement mentioned by Keogh in his observations on this John Smith (aka John Thomas) incident was itself inspired and driven, not just by those whose convictions derived from the Enlightenment, but by Christian believers imbued with specifically religious conceptions of human beings and human relations. The Society of Friends, the Quakers, were exemplary in the exercise of Christian charity towards all, irrespective of race, gender, class or creed. The Anglicans, too, however, emphasized the need for charitable deeds, and the Book of Homilies – which acquired status alongside the BCP [the Book of Common Prayer] and the Thirty-Nine Articles as a repository of Anglican doctrine – includes 'An Homily of Almsdeeds and Mercifulness towards the Poor and Needy' (1864) and in the eighteenth and nineteenth centuries, Charity Sermons – themselves often the occasion of immediate fund-raising, urging people to be generous in supporting one good cause or another, including Charity Schools – were a feature of Anglican life. Such specifically religious perceptions and principles underlay many of the philanthropic initiatives and corresponding institutions in these islands in the eighteenth and nineteenth centuries and must be regarded as important, indeed definitive, constituents of the general world-view of Nano Nagle, Edmund Rice and their respective contemporaries, Catholic, Protestant and Dissenter alike.

Our focus here, though, is on Catholic tradition which is likely to have influenced Edmund most immediately. In negotiating Black Johnnie's freedom, he would have been seen by himself and by his co-religionists as 'redeeming the captive.' *Redemptio captivorum*, the redemption of captives, was, in fact, commonly presented as one of the Seven Corporal Works of Mercy. From the time of the Fathers of the Church, right through the Middle Ages and on into modern times, these were often listed thus: 'Feed the hungry. Give drink to the thirsty. Shelter the homeless. Clothe the naked. Visit the sick. Visit the prisoner. Bury the dead'. In the case of the Sixth of these Seven Works, many sources refer to *visiting* prisoners. In the course of the Middle Ages, and especially in the context of the Crusades and their consequences, the notion and the practice of ransoming Christians held captive by Muslims emerged. There were, in fact, religious orders dedicated to this mode of beneficence, including the Trinitarians, whose members were committed by vow to offer themselves as substitutes for fellow Christians whose liberty could be achieved by no other means. In this *milieu* and against that background, catechetical and other writers and preachers recast the Sixth of the Corporal Works of Mercy to accommodate and to advocate redeeming captives as well as, or, indeed, instead of, visiting, and otherwise assisting, prisoners.

In Catholic teaching, there are three main virtues which govern our relations with others, Justice, Mercy and Charity. The Cardinal Virtue of Justice requires the faithful to give each her/his own; to give to both God and to our human brothers and sisters whatever they are, respectively, entitled to; worship and obedience to God, whatever is rightfully theirs to others. It is worth noting that, from the time of the Fathers of the Church, through the Middle Ages to today, the Church has accepted and taught the doctrine of the universal destination of goods, which, without either renouncing or denouncing the right to private property, insists, nevertheless, that the Creator intended the world, and all that is in it, for the benefit, not of the few, but of all. In this context, the Church has insisted that, in the matter of *bona temporalia*, of temporal, material goods, whatever is superfluous to one's need to support one's self and one's dependents in accordance with one's state is morally and actually the property of the poor. This radical doctrine is dealt with in this way by the influential Augustinian, William Gahan, in his Sermon for the First Sunday after Pentecost, 'On the Necessity and Signal Advantages of Alms and Works of Mercy'.[5] Whilst indicating clearly and emphatically that one is rich or poor by the disposition of God's Providence, and must, in effect, be satisfied with one's lot in life, Gahan – whose Sermons were recommended for parish libraries by Bishop James Doyle of Kildare and Leighlin in 1822 – says:

> [God] has appointed the rich to be the trustees, stewards and co-operators of his Providence, and has absolutely commanded them, as Sovereign Lord and Master of all they possess, to relieve the distressed poor by alms-deeds, according to their respective abilities and wants.[6]

In effect, therefore, the poor were entitled to one's superfluities, to that part of one's wealth which was not necessary to maintain self and family and other dependents in a status-appropriate manner, it being accepted that prince and prelate needed more than pauper to live in a socially and politically becoming level and style. The poor also had a claim on *bona temporalia* held by the Church. According to the canonists, the temporal goods of the Church were the patrimony of the poor and it was, in fact, its duties to the poor that permitted the Church to get, hold and use its wealth. Charity is the theological virtue by which God is loved above all for his own sake and the neighbour – in effect, any human being, 'even those who injure us or differ from us in religion' – as one's self for the love of God. In this two-fold love lies all the Law and the Prophets and, in classic Catholic theology, Christian perfection – the object of all human and, especially, of all religious, life – is perfection in Charity. Whoever loves God above all for his own sake and the neighbour as her/himself for the love of God, is, in God's eyes, a saint, whether known or not, whether canonised or not. Charity, in fact, inspires and suffuses all dealings with the neighbour and, in practical terms, it can be difficult to distinguish acts of the virtue of Charity from those of the virtue of Mercy.

A classic treatment of the Virtue of Mercy is that of St Thomas Aquinas. In the *Secunda Secundae*, the Second Part of the Second Part, of the *Summa Theologiae*, he devotes the four articuli of Quaestio 30 to that virtue.[7] In the concise translation of this section of the *Summa* by McDermott, *Misericordia* is rendered as 'Compassion' and is presented in the following terms: 'Compassion is heartfelt identification with another's distress, driving us to do what we can to help.'[8]

Mercy, therefore, is 'com-passion'. It is 'suffering with' the neighbour in her/his misfortunes. It is, in effect, an identification with, and appropriation of, the hurt of others, a manifestation of our recognition of our common fragility and vulnerability, including and requiring our reaching out in solidarity to relieve the ills, and supply the deficiencies, of others.

St Thomas goes on to treat of Almsgiving, in the ten *articuli* of *Quaestio* 32 and this treatment is thus summarised by McDermott:

> We give alms to relieve need, so almsgiving is an activity of the virtue of compassion ... Traditionally seven bodily and seven spiritual acts of almsgiving have been distinguished. The verse sums them up as: [the Corporal Works] *visit, sup, feed, clothe, ransom, shelter, bury*; [the Spiritual Works] *teach, advise, reprove, comfort, forgive, support and pray*. These acts answer to the various bodily and spiritual needs of our fellowmen.[9]

The Virtues of Justice, Charity and Mercy were presented and explained in the catechisms and spiritual books of the day. The influential Donlevy catechism, of which there were versions in both Irish and English, has the following series of Questions and Answers in The Sixteenth Lesson of Part Two, Of the Christian Virtues, and Good Works:

Q. What is Charity?
A. It is a virtue we receive from the Holy Ghost, which makes us love God above all things, for his own sake; and likewise our neighbour as ourselves, for God's sake.

Q. Are we bound to have this virtue?
A. Yes, most certainly: for no one can be saved without it. 1 *Cor* 13: 1, 2, &c.

Q. How shall we know that we have the love of God above all things?
A. There is no better sign of it, than to love our neighbour as ourselves; for it is false to say that we love God, when we love not our neighbour. 1 *Jn* 4: 20.

Q. How yet shall we know that we love God and our neighbour?
A. We shall know it by our good works: for as the tree is known by its fruit, so shall the righteous man be known by his obedience to the Church, and by his good works. *Mt* 7:16, &c.

In *The Poor Man's Catechism*, one of the most popular works of its kind in Ireland in the eighteenth and nineteenth centuries, recommended for parish libraries by Bishop James Doyle and included amongst the books in the library of the Brothers' school at Hanover Street in Dublin in 1825, having listed both the Seven Corporal, and the Seven Spiritual, Works of Mercy, the English Benedictine, John Mannock writes:

> Great is the obligation of every Christian to relieve, as in his power, his distressed brethren. 'Tis the duty of charity to love your neighbour as yourself; and this not in word only, but in work ... As many ways as our neighbour may be in need, so many ways there are of relieving them, so many works of mercy; as to feed the hungry, to give drink to the thirsty, to clothe the naked, &c. Of the six first we read in St Matthew (c. xxv), of the seventh much is said in the book of Tobias ... There is no virtue more noble than to give charities to others; in this you resemble the great God of nature, *who opens his hand, and fills every creature with blessings.*[10]

As the scriptural citations attest, the Parable of the Sheep and the Goats was both the inspiration and the engine for performance of the Works of Mercy (Mt 25:31-40). On those on his left hand, those who, in not giving food to 'the least', denied it to the king will be pronounced this awful judgement: 'Depart from me, you cursed, into everlasting fire, which was prepared for the devil and his angels' (Mt 25: 41-46, esp. 41).

This Gospel text has engaged the European religious imagination for centuries. Of the many references, direct or indirect, to this pericope, one has proved enormously influential. In his *Vita* of St Martin of Tours, itself of major and enduring consequence in the history of hagiography, Sulpicius Severus recounts an episode in which St Martin, a soldier and still a catechumen, encounters a beggar at the gates of the city of Rheims. It is mid-winter and the beggar is naked. No one responds to the beggar's plight. Martin takes his sword and divides his military cloak in two, giving half to the beggar

> The following night ... when Martin had fallen asleep, he saw Christ clothed in the part of his [Martin's] cloak which he had used to cover the beggar. He was told to look very carefully at the Lord and to recognize the clothing which he had given. Then he heard Jesus saying in a clear voice to the host of angels standing all around, 'Martin who is still a catechumen covered me with his cloak' ...[11]

This incident became a homiletic common-place and, in one version or another, survived in folklore across Europe. It is, for instance, re-told in the often re-printed and widely disseminated – there was a copy in the Hanover Street school library – Butler's *Lives of the Saints*.[12] Under the entry for 11 November, the Feast of St Martin, is summarised in the Fourth Lesson, a part of the Second Nocturn of Matins for Martinmas in the Roman Breviary. It is adumbrated in a kind of folk-tale which presents Christ in one guise or another seeking alms, whether food or shelter, and being accepted or rejected as the case might be, rewarding or punishing the people's compassion or lack of it. The teaching of the catechisms was augmented by that of the spiritual classics of the day. In his letter of 1810 – the earliest of his extant letters – Edmund Rice outlined for Archbishop Bray of Cashel and Emly the conduct of the school at Mount Sion, Waterford, the first establishment and the mother house of the then undivided Society of the Presentation. With particular and immediate reference to provision there for Religious Instruction, Edmund writes:

> At the half hour before twelve o'clock the bell rings for giving general moral instruction, at which time one of the masters

whose turn it is, having the boys all assembled about him, explains the Catechism or out of *Gobinet*, or other books that are deemed fit, gives instruction suited to the capacity of the children.[13]

Normoyle states that the reference to Gobinet is to 'Dr Charles Gobinet of the Sorbonne, author of *The Instruction of Youth in Christian Piety*, written in 1655'. This book was translated into English, was recommended by Bishop Doyle and is included in the Hanover Street library.[14] Under the heading 'Of Charity towards the Poor', Gobinet writes:

> But of all that is said in the Scripture concerning the giving of alms, nothing more clearly evinces the obligations of it, than what the Son of God will say at the day of judgement, to the elect and to the reprobate. To the first he will say – 'Come, ye blessed of my Father, possess the kingdom prepared for you, for I was hungry, and you gave me to eat; I was thirsty, and you gave me to drink; naked and you clothed me, &c'. To the reprobate he will say – 'Depart from me, you cursed, into everlasting fire; for I was hungry, and you gave me not to eat; I was thirsty, and you gave me not to drink, &c'. He adds that what is given or refused to the poor, is given or refused to himself. (Mt 25)[15]

The spiritual classics most widely read in the day impressed on their readers – on, most especially, those blessed by Providence with the goods of this world, such as, for instance, the surviving Catholic landed gentry to which the Venerable Nano Nagle belonged, or the emerging Catholic mercantile class to which Edmund Rice belonged – their obligation to perform the Spiritual and the Corporal Works of Mercy. It was, indeed, by so doing that these, rich in fact, might still be poor in spirit. In his often-translated, widely-disseminated and hugely influential *Introduction to the Devout Life*, also recommended by Bishop Doyle and available at Hanover Street, St Francis de Sales writes:

> Love the poor, and poverty, for so shall you become truly poor, since as the Scripture says, *We are made like the things which we love*. Love makes lovers equal; *Who is weak (saith St. Paul) with whom I am not weak?* He might have said likewise, Who is poor, with whom I am not poor? For love made him like to those whom he lov'd. If then you love the poor, you shall be truly partaker of their poverty, as poor as they ...[16]

Jesus urged his followers to lay up treasure, not on earth, but in heaven (Mt 6: 18-21). From the time of the Fathers, it was accepted that this storing of wealth in heaven could be achieved by means of almsdeeds. In his sermon for the Saturday of Ember Week in Lent, John Gother or Goter,[17] a writer held in high esteem by Nano Nagle,[18] recommended by Bishop Doyle and available at Hanover Street thus urges his readers:

> Let us now then resolve on a better management [of temporal goods], and never throw away that, which, if rightly placed, would serve to purchase heaven. *Whilst thou spendest anything idly, the poor lay claim to it, and say, it is theirs*: they cry aloud, *It is inhumanly taken from them, whatever is thus mispent [sic]*.[19]

In his Consideration, or Meditation, for the Wednesday within the Octave of the Ascension, Richard Challoner, Vicar Apostolic for the London District, 1741-1781 and 'by far the most popular author among eighteenth-century Catholic Dubliners', treats of charity to the poor and, in so doing, highlights the fate of those who, by ignoring the claims of the poor, find themselves before the Judgement Seat of God bereft of the treasure in heaven which almsdeeds would have gained for them:

> Alas! What a figure will their extravagant expenses then make! What account will they be able to give, of all that they have sacrificed to pride, and vanity; to luxury and intemperance; to gaming and criminal diversions! Will not all these robberies of the substance of the poor cry to heaven against them for vengeance at that day?[20]

There is evidence to suggest that compassion towards the afflicted and deprived was a feature of Irish life in the eighteenth and nineteenth centuries. It was, though, the practical compassion of better-off Catholics – such as the Nagles and the Rices – which, from the mid-eighteenth century onwards, established and sustained a whole range of charitable initiatives and institutions for the benefit of their less-well-off compatriots and co-religionists. As lay people, both Nano Nagle and Edmund Ignatius Rice were concerned at the plight of the Catholic poor. Subsequently, as religious, both devoted their lives to supplying the needs of the afflicted and deprived. One of the earliest Annalists of the Sisters of the Charitable Instruction of the Sacred Heart (later the Presentation Order) summarises Nano's over-riding objective thus: 'She intended its members to be devoted solely to works of charity among the poor; and in fine to seek them out in their hovels of misery and want and woe.'²¹ In terms in which her own respect is clearly discernible, Nano herself wrote to Teresa Mulally on 30th October 1779 regarding the Grey Sisters, the Hospitaller Sisters of the Society of St Thomas of Villanova, whose rule was under consideration as a possible template for that of the Sisters of Charitable Instruction of the Sacred Heart, the Presentation Sisters:

> They have different houses for these charities which are most useful. In some houses they take care of the sick, there are others where they instruct orphans, others where they have boys and girls separately, others where they take care of old men and women, others ladies of distinction. They have houses for penitents and in some places, she says, they are of great service to prisoners.²²

Nano herself risked derision and dismissal as a 'galloping nun' (see the Sermon preached by Nicholas Barron SJ, November, 1782)²³ because she wished not to be a cloistered nun so that she and her companions might the better provide, religious education certainly, but also a range of other services to the poor of Cork. Edmund, likewise, was involved in charitable work in Waterford in the 1790s.²⁴ As a 'poor Presentation monk', he did, of course, focus on his schools but, as well as teaching, he also fed and clothed his pupils at Mount Sion and he and his early Brothers were remembered as being zealous in visiting the prisons and in accompanying the condemned to the gallows.²⁵

It was, of course, one of the Seven *Spiritual* Works of Mercy, 'To instruct the ignorant', which emerged as the principal objective of Catholic philanthropy in the period in question. Standard doctrine insisted that, as the soul excels the body, so the Spiritual Works of Mercy excel the Corporal. The tradition recognised and confirmed that, if the neighbour were dying of hunger, one's immediate Christian duty would be, not to teach, but to feed him. In and of itself, though, it was deemed more excellent to instruct the ignorant than to feed the hungry. Throughout the eighteenth and nineteenth centuries, one of the great fears of the Catholic Church in Ireland was that of losing members of the faithful to other Christian denominations. There was a suspicion – not always unsubstantiated – that those other denominations were prepared to go to considerable lengths – often with State support – to draw the faithful from their allegiance to Rome. It was considered that the education, including, above all, the religious education, of the Catholic masses was a *sine qua non* of any effective response by the Hierarchy to what one historian has called 'The Protestant Crusade'.

Those who provided, and those who supported, Catholic education for the poor of Ireland at this time were attempting to address what they saw as the single most serious threat to the spiritual welfare – and, so, to what they would have deemed the highest welfare of all, the eternal welfare – of those they sought to serve by works of mercy and charity. All involved in religious instruction, in particular, clerics, religious and, it bears re-iteration, the hundreds of lay people who, in parishes across the country, taught Christian Doctrine classes before and/or after Mass on Sundays, would have heard or read that 'those who instructed others unto justice would shine like stars for all eternity'. This verse from the Book of Daniel (12:3) was and is adumbrated iconographically in the star incorporated in the institutional crest of some teaching congregations, including those of the Ursulines, the Brothers of the Christian Schools (i.e. the De la Salle Brothers), and, up to comparatively recently, the Brothers of the Christian Schools of Ireland (the Christian Brothers). In its Latin version it was the institutional motto of the Ursulines. It was invoked in sermons, including the Barron sermon of November 1782, at which Nano herself may have been present. It was quoted in the 1832 Rules and Constitutions of the Religious Society of Brothers, i.e., the Christian Brothers.[27]

Instructing the young unto justice was deemed especially praiseworthy. The 1793 version of the Rules and Constitutions of the Sisters of the Congregation of the Charitable Instruction (i.e., the Presentation Sisters) opens thus:

> The principal end of this Religious Institute is the Instruction of poor Girls in the principles of Religion and Christian Piety. In undertaking this very arduous, but most meritorious, task, the Sisters, whom God is graciously pleased to call to this state of perfection, will encourage themselves and animate their zeal by the example of their Divine Master, who shew'd [sic] on all occasions an ardent love for little Children, expressed the greatest pleasure on seeing them approach him, and declared that *whosoever receiveth one of the little ones in his name receiveth him.* [Mt 18:5; italic in original]

Adopted more or less verbatim by Edmund and his first companions in the 1809 Rule of the original and undivided Society of the Presentation, this saying of Jesus was understood to indicate that to welcome a child into one's school was to welcome Christ himself.

In this regard, alone amongst the Spiritual Works of Mercy, that which urged the instruction of the ignorant, established, at least in the case of the child, an identification of the Saviour and the object of one's compassion in a way otherwise associated with the Corporal Works. Just as when one feeds the hungry, one feeds Christ, so when one receives the child, one receives Christ. In effect, in admitting the child, the poor child in particular, to one's school, one admitted Jesus and it was, by implication, Jesus himself who was thus served by those who founded, by those who conducted, and by those who, by their alms and other assistance, supported, schools in which the poor especially were instructed in the Catholic faith.

'You did it to me' is a clear and direct assertion of Jesus which may be taken to indicate and summarise a mind-set, a way of seeing the world, which evoked and guided Catholic philanthropy in Ireland in the eighteenth and nineteenth centuries.

Endnotes

1. M.C. Normoyle, *Memories of Edmund Rice* (Dublin: Christian Brothers, 1977).
2. Normoyle, *Edmund Rice*, 267.
3. Daire Keogh, *Edmund Rice and the First Christian Brothers* (Dublin: Four Courts Press, 2008), 64-9.
4. Maria Luddy, Foreword, in M.H. Preston, *Women and Philanthropy, and the Language of Charity in Nineteenth-Century Dublin* (London: Praeger, 2004), x.
5. Daire Keogh, 'Gahan, William', *Dictionary of Irish Biography* (Cambridge: Cambridge University Press for the Royal Irish Academy, 2009).
6. W. Gahan, *Sermons and Moral Discourses for all the Sundays and Principal Festivals of the Year* ... In Two Volumes, Third Edition, Revised and Corrected (Dublin: Richard Coyne, 1825), 285-6.
7. Thomas Aquinas, *Summa Theologiae* in 60 vols, Vol.34, R.J. Batten (ed.) (London: Eyre and Spottiswoode, 1975), II-II, Q 30.
8. Thomas Aquinas, *Summa Theologiae: A Concise Translation*, Timothy McDermott (ed.) (Notre Dame, IN: Ave Maria Press, 1991), 360.
9. Aquinas, *Summa Theologiae*, McDermott (ed.), 362.
10. J. Mannock, *The poor man's catechism; or, the Christian doctrine explained. With short admonitions. This edition is newly revised, and much amended, by the Rev. B. McM.* (Dublin: MDCCXCIV), 261-2.
11. C. White (ed.), *Early Christian Lives* (Harmondsworth: Penguin, 1998), 137-8.
12. A. Butler, *Lives of the Saints* (Dublin: 1779), 204-28.
13. Normoyle, *Memories of Edmund Rice*, 3.
14. O'Toole, *A Spiritual Profile*, 299.
15. C. Gobinet, *Instructions for Youth in Christian Piety* (Dublin: James Duffy & Sons, 1872), 208.
16. Francis de Sales, *An Introduction to a devout life* ... *Faithfully rendered into English* (Dublin: 1705), Part III, Ch. 15 iv-vi, 1705, 205-26.
17. S. Handley, 'Goter, John (d.1704), *Oxford Dictionary of National Biography* (Oxford: Oxford University Press, 2004).
18. Raphael Consedine, *Listening Journey: A Study of the Spirit and Ideals of Nano Nagle and the Presentation Sisters* (Victoria, The Congregation of the Presentation of the Blessed Virgin Mary, 1983), 81.
19. Gother, J. (1704-1740?), *The Spiritual Works of John Gother* 16 vols (Dublin: Wogan and Cross, 1792), III, 96-7.
20. R. Challoner, *Considerations upon Christian truths and Christian duties digested into meditations for every day of the year*, 2 vols (London: 1754), 297-8.
21. T. J. Walsh, *Nano Nagle and the Presentation Sisters* (Dublin: M. H. Gill and Son, 1959), 99.
22. T. J. Walsh, *Nano Nagle*, 363.
23. Mary Pius O'Farrell, *Nano Nagle Woman of the Gospel* (Cork: Cork Publishing, 1996); idem, *Breaking of Morn Nano Nagle (1718-1784), Francis Moylan (1735-1815)* (Cork: Cork Publishing, 2001), 92-9, esp. 97.
24. Keogh, *Edmund Rice*, 68-9.
25. Keogh, *Edmund Rice*, 99.
26. O'Farrell, *Breaking of Morn*, 92-9.
27. E. R. Hickey, Rule and Constitutions of the Society of Religious Brothers 1832, *Inheritance: Collection Two*, (Rome: Congregation of Christian Brothers. For private circulation, 1982), 395.

Part Three

Presentation Vision

'Consider the Mustard Seed': From Nano's Humble Beginnings to Disproportionate Growth

Mary T. O'Brien PBVM

One of the most powerful ways of entering into the spirit of Nano Nagle is to read her own words as we find them recorded in her sixteen letters, plus a fragment of another, which are accessible to us today.[1] Seven of these letters and the fragment were addressed to one person, an Ursuline novice in Paris, Sister Angela Fitzsimons between July 1769 and December 1770. These are addressed to Miss Fitzsimons (as distinct from the title, Sister) by Nano because of the Penal ban on anything that could be interpreted as related to the Catholic faith. The other nine were addressed to Nano's friend, Teresa Mulally, in Dublin between September 1776 and January 1783. Eight of these letters are in the archives at George's Hill, Dublin. The other, dated August 1770, is in the Presentation Convent at Newburgh, New York. How it got there is not certain, but Newburgh and St Michael's on 33rd Street can trace their origins to Dublin.

The letters addressed to Miss Fitzsimons, while they carry a lot of valuable information about Nano herself, her concerns and dreams and also about the poverty and suffering of people in Cork city in Penal times, are focused largely on encouraging the three Ursuline novices destined for Nano's apostolate in Cork. The nine letters addressed to Teresa Mulally are concerned more with the economics of a possible foundation in Dublin and the beginnings of Nano's new Congregation in Cork, the Sisters of Charitable Instruction of the Sacred Heart of Jesus. Although these letters are scant in many respects, they cover a most important segment of Nano's life and the beginnings of our Congregation. Of course we wish that we could access the many other letters she must have written and received. We would love to discover the contents of Nano's desk as well as the trunk of documents appropriated after her death by her agent, the Cork merchant Thomas Roche.[2] Nevertheless, we can assemble, from the letters available to us, some significant elements, if not a complete portrait of Nano Nagle, woman of astounding faith and courage.

The first thing that strikes one on reading her letters is the recurrence of certain images and themes from Scripture. From other evidence, and particularly from the fragment of her Bible now on display in the South Presentation Convent in Cork, it is clear that Nano made the Word of God her guiding light in a very particular way. That relic (part of her personal Bible) in South Presentation shows many well-used, well-fingered pages. This gives us some important clues to her spirituality. We can say with confidence that her spirituality was biblically influenced. While she does not quote Scripture directly in her letters, images and phrases from the New Testament in particular are obvious on almost every page. One of these is the image of the mustard seed. It must have been a kind of life-line for her, a mainstay of her firm belief that God could bring growth – even disproportionate growth – from tiny and humble beginnings.

Before dealing directly with Nano's reference to the mustard seed, it will be well to begin by recalling its source in the New Testament. There are five references in all in the gospels, two in Matthew, two in Luke and one in Mark. The women and men who listened to Jesus building a parable around the mustard seed would have been well aware that the mustard seed is tiny, as small as the head of a pin, and that its growth from tiny seed to mature plant is swift, and its capacity to spread is quite phenomenal. Some would have been very slow to plant it in their gardens. A second-century Jewish document, known as the Mishnah, actually forbids the planting of mustard seed in Palestinian gardens because 'it grows wild, gets out of control and attracts unwanted birds, who disturb the gardens.'[3] Once you plant that mustard seed, you cannot control its growth.

Three of those New Testament references to the mustard seed occur in the parables section of the Synoptic Gospels referring to the Kingdom of Heaven (Mt 13:31–32; Mk 4:30–32 and Lk 13:18–19). The settings in all three contexts are similar. Jesus is teaching about the 'mysteries of the Kingdom'. 'What is the Kingdom of God (Reign of God) like?' asks Jesus in Mark and Luke. No such question precedes the teaching in Matthew. The word-picture and simile follow in all three cases, with slight variations. Nano must have pondered the parable well, with its many implications.

Mt 13:31–32 reads in the New Jerusalem Bible translation:

> The Kingdom of Heaven is like a mustard seed, which a man took and sowed in his field. It is the smallest of all the seeds but when it has grown it is the biggest shrub of all, and

becomes a tree, so that the birds of the air come and shelter in its branches.

Mk 4:30–32 reads:

He also said, 'What can we say the Kingdom of God is like?' What parable can we find for it? It is like a mustard seed, which at the time of its sowing in the soil is the smallest of all the seeds on earth. Yet once it is sown it grows into the biggest shrub of them all and puts out big branches so that the birds of the air can shelter in its shade.

Lk 13:18–19 reads:

He went on to say, 'What is the Kingdom of God like? What shall I compare it
with? It is like a mustard seed which a man took and threw into his garden; it
grew and became a tree, and the birds of the air sheltered in its branches.

It appears likely that Nano pondered the implications of this parable for her and for her dream. We have reason to assume that the conviction grew in her that small steps taken, like sowing a tiny seed in faith, could bring results out of all proportion. She worked to this parable, drawing strength from it as we shall see, and she wrote confidently about it as well.

Two other references to the mustard seed in the New Testament are worth considering, before we return to Nano's own writings. In the following two examples the context is different. We are dealing with the Sayings of Jesus, but with these as related to a particular action. The issue in both cases is faith. In the case of Mt 17:20, Jesus has healed an epileptic, where his disciples had failed to do so. Afterwards the disciples come to the Master privately to ask why they could not succeed. His answer is a little surprising:

I tell you solemnly, if your faith were the size of a mustard seed, you could say to this mountain, 'Move from here to there' and it would move. Nothing would be impossible for you.

Lk 17:5–6 presents the mustard seed in a slightly different context, but with a similar message. That context is the seemingly impossible task of repeatedly forgiving an offending brother. The disciples ask

Jesus: 'Must we forgive seven times a day?' In other words, 'Must our forgiving be never-ending?' They must have been hoping for a 'reasonable' answer. But they were in for a shock. Jesus gives a very surprising answer, which seems in fact to be the answer to another question. He replies: 'Yes, and seventy times seven'. They rightly surmise that this is beyond them, indeed well nigh impossible, so they make a plea: 'Increase our faith'. They want more of whatever it takes to forgive like that. And Jesus says in effect: No, you do not need more. You do not need large quantities ... You just need a tiny bit of the real thing. And this is where the mustard seed appears again:

> Were your faith the size of a mustard seed, you could say to this mulberry tree, 'Be uprooted and planted in the sea' and it would obey you.

From these two latter examples we note that the mustard seed image is linked very much to doing things that are perceived as impossible – healing of an incurable disease and forgiving without limit.

For Nano Nagle, promoting the reign of God in a particular way in the dangerous circumstances of Penal Ireland surely involved facing the impossible – or, as one of our Chapter documents expresses it – 'moving beyond the possible'. It meant acting with a faith that could overcome all obstacles. The gospel image of the mustard seed, understood in both senses – as image of disproportionate growth and as image of powerful faith that moves mountains – informed her thinking and her acting. This she loves to address in her letters.

In her Letter of 1770 to Miss Fitzsimons, the Ursuline novice in Paris, relating to plans for the Cork foundation and the prospect of a possible leader for the group, Nano writes: 'She may be compared to the grain of mustard seed in the gospel ... and the good seed she will sow will spread.' We note the confidence here. There is no 'perhaps' no 'maybe' but utter assurance: 'The good seed she will sow *will* spread.'[4] The little step taken in faith will surely yield results. In her Letter of 29 April 1770 to the same Miss Fitzsimons, Nano speaks in the same vein, as if foreseeing the future growth of her project:

> I build more on the success of it [the project] from that poor way [in which] it first took its rise than any means [wealth] it has pleased God to give me at present to carry it on ... as in all appearance several [establishments] may spring from this.[5]

Again to the same person in another letter dated 13 May 1770, referring to the good work (the establishment of the Ursuline foundation in Cork), Nano writes with amazing assurance of the disproportionate growth that is to attend her seed-sowing: 'You will see it prosper far beyond what one has a right to expect in a country such as this.'[6]

In her letter to her friend, Teresa Mulally, in Dublin in 1783, Nano expresses a similar sentiment:

> Though neither you nor I should live to see it [the Presentation foundation] prosper in our time, yet I hope to see it prosper hereafter [later on] and be of service to the Kingdom.[7]

In another letter to Teresa Mulally, 29 September 1776, Nano speaks characteristically of her inadequacy as she invites three persons to help her in the work: 'The Almighty makes use of the weakest means to bring about his works.'[8] She has a preference for humble, small 'noiseless' beginnings. Twice she states that she does not want 'to make a noise' about what she is doing. One would expect such discretion in the climate of Penal times, and one would expect that Nano would mention such a reason. But she does not. Her declared reason for choosing small and 'noiseless' beginnings is 'to show that it is God's work and has not been effected by human means'.[9] Regularly in her letters she mentions 'growth by degrees': 'By degrees, with the assistance of God, we may do a great deal.'[10]

One of the most inspiring traits in Nano Nagle is her courage. Just think of her, laying her life on the line, the 'reluctant prophet' as Sr Mary Pius O'Farrell describes her,[11] taking the first tentative steps in faith as she left an attractive lifestyle in Paris, then a possible haven of peace in a French (or Flemish) convent, to set up her first school for thirty poor and ragged children in Cove Lane in Cork. 'Though the laws might prevent her from doing as much as she wished, they could not prevent her from doing what lay in her power.' She did 'what lay in her power'[12] even when, as she states in her letter of July 1769[13] she 'had everything to fight against'. At this stage she did not have the support of family or church or friends. The odds were stacked against her, but she stood firm, ready to give all – her personal gifts, the good life of Paris, her entire fortune: 'The Almighty makes use of the weakest means to carry out His work. Gradually ... we may do a great deal.'

And so it happened. Nano knew herself to be engaged in a divine project and she had more than a premonition that the work would prosper. The phrase, 'all in my power' is a very interesting one. It occurs at least ten times in her letters. I think it is not unrelated to the mustard seed image. Doing 'all in one's power' may simply mean planting a tiny seed. Growth is automatic if the conditions are right. But the act of planting it in the soil is vital. This is the risk-taking act of faith. Of this Nano was sure, and the story of Presentation beginnings is linked with her practical faith - a faith which led her to do 'all in her power' at a given time, to plant the mustard seed available to her, trusting the outcome and the growth to Divine Providence.

Gradually Nano found herself in the midst of a self-fulfilling prophecy. The growth came in abundance. Requests came pouring in for more of 'Miss Nagle's schools'. Gradually too, her family came to see and understand her mission. Her uncle Joseph, while objecting at first because of fear for his life and for that of the entire family, eventually came to admire the courage and determination of his niece and put all his considerable wealth at her disposal. Gradually the poorest of the poor, in school and street and hovel, saw their dignity respected as a future of a different kind – a future full of hope – loomed out before them. Soon Cork city had five schools for girls and two for boys. The mustard seed was sprouting. Because of the many trade links between Cork and the New World, soon there were boys being educated in the West Indies, because, in Nano's own words: 'My views are not for one object alone.'

Then there were homeless and sick women in Cork who needed compassion and healing. Nano responded by visiting these in their homes and attics and mud cabins, bringing what medical and spiritual comfort she could, often putting her own life at risk as she trod the unlit alleyways at night, guided only by the light of a flickering lantern. Building a hostel for homeless women had been her life's dream. Eventually, before she died, this was to be accomplished. 'Not words but deeds' – the motto of the Nagle family – became the motto of this courageous Lady of the Lantern. Echoes of the Letter of St James about 'doing what the Word tells you' may well have merged in her imagination with the mustard seed parable to provide motivation and inner strength. 'Not words but deeds.' Nano surely took that motto to heart, acting on it with tiny faith-inspired steps, taking in children 'by degrees' as she says, 'not making a noise about it', going wherever the Spirit led her, always in the awareness that her small steps in faith would yield a hundredfold in due time.

Planning for the future became necessary. Setting up her fledgling ministry on a stable footing caused her much agony and a lot of extra work. To this end, enlisting the help of Dr Moylan, and assisted ably by his uncle Fr Doran SJ, who had many connections in France, Nano set about establishing the first Irish Ursuline foundation in Cork. The difficulties associated with this project were immense.

When eventually three Irish candidates were found (one of whom was Eleanor Fitzsimons – the Miss Fitzsimons who features so much in Nano's Letters) – candidates who would undergo Novitiate training in France and then return to Ireland, Nano could not find a professed Religious who was willing to head up the foundation. At the end of an intensive search on the part of both Nano and Dr Moylan, one Sister Margaret Kelly of Dieppe/Rouen agreed. On many occasions it must have seemed as if the dream was doomed to failure, as if the mustard seed had perished and the future was very uncertain. But Nano's faith never flagged: 'We do not know what is best for us ... and so we ought to be resigned to the divine will.'

Eventually the Sisters came, having travelled by boat from Le Havre to Cork. Nano welcomed them to the convent she had prepared for them in Cove Lane. It seemed her troubles were over now. It was presumed that she would join the new community and profess religious vows. Instead she chose to live in a little cell on the grounds, while continuing to teach the catechism in her schools by day and visit the sick poor in their homes at evening time. This must have been an agonizing time for her as she tried to discern the next steps.

Her refusal to join the Ursuline community caused a temporary but strong disagreement between herself and Dr Moylan. The Ursuline Rule of enclosure put limits on the availability of the Ursuline Sisters for the kind of ministry Nano envisaged. She would start all over again, even if she had to leave the diocese and move elsewhere, trusting in 'the power of the Almighty', plant another mustard seed, and seek out helpers who would be free to share her vision and her strategy.

Once again, the search for such helpers was beset by difficulties on all sides. Prospective candidates for the ministry came and soon departed, their health unequal to the task in hand. A person of less courage than Nano would have given up the struggle. After all she was now fifty-seven-years-old, and 'listening to the will of heaven' was a painful process. Could she dare to begin to open another path? Could she plant another tiny mustard seed? Yes, this is exactly what she did, as eventually, in 1775, with three companions, Mary Fouhy, Elizabeth Burke, and Mary Ann Collins, she laid the humble foundations of a new religious congregation in Cove Lane in Cork. We are told that 'few wished to join her rag-tag establishment, her walking nuns' (some called them rather disrespectfully, 'the galloping nuns'), but Nano would not be diverted from what she perceived as the divine call. She professed simple vows on 24 June 1777 in the presence of Bishop Butler and her three novice-companions. The Annalist tells us: 'Thus did she devote her person and her wealth to the gratuitous instruction of the poor and destitute little ones of the Lord.'

Her three companions were professed on the same day. The beginnings of this new Congregation were humble indeed, and it was appropriate that the first Christmas for Nano's family should be marked by celebrating dinner with fifty beggars – the poorest of Cork's poor. Nano herself, we are told, was first to serve the food, and she stood in joy behind the beggars' chairs as they relished the Christmas meal.

From the humblest of beginnings and many trials the Congregation became known 'by degrees' as a work of God. Soon, because of Cork's many trade-links in other countries, bishops from around the world began to seek Sisters to begin the work of Catholic education in their dioceses. Among the earliest of these requests was one which came from Nano's adviser and friend, Bishop Moylan, now Bishop of the neighbouring diocese of Kerry. He requested two sisters to begin a good work in Killarney. Of course she had to refuse – though a foundation in Killarney was made some seventeen years later. After all there were only four sisters in her small Cove Lane community. Gradually, however, by the last decade of the eighteenth century, within a few years of Nano's death, small groups of Presentation Sisters moved to other towns and cities, and eventually across the globe, to carry the torch already lit in Cork:

- › 1793 Kilkenny
- › 1793 Killarney
- › 1794 Dublin
- › 1798 Waterford
- › 1833 Newfoundland (the first outside Ireland)
- › 1836 England
- › 1841 India
- › 1854 San Francisco
- › 1866 Tasmania
- › 1873 Australia
- › 1874 Dubuque Iowa
- › 1874 New York
- › 1886 Fitchburg MA, Fargo, North Dakota and Aberdeen, South Dakota
- › 1895 Pakistan
- › 1949 Zimbabwe
- › 1950 New Zealand
- › 1952 San Antonio, Texas
- › 1960 Philippines

- 1966 Papua, New Guinea
- 1967 Alaska
- 1970 Scotland and Zambia
- 1974 Bolivia
- 1981 Chile
- 1982 Ecuador
- 1990 Peru
- 1992 Slovakia and Eastern Europe
- 2013 Holy Land
- 2016 Cambodia[14]

That list is not complete, but the story goes on. The mustard seed still continues to spread across the globe as a charism evolves.

The story of growth from humble beginnings, trusting as Nano did, in the 'power of the Almighty' continued worldwide in the century which followed. It continues to the present day. Each of us, from our own local scene, can tell our mustard seed story and marvel at the way the Providence of God has been guiding the evolution of the charism of Nano down the years – to ministries and places where the light of the Gospel shines through the ministry of other Ladies of the Lantern. Each one of us can choose and ponder on a Presentation mustard seed story that is familiar to us. Think of the many foundations that were made in America, India, Australia, Tasmania, Africa, Latin America, Central America, The Philippines, and elsewhere since 1793. Mother Vincent Hennessy and her companions left Mooncoin, County Kilkenny, for an unknown land in faraway Dubuque in 1874. It took them weeks of travelling by sea and land to get there. A small beginning indeed, but what an outcome! Consider the growth from the day of their arrival – 'with no convent, no place of reception ...' only the hospitality of the Visitation Sisters, and later a borrowed rectory home in Key West. A small convent parlour was the first Presentation school in Iowa. The story of the Hughes sisters on mission to the Dakotas strikes a similar note. They arrived expecting a residence and school and found neither. A tiny log cabin became their classroom by day, their sanctuary, kitchen and sleeping quarters by night. Such stories can be multiplied. They fill the pages of our Annals and archives. Pondering these precious mustard seed stories can be instructive and encouraging.

Nano was creative and courageous in 'reading' the call of God to her through her experience. In the plight of the poor and deprived of her time she heard the call of God. We, her followers, and all who are inspired by her example and her spirit, are called to be no less creative, no less courageous and no less discerning in our time and place. We hold on to the powerful gospel image of the mustard seed, as Nano did, knowing that 'the Almighty makes use of the humblest means to carry out His work'[15] and this, in Nano's words, 'to show that it is His work and is not effected by human means.'[16]

Her vision has the potential to inspire us, and that vision is not narrow. It is broad as the universe:

> My views are not for one object alone. If I could be of any service saving souls in any part of the world, I would willingly do all in my power.[17]

That latter phrase 'all in my power' may best be understood when linked with the Kingdom image of the mustard seed. Nano's determination, her unwavering faith in Divine Providence and her awareness of limitation somehow found their expression in the humble, mighty mustard seed. A beautiful connection between Nano's 'all in my power' and 'the power of the Almighty' finds its exemplification in the powerful metaphor of the mustard seed. They also merge in her life-story, as in that of the Apostle Paul:

> One does the planting, another the watering,
> but it is God who makes things grow. (1 Cor 3:6)

Out of such a theology, Nano lived and prayed and worked. She generously gave her all, 'all in her power', trusting that her efforts in planting seeds would one day yield a harvest blessed by 'the power of the Almighty', with unforeseen success. We have reason to be inspired and encouraged as we reflect on our humble beginnings and on the outcome. Nano would acknowledge that 'it is all God's work and has not been effected by human means'.[18]

This invites a reflection on 'The Power of One', on the difference that one person, one courageous act of faith, one simple planting of a seed can effect. Not words but deeds! The story of Presentation is a truly amazing founding story. It has been repeated in different ways in differing climes and cultures since 1776 as the charism of Nano evolved in new situations. As we reflect on and share our mustard seed stories, we rejoice in our humble beginnings, in our founder's vision and faith and in the vision and faith of the Sisters who have gone before us, on whose shoulders we stand. The mustard seed carries a rich and powerful Kingdom message, a message of hope. Little steps taken in faith do matter. One person's contribution can have repercussions across the globe. In God's great plan of love the

Power of One can change the world for the better. A tiny Mustard Seed planted in faith can grow into something quite surprising and beautiful. The Presentation story is laced with examples of miracle growth from humble beginnings. The Mustard Seed speaks of potential being realized, of a charism in evolution. It gives reason to celebrate and to give thanks.

Endnotes

1. Transcripts of the original letters are now held in the Ursuline Convent, Blackrock, Cork, and in Presentation Convent, George's Hill, Dublin. See T.J. Walsh, *Nano Nagle and the Presentation Sisters* (Dublin: M.H. Gill & Son, 1959), Appendices.
2. Sr Mary Pius O'Farrell, *Nano Nagle, Woman of the Gospel* (Cork: Cork Publishing, 1996), 197–8.
3. J.D. Crossan, *Jesus, A Revolutionary Biography* (New York: Harper Collins, 1994), 66–7.
4. Nano Nagle to Miss Fitzsimons, AL early in 1770, par 1, in Walsh, *Nano Nagle*, 347.
5. Nano Nagle to Miss Fitzsimons, AL 29 April 1770, par 2, in Walsh, *Nano Nagle*, 349.
6. Nano Nagle to Miss Fitzsimons, AL 13 May 1770, par 7, in Walsh, *Nano Nagle*, 352.
7. Nano Nagle to Miss Mulally, AL 31 January 1783, par 2, in Walsh, *Nano Nagle*, 366.
8. Nano Nagle to Miss Mulally, AL 29 September 1776, par 1, in Walsh, *Nano Nagle*, 357.
9. Nano Nagle to Miss Fitzsimons, AL 17 July 1769, par 12, in Walsh, *Nano Nagle*, 347.
10. Nano Nagle to Miss Fitzsimons, AL 28 September 1770, par 4, in Walsh, *Nano Nagle*, 355.
11. Sr Mary Pius O'Farrell, *Nano Nagle, Woman of the Gospel* (Monasterevin: Presentation Sisters 1996), 64.
12. ibid. citing Bishop Florence McCarthy, Anniversary Sermon.
13. Nano Nagle to Miss Fitzsimons, AL 17 July 1769, par 12, in Walsh, *Nano Nagle*, 347.
14. The list of foundations mentioned here refers only to a sample of those in the records of the Union of Presentation Sisters. It is not a complete list. It does not include the multiple foundations linked with the Presentation Society of Australia and Papua New Guinea or of the Conference of Presentation Sisters of North America.
15. Nano Nagle to Miss Fitzsimons, AL 28 September 1770, par 3, in Walsh, *Nano Nagle*, 354.
16. ibid.
17. ibid.
18. Nano Nagle to Miss Fitzsimons, AL 17 July 1769, par 3, in Walsh, *Nano Nagle*, 345.

Edmund Rice and the Presentation Sisters

Beth Hassel PBVM

Nano Nagle and Edmund Rice never met. In fact, Nano was forty-four-years-old when Edmund was born. Because she was so deeply attuned to the needs of the Church in Penal Ireland, and because she met those needs so creatively and effectively, her influence on her fellow visionary was extraordinary. The charism of the two Congregations stemming from Edmund Rice – the Presentation Brothers and the Christian Brothers – can largely be traced to the inspirational vision and evolving charism of Nano Nagle, which Edmund Rice experienced first-hand through his contact with the Presentation Sisters in Waterford. The relationship that was forged between Edmund Rice in Waterford and the charism of the Presentation Sisters in the legacy of Nano Nagle forever changed the Catholic model of education and the sharing of Catholic values in Ireland.

The story of Edmund Rice is largely a story of choices that mattered and relationships that were formed in eighteenth-century Ireland, choices which have informed and transformed the understanding of faith-based service in our world today. He was educated by an Augustinian priest, Fr Patrick Grace[1] and trained in business in Waterford, interning with his Uncle Michael when he was seventeen, a training which would eventually make him a millionaire in today's terms.

At significant points in his life women – such as his mother, wife, daughter and more – played a critical role, appearing to be instruments of God in fashioning his destiny.[2] He became an exemplary leader in his own time, and a real example for the Church in the twenty-first century. Edmund Rice made choices that mattered to him, to his native Ireland, to the Church and to the world. The legacy of Nano Nagle was the reason for a number of significant choices which he made. Inspired by the Presentation Sisters in Waterford, he founded the Society of the Presentation in 1802. The members of this religious Brotherhood were also known as 'Gentlemen of the Presentation'.

Margaret Tierney, his mother, was from a rich family, and taught him to care for others. This sense of care and concern was to be a hallmark of his life:

> My mother was very kind and she never tired of helping other families. She was always caring for the needy traveler or sending us to some poor family's house with a basket of food for them to eat. Prayer was always part of our daily life.[3]

Among the other influential women in his life was a Mrs St Ledger about whom we know little – except that she had two sons who became Jesuit priests. Edmund was a frequent visitor in her home in Waterford and often sought her advice: 'The conversation of this pious lady made a deep impression on him at age seventeen in Waterford'.[4]

His deepest relationship was with Mary Elliott whom he married at age twenty-three in 1785. The historian, Daire Keogh, has described her as a 'fun-loving and hospitable teenager'[5] who shared Rice's sensitivity and compassion for the poor. Keogh, in his volume entitled, *Edmund Rice and the First Christian Brothers*, refers to their home at Ballybricken, Waterford city, as Rice's first school, where the couple fed and clothed poor children, fifteen years before he started his education enterprise in Mount Sion'.[6] Mary died tragically in 1789. It is unclear whether it was by accident or through illness. Keogh has noted that, 'Ironically, Rice's most intimate relationship is the one about which we know the least … no details of his short-lived marriage survived other than the newspaper announcements of the tragic death …'[7] The tragedy of his wife's death played an enormous part in his sense of purpose in life. From this period onwards, Edmund Rice developed a heightened religious and social conscience coupled with a growing sense of a vocation to religious life.[8] He deeply felt this call to mirror the way of life of the Presentations Sisters in Waterford, not only in terms of consecrated life, but also in terms of service to the poor and needy. At the time of his wife's death, their daughter, Mary, was born prematurely. We know little about her and the record is uncertain, but apparently she was delicate or handicapped in some way.[9] According to Keogh, Edmund entrusted his daughter to his brother Patrick.[10] When Patrick died in 1833 Mary moved and remained in the care of cousins until her death in January 1859. Nothing further is known about Rice's relationship with his daughter except that he provided generous financial support for her. After his death the Brothers supported her simply yet adequately.[11]

In 1790 at age twenty-eight, just two years after his wife's death, Edmund Rice collected a group of men in Waterford to form a pious, holy, association. He practiced his faith at daily Mass and embraced the exacting spirituality of the Catholic Counter-Reformation, which was characterized by sacramental devotion, meditation, prayer and the exercise of good works.[12] In 1791, he purchased a Bible, an unusual purchase for a Catholic in Penal Ireland, and immersed himself in the study of it. This Bible survives and is well worn. It contains his original annotations and twelve quotations from Scripture, which he transcribed in the flyleaf.[13] All of these quotations are texts against usury. He was thus obtaining guidance from the Bible as he sought to integrate his excellent business skills into his Christian life. He grew to measure his life against the parable found in Matthew 25[14] (cf. Steele chapter six above).

At this point we see Rice's priorities changing from sharpening his business acumen to the alleviation of the misery of others. He first considered 'fleeing from the world' and becoming an Augustinian Friar as his brother John had done. However, the influence of the legacy of Nano Nagle visible in the life of the Presentation Sisters helped him to make another choice.

He was a close friend of Father John Power, who was later to become Bishop of Waterford and Lismore (1804–1816). A text from the history of the Presentation Sisters illuminates the source of their influence on Edmund's friend:

> The incident that led to the establishment of the Presentation Sisters convent in Waterford was in itself very trifling, but it showed the many wonderful and seemingly insignificant means which God makes use of to bring about his designs. A poor girl, reared up in our school, that is to say, educated in Nano's own foundation, one of the schools in Cork, was obliged to leave home and find work in the city of Waterford. She was poor indeed in this world's goods but she was taught early in youth to live a life of virtue, the advantages of which would last her for all eternity. Even though there is no evidence that she was supervised by relatives she never failed in her religious duties. She received the Sacraments as frequently as ever and she seemed so thoroughly instructed in the necessary form of Confession (such instructing was, at that time, confined to the better classes) that the priest asked her where she was from and how it came about that she was so well informed in all that related to her duty of serving God. She said she was from Cork and it was at the convent school where she received

instruction in the Faith. In this almost accidental manner, the Parish Priest, Fr John Power came to know about the convent school in Cork for the instruction of the poor Irish. Delighted with the standard of religious instruction, he thought of getting a similar foundation in Waterford.[15]

This seemingly casual encounter of Fr John Power with that anonymous poor girl was one of the seminal events which, in the providence of God, made Edmund Rice the apostle of poor Irish boys.[16]

In 1795, Fr Power appealed to the Presentation Sisters in Cork to come to Waterford to begin schools to educate poor girls. Nano Nagle had died in 1784 and her successor, Mother Angela Collins, replied that she had no Sisters to send but would gladly train postulants, if sent, from Waterford.[17] Three women volunteered – Fr Power's sister, Ellen (or Eleanor); his sister-in-law Margaret Power, a widow; and Mary Mullowney. They entered the Cork novitiate in 1795 so that they would be able to return to Waterford as Presentation Sisters to begin a school there. Ellen and Margaret Power offered their property to establish the first school for the instruction of the poor girls of Waterford.

At the same time, Edmund Rice had been searching for ways to remedy the massive ignorance of Catholic youth stemming from the Penal Laws. He had long felt that God called him to such work. The call grew stronger with the proposed establishment of the Presentation Sisters in Waterford. He offered financial support to Father Power and leased a site for the new buildings. The three newly-professed Presentation Sisters came to Waterford in September, 1798 and Rice took on the financial responsibilities of the school and the fledgling Presentation community: 'I acknowledge the lease to be taken by me in trust and of the sole use and benefit of Miss Ellen Power, Mrs Margaret Power and Miss Mary Mullowney – Westcourt, 1 June 1799'.[18] His substantial success in business enabled him to support all of these educational endeavours. At the same time he was still exploring a vocation to religious brotherhood or priesthood. The following incident illustrates his struggle:

> He was one day travelling with a holy Friar who was evidently a man of prayer. Both slept in the same room. Brother Rice's companion on the occasion, employed so much of his time, not as it occurred to Brother Rice in asking God for favour, but in prayers of praise and in blessing God, that the future founder of the [sic *Presentation Brothers and the*] Christian Brothers asked himself why he was not as devout as the Friar seemed

to be. He resolved to give himself more to prayer, and to lead a Friar's life of reflection and contemplation.[19]

According to tradition, this friar was Fr Lawrence Callanan OFM, Nano Nagle's confessor, who completed the draft Rule and Constitutions of the Presentation Sisters in 1793.[20] If so, Rice had an invaluable source for the founding of a lay teaching brotherhood inspired by the charism of Nano Nagle and that of the Presentation Sisters. The influence of Nano and the Sisters on Edmund Rice was thus both organizational and inspirational.[21] His experience with the aforementioned Friar and the Presentation Sisters in Waterford, reinforced his desire to pursue his incipient faith-based educational vision. He had the opportunity to directly observe the good effects of the moral and religious education of the poor, in the conduct of the female children, who were instructed by Presentation Sisters.

Ellen Power, a member of the founding Presentation community, is credited with Edmund Rice's ultimate decision to dedicate his life to God in service of the poor of his adopted city. Based on the recollections of the Presentation Sisters in Waterford, Ellen Power confronted the thirty-one-year-old wealthy businessman, reprimanding him for his intention to leave his native country to enter religious life abroad. Keogh recounts the following narrative:

> It would be a strange and inconsistent thing for you to travel leagues of land and sea, and shut yourself up in a monastery in some distant place while the sons of your poor country men at home are, owing to untoward circumstances, utterly unacquainted with the rudiments of divine or human knowledge, and running wild through the town without a school, or a teacher, or any possible means of acquiring the most elementary education ... Would it not Mr. Rice ... be far more meritorious work and far more exalted to devote your life and your wealth to the instruction of these neglected children in the principles of religious and secular knowledge, than to bury yourself in some continental religious house where you will have no scope for the exercise of active benevolence.[22]

And so the challenge of a Presentation Sister to do for the poor boys of Waterford what Nano Nagle had first done for the poor of Cork provided the illumination Edmund was seeking. The challenge sank deep in his heart. His response changed the map of religious brotherhood and Catholic education in Ireland and later, across the globe.

Edmund Rice's financial and managerial support of the Presentation Sisters was substantial and ongoing, since he shared the vision of education he had learned from them. The three Sisters who arrived in 1798 had grown to six by 1801, and he came to their assistance, granting them a life annuity from land which he had purchased. He thus devised a means of investing their capital to provide maintenance for the six Sisters, while keeping their funds free from any danger of confiscation.[23] His generosity extended to paying the expenses for the thrice-repeated novitiate of a woman who was to become Mother Magdalene Sergent.[24]

In consultation with his bishop, and his brother Father John Rice, OSA, Edmund retained his assets (estimated at fifty thousand pounds with considerable property and other investments) in order to continue supporting the Sisters, and to initiate and provide long term financial viability for his own new educational efforts.[25] No doubt, the prolonged negotiations needed to establish the Waterford Presentation Convent and school and the problems of providing for the ongoing maintenance of the Sisters offered Edmund salutary experiences that would guide him in his own initiative. Likewise, he would have appreciated and learned from the Presentation Sisters, their approach to teaching large groups of children, adapting it over time to his evolving vision for his own educational mission. Right from the beginning of his first foundation of Mount Sion, Waterford, Edmund established a two-school system. There was a lower school to teach the basics and an upper school to teach the vocational subjects.[26]

Edmund Rice is an example of charismatic leadership, influenced by an unnamed woman who was educated by Presentation Sisters in Cork. Thus, Nano Nagle's legacy influenced Edmund Rice and also several others involved in the establishment of religious orders, for example, Priscilla Beale (1822–1878) who brought the Sisters of Saint Louis to Ireland; and Mary Martin (1892–1975), founder of the Medical Missionaries of Mary. The Sisters of Mercy are regarded as 'cousins' since Catherine McAuley (1778–1841) did her novitiate with the Presentation Sisters, George's Hill, Dublin. Katherine Drexel (1858-1955) founded the Sisters of the Blessed Sacrament. Maurice Leahy writes of her: 'the good Mother Katherine Drexel ... regards Nano Nagle as a spiritual grandmother ...'[27] More recently, the Missionary Sisters of the Eucharist, an indigenous Guatemalan community, were founded by Sister Kathleen Curtin, a Presentation Sister from San Francisco.

The Presentation Sisters in Waterford offered Edmund Rice a pattern for a way of life. However, in the absence of any known statement from him, it is impossible to know the extent to which the community, still less their individual personalities, influenced his thinking.[28] It is, however, very significant that, in 1808, Edmund and seven companions chose to make simple vows as the Society of the Presentation in the Chapel of the Presentation Sisters, Waterford.[29]

The life of Edmund Rice reveals the potency of the combination of receptivity to Spirit-led influences and the creative adaptation of these to new and varied contexts. As such, his story inspires a new generation of faith-inspired social entrepreneurs.

Endnotes

1. Daire Keogh, *Edmund Rice 1762–1844* (Dublin: Four Courts Press, 1996), 25.
2. A Christian Brother, *Edmund Ignatius Rice, Founder of the Christian Brothers* (Dublin: Catholic Truth Society of Ireland, 1914), 1–30.
3. Gregory Smyth, *Blessed Edmund Rice 1762–1844* (New York: Christian Brothers Foundation, 2005), 4.
4. A Christian Brother, *Edmund Ignatius Rice*, 9.
5. Daire Keogh, *Edmund Rice and the First Christian Brothers* (Dublin: Four Courts Press, 2008), 60.
6. Keogh, *The First Christian Brothers*, 60.
7. Keogh, *The First Christian Brothers*, 58.
8. Keogh, *1762–1844*, 31.
9. Keogh, *The First Christian Brothers*, 62. Desmond Rushe, *Edmund Rice: The Man and His Times* (Dublin: Gill and Macmillan, 1981), 24.
10. Keogh, *The First Christian Brothers*, 62.
11. Keogh, *The First Christian Brothers*, 63.
12. Keogh, *The First Christian Brothers*, 64.
13. Keogh, *The First Christian Brothers*, 65
14. Keogh, *The First Christian Brothers*, 67.
15. Congregation for the Causes of Saints, *Cork and Ross Cause of Nano Nagle, 1718-1784, Book 1* (Rome: 1994), 652.
16. Sr M. Camillus Galvin, *From Acorn to Oak* (Fargo, ND: Presentation Sisters, 1969), 97.
17. T. J. Walsh, *Nano Nagle and the Presentation Sisters* (Dublin: M. H. Gill and Son, 1959), 152.
18. Sr Mary Pius O'Farrell, *Nano Nagle, Woman of the Gospel* (Cork: Cork Publishing, 1996), 274.
19. Rushe, *Edmund Rice*, 31. See also Keogh, *The First Christian Brothers*, 90.
20. ibid.
21. Denis McLaughlin, 'The Education Charism of Blessed Edmund Rice', *Australian eJournal of Theology* 7 (June 2006): 12. aejt.com.au/.../AEJT_7.6_McLaughlin_Education_Charism.pdf
22. Keogh, *The First Christian Brothers*, 73–4.
23. M. Raphael Consedine, *Listening Journey* (Victoria: Congregation of Presentation Sisters, 1983), 132.
24. Magdalene Sergent made her first novitiate in Waterford but could not take profession because her father would not pay her dowry. She went to South Presentation Convent and made a second novitiate. Again, at Profession, her father refused to pay her dowry. Finally, she moved to Clonmel, Co Tipperary, where she did a third novitiate, at which time her father relented and paid the required dowry. She was one of the three founder of Presentation Convent, Manchester, England in 1836. M. Raphael Consedine, *Listening Journey*, 265.
25. Denis McLaughlin, 'The Founding of the Irish Christian Brothers: Navigating the Realities Through the Myths,' *Australian eJournal of Theology* http://dlibrary.acu.edu.au/research/theology/ejournal/aejt_5/denis.htm
26. ibid.
27. Maurice Leahy, *The Flower of Her Kindred* (New York: Maurice Leahy, 1944), 51.
28. M. Raphael Consedine, *Listening Journey*, 133.
29. One year later, Edmund and his companions professed their perpetual vows, according to their Rule and Constitutions which they adapted from that of the then Presentation Sisters. Congregation for the Causes of Saints, *Nano Nagle*, 655; Keogh, *The First Christian Brothers*, 101.

The Presentation of Mary: Returning to the Protogospel of James

Anne M. O'Leary PBVM

The tradition of the Presentation of Mary in the temple is recorded in a second-century apocryphal gospel, entitled the Protogospel of James (PJ, c. 140 CE).[1] Did Nano Nagle (1718–1784), and her early companions – who became part of the religious congregation, the Sisters of the Presentation of the Blessed Virgin Mary in Cork – have access to a copy of this manuscript? It is highly unlikely. As with most Catholics in the West then, as perhaps now, the tradition would have been communicated primarily through, 'church doctrine or preaching or the rendering of artists and poets rather than the reading of the Protoevangelium itself.'[2] Theologian, Thomas O'Loughlin's research demonstrates the key role liturgy played in retaining the collective memory of the narrative found in Protogospel and the theological insights that are reflected there, even, paradoxically, while the explicit use of this same text in the liturgy largely disappeared.[3]

In his comprehensive study of Nano, historian T. J. Walsh notes that, 'The veneration of the Mother of God under the title of her Presentation in the Temple was, like the devotion to the Sacred Heart of Jesus, a legacy of French piety that Nano treasured'.[4] We know from the Annals of South Presentation Convent, Cork, that Nano and the Sisters celebrated the Feastday of the Presentation of Mary. In a letter from Nano Nagle to Teresa Mulally in Dublin in 1783, she recalls the occasion of the reception of a Novice on 21 November of the previous year, an occasion of joy, a moment of light set against the great shadow cast by the Penal Laws of the day: 'We received a novice on the [Feast of the] Presentation of our Blessed Lady. We had a very fine sermon at the reception. There was only a few friends and the clergy present, as our chapel is small, nor did I choose [that] it should make a noise in the town'.[5]

The Protogospel of James begins with an account of the birth of Mary to Joachim and Anna, and ends with an account of the birth of Jesus, and the reign of terror wrought by King Herod (d. 4 BCE) who orders the killing of all male children under two years of age upon hearing predictions of the birth from the Magi (Mt 2:1–12, 13–18). It is called 'The Protogospel' because it provides information on the birth and youth of Mary, material which is not found in the canonical Gospels.[6]

There is strong evidence that copies of the document were widely circulated and well received in antiquity. This is suggested by the fact that that there are more copies extant from the Patristic period – about one hundred and forty – than some of the New Testament writings.[7] It is also supported by the frequent occurrence of citations from and references to it in the writings of many of the early Fathers of the Church – for example, Justin, Martyr (b. 100), Clement of Alexandria (d. c. 215), Origen of Alexandria (185–232), Gregory of Nazianzus (b. c. 325–389) and Gregory of Nyssa (d. c. 385). Many of the Fathers, especially in the East, regarded it as a very valuable witness to early traditions and theological insights in relation to Mary. In fact, the Eastern Church 'celebrates the entry of Mary into the Temple at Jerusalem as the moment of exchange between the Old Covenant and the New Covenant [whereas] in the Western Liturgy the ending of the old dispensation and the beginning of the new is celebrated on 2 February, the Feast of the Presentation of Jesus in the Temple by his parents, Mary and Joseph' (Lk 2:22).[8] It is also worth noting that while, relatively early on, there had been widespread consensus among the Christian communities regarding what constituted the canon of the New Testament, it was not formally recognized as complete until around the time of Augustine (354–430 CE).[9] While the Protogospel was not finally accepted into the canon, the tradition of the Presentation of Mary spread and was elevated to the status of a liturgical Feast in the following century. According to John Baggley, 'The historical origins of the Feast appear to be linked with the dedication of the Basilica of St Mary the New in Jerusalem on 21 November 543 CE; by the late seventh century it was celebrated throughout Jerusalem, and in Constantinople by the early eighth century'.[10] It was introduced in the West through the Greek monasteries that were erected in Italy in the tenth century.[11]

The Protogospel of James: A Theological Narrative

As with the canonical Gospels, Mathew, Mark, Luke and John, the Protogospel of James is intended to be read primarily as a theological narrative that arises out of a particular historical context. In other words, the primary objective is theological rather than historical. The main focus in reading a narrative theologically is to discern what it communicates about the nature of God and the impact of God's revelation in history.

Relative to the four canonical Gospels, 'the background and foreground are reversed' in the Protogospel of James.[12] In the Gospels of Matthew, Mark, Luke and John, Jesus is the primary subject and accounts about him occupy most of the verses, while the accounts about Mary, his mother, occupy relatively few. In the Protogospel, Mary is the chief subject, and we hear little about her son, Jesus, and nothing about him beyond his infancy.

The Protogospel presents the narrative of the Presentation of Mary thus: A certain Jewish couple, Joachim and Anna, have a great need. They have health, they have wealth, but they do not have an offspring. They petition God for this apparent curse to be reversed. An angel communicates to them separately that the womb of the barren woman, Anna, will be filled with life and that this 'offspring shall be spoken of throughout the whole world' (PJ 4.1).[13] The elated Anna makes a promise to the angel: 'If I should give birth to a boy or girl, I shall present the child as a gift to the Lord my God and it shall be a servant to God all the days of its life' (PJ 4.1).[14] A baby girl is born to the couple, and she is called Mary. Her mother makes a sanctuary for her in her bedroom and does not let any impure food pass through her lips. When the time comes that she is three years of age, that is God's *kairos* time, her parents bring her to the Temple to fulfill the promise made. She remains there until she is twelve years old.[15] The priests then arrange for her to be betrothed to a certain man named Joseph. While in his care, she in turn has a spiritual annunciation. An angel brings news of the unusual mission for which God has been preparing her: 'Cease being afraid, Mary, for you have found favor before the Master of all and you will conceive by his word' (PJ 11.2).

When Mary becomes visibly pregnant, Joseph is terribly angry and ashamed. Mary protests thus: 'I do not know a man' (PJ 15.2). An angel reveals to him that his betrothed speaks the truth. However, when news gets out about the pregnancy of this as yet unmarried woman, the priests are alarmed. They call the couple to the Temple to administer the water-test required by the Law of Moses to discern if Mary has been unfaithful (Num 5:14–17, 27–28). In Mary's case, the test comes up negative. The narrative tells us that Joseph then takes her 'to his home rejoicing and giving glory to the God of Israel' (PJ 16.2). Joseph then goes and secures a midwife to assist Mary. Upon finding one, he informs her that his betrothed has 'conceived by a holy spirit' (PJ 19.1). Mary gives birth in a cave to an infant boy whom they call Jesus. The midwife, discerningly recognising the child as the Infant-Messiah, is overjoyed. She cries out: 'My spirit is uplifted today for my eyes have seen wonders, for salvation is born to Israel' (PJ 19.2). When the midwife leaves the cave she meets another woman, Salome, and tells her of the miraculous virgin birth. Salome does not believe the account. She goes to see for herself, and is daring enough to use her finger to test Mary's condition and establish the truth of the midwife's claim. Upon doing so, it burns as if with fire. An angel scolds Salome for her disbelief, but tells her to place the offending finger against the Christ-child. She complies and, immediately, she is healed (PJ 20.1–4).[16]

Thus, the account portrays how intimate God's involvement is in the life of human beings. In particular, it traces three key theological insights: First, how deeply interested God is in the lives, first, of Anna and Joachim, and then, in the life of their daughter, Mary, whose purity is cherished by all who know her. Second, it relates how kenotic God is that God's son would be born of a woman, Mary. And, thirdly, it indicates that nothing is impossible with God: Mary's child is conceived apart from intimate relations with her betrothed, Joseph. Moreover, in an extraordinary way, she does not lose her virginity in the process.[17]

Toward a Pattern of Presentation Spirituality

What is common to the portrayal of Mary in both this apocryphal gospel and the canonical Gospels is the pattern of spirituality: *There is an acute need; there is a petition to God; the need is met after a time of waiting and testing.* In the Protogospel, Anna and Joachim need a baby; at Cana, the wedding party have run out of wine (cf PJ 1–3; Jn 2:3); in the Protogospel, the couple both beg the Lord to answer their prayers for an offspring; at Cana, the mother indirectly entreats Jesus, her son, to answer the need of the family (PJ 2; Jn 2:3); in the Protogospel, after years of waiting and testing, fertility replaces infertility, joy and honor replace shame when Anna gives birth; at Cana, after years of waiting and testing, the Messiah has come; full jars replace empty ones, and joy and honor replace shame when the wine is topped up (PJ 5.2; Jn 2:4–11).[18] We also find this pattern of spirituality in scriptural narratives that tell of the experiences of other barren couples: Abraham and Sarah (Genesis 17:1–19) and Hannah and Elkanah (1 Samuel 1:1–2:11) in the OT; Elizabeth and Zechariah (Luke 1:5–25, 57–58), in the NT.[19]

The Protogospel also draws greatly upon other traditions found in both the Old Testament or Hebrew Bible and the New Testament.

When the time for Mary to leave has come, and the high priest is trying to discern who among the widowed men should be her husband, 'an angel instructs the high priest to take the staff of each man and wait for a sign' (PJ 8.3). Similarly, God had instructed Moses 'to have each of the ancestral houses [tribes] present a staff and wait for a sign from God indicating which house should serve as Israel's priests (Num 17)'.[20] In the Book of Numbers, we are told that 'Aaron's staff, representing the house of Levi, had sprouted and put forth not only shoots, but blossoms as well, and even bore ripe almonds' (Num 17:23). In the Protogospel, we are told that 'a dove came forth from the staff and it alighted upon Joseph's head' (PJ 9.1). This was the sign that he was to be betrothed to Mary. Some of the popular paintings of Joseph with blossoms, usually lilies, are the result of the conflation of the two accounts in tradition.

The pattern of spirituality outlined above can be traced many times over in the life of Nano Nagle. There is an acute need in Cork: There are so many poor illiterate people living in slum conditions in the city, ignorant of their faith, disenfranchised and degraded under the burden of eighteenth-century Penal Laws. There is a petition to God: Nano entreats the Almighty, first, to send her candidates to train in Paris for the hoped-for Ursuline foundation in Cork – to be established for the continuation of the charitable works into the future which she had begun, and later, for a professed Sister to be superior of the fledgling community. The need is met after a time of waiting and testing: Her hopes having been dashed so often, Nano finally secures four women – Eleanor Fitzsimons, Margaret Nagle, Elizabeth Coppinger and Mary Kavanagh – to become the nucleus of the Ursuline foundation in Cork. Moreover, only with the most persistent help of Bishop Moylan, is the Irish-born professed Ursuline at Dieppe, a Mother Margaret Kelly, secured to come to Cork to fill the role of Superior. The community is established on 18 September 1771.[21] This blessing, which Nano attributes to Divine Providence, surprisingly leads, in turn, to another time of waiting and testing of her faith and vision: the Ursuline Sisters choose to observe the practice of enclosure. This means that they cannot teach in the schools beyond the convent walls. There is again an acute need: How might she ensure the care of the schools and the poor across the city outside the convent walls? This need provokes Nano into beginning her own religious order or Congregation, after her death called the Sisters of the Presentation of the Blessed Virgin. She founds the Congregation in 1775 with just three candidates. More come but do not stay. Her plenitude of financial resources gets depleted due to great demands on her generosity. She has to beg in order to sustain her schools and good works, suffering the taunts of being taken for an impostor, and her schools, seminaries of vice or prostitution.[22] In time, however, holistic education replaces woeful ignorance; catechesis and faith-based practices replace pernicious superstition; and gainful occupation replaces idleness and violence of the worst kind.

Theological Treasures in Relation to Mary

The author of the Protogospel also draws from the same stock of theological traditions that lie behind the Sacred Scriptures, particularly in relation to Mary. The most striking theological comment on Mary in the Protogospel has to do with her purity. As a child, she is guarded by her mother, Anna, who, as noted above, creates a sacred space for her to dwell in her bedroom (sanctuary). She ensures that her daughter does not eat anything impure and has only for company some undefiled daughters of the Hebrews. After Mary is presented to God in the Temple she is taken to the inner sanctuary, the Holy of Holies, where she is fed pure food by an angel and contemplates God.[23] As an adolescent, she cannot be found to make the Temple impure, so she is asked to leave and is betrothed to Joseph. As a young woman, contrary to Joseph's first suspicion, she has not made herself impure according to the Law of Moses by committing adultery. Beverly Roberts Gaventa suggests that, 'Mary's purity so dominates this story that she herself is almost a function of that purity rather than the purity being a characteristic of Mary.'[24]

In the Hebrew Bible, the term 'virginity' is a polyvalent metaphor. While the Law of Moses promotes the value and requirement of biological virginity up to the point of marriage (Ex 22:15-16; Dt 22:13-29), more often, the term is used as a metaphor to refer to theological virginity or purity of heart. Such purity implies a sinlessness, a desire to be sin-free. When Israel is faithful and does not sin against God, her Lord, she is described as a virgin. Sometimes Israel is mocked by the other nations precisely because of her unwavering fidelity to her God. This purity of heart is reflected when Israel is called by the title, 'Virgin Daughter of Zion'. When Israel is unfaithful and breaks her covenantal bonds through sin and the worship of other gods, she is compared to a whore and a prostitute, perhaps most famously by the prophet Hosea (Hos 2:4-15; cf. Jer 18:13-17; Ezekiel 16).

New Testament scholars find the matter of Mary's theological virginity (variously called spiritual purity or sinlessness), reflected particularly in the Gospel of Luke where she accepts, with wonderment but without doubt, the mission from God to her spoken of by the angel, Gabriel. Mary reflects a purity of heart also when, after the mission is fulfilled and she brings forth the fruit of her womb, she 'kept all these things, reflecting on them in her heart' (Lk 2:19). It is, however, the words of the angel about Mary that provide the strongest theological insight into her purity of heart, her ability to 'see God' and see God at work in her life (Matt 5:8). Gabriel greets her with these words: 'Hail, favored one (Gk, *kecharitōmenē*). The Lord is with you' (Lk 1:28). Here, she appears in right relationship with God, often rendered as 'full of grace'. We get no indication from Luke (or any other NT writing) that there was a time before the annunciation or after the birth of Jesus when she was only partly favored or partly graced.

Through the description of her childhood sanctuary at home and her dwelling in the Holy of Holies at the Temple of the Lord, the author of the Protogospel conveys that her life from the outset was wholly given to God. At no point in the apocryphal narrative is there any indication of impurity of heart or body. Moreover, soon after the Gospels and the Protogospel were completed, 'it was customary for the Fathers to refer to the Mother of God as all holy and free from every stain of sin, as though fashioned by the Holy Spirit ... as "full of grace" ...' (*Lumen Gentium*, art. 56).[25]

Thus, we are doubly alerted, that is, through Scripture and Tradition, to a stunning reversal beyond anything ever thought of or imagined prior to this in human history: She who dwelt in God's presence in the Temple, now has God's presence come dwell in her womb. Her womb becomes the temporary sanctuary and her offspring, in turn, the new and ultimate sanctuary of God (Jn 2:13-22). Gregory of Nazianzus (329-289/90 CE) noted that, 'They are not few in number who say that the God-man was born from the Virgin's womb, which the Spirit of the great God formed, constructing a pure temple to house the Temple. For the Mother is the temple of Christ, while Christ is the Temple of the Word'.[26]

Theologians and tradition through the centuries have safeguarded in the deposit of faith the deep conviction about Mary's virginity. Her purity of heart, her sinlessness since the moment of her conception, and her perpetual virginity have been treasured tenets of the Christian faith through the ages.[27] The belief in Mary's Immaculate Conception was finally promulgated as dogma by Pope Pius IX on 8 December 1854.[28]

In the NT, both Matthew and Luke testify that Jesus was born of a virgin called Mary, understood in the biological sense as well as the theological sense, through the power of the Holy Spirit (Mt 1:23; Lk 1:27).[29] The Protogospel supports and supplements the Gospels.

Moreover, the Protogospel records the mixed reaction of those who heard the news of the miraculous birth. In the Protogospel, as in Matthew's Infancy Narrative, Joseph is utterly skeptical of Mary's explanation until an angel appears to him and confirms it to be true (PJ 13.1; Mt 1:20–24). The Protogospel also includes an even more skeptical character than Joseph, namely, Salome. Like the mockery by some foreign nations of the 'Virgin Daughter of Zion', or Israel, because of her faithful love for God, Salome mocks the daughter of Anna and Joachim upon first hearing the news of the virgin birth (PJ 19.3).[30] Her response to the news contrasts with that of the unnamed midwife who, upon attending the virgin birth, believes the news of God's extraordinary intervention in Mary's life and rejoices, as does Elizabeth, in Luke's Infancy Narrative (Lk 1:43).

More importantly, the Protogospel 'is the first writing to delineate clearly the perpetual virginity of Mary'.[31] The canonical Gospels comment explicitly about the question of Mary's physiological virginity only to the point of Jesus' birth. However, the Protogospel not only supports the tradition that Mary was a virgin, in the physiological sense, before the birth of Jesus, but also during and after – *ante partum, in partu, post-partum*. The level of detail provided to assure the hearer/reader of the virginity of Mary after the birth suggests an apologetic purpose. We know that at the time it was written some, like Celsus a second-century Roman philosopher, 'impugned the virginity of Mary'[32] by proposing that Jesus was born of Mary and a Roman soldier named Pantera.[33] The declaration of the Perpetual Virginity of Mary as a dogma at the Ecumenical Council of Chalcedon (451 CE) secured the safe deposit of this belief in the tradition of the Church for all times.

A story from the time of the first Presentation Sisters is apt in this context. For more than a decade, Francis Moylan (1735–1815), the then Bishop of Cork, had petitioned Rome for Apostolic approval of the religious order founded by Nano Nagle. Rome, however, refused the Sisters permission to take solemn vows unless they concomitantly accepted the practice of enclosure. Moylan made the case that the two need not be tied together – solemn vows need not be tied to enclosure. His hope was that, if granted, solemn vows would bring the much needed elevated status and security to the Congregation; while the omission of the usual requirement of enclosure would provide the Sisters with the equally needed freedom to go wherever the needs cried loudest around the city of Cork or elsewhere.

In one of Bishop Moylan's responses to the Congregation in Rome he protested (1789): 'Again it must be observed that our women, not only religious but those recognized as pious, are much attached to chastity and adverse to worldly cares. *Enclosure and iron grilles are not more staunch than their sterling dispositions*'.[34] (Italics added) Moylan clearly fears what might happen to the mission if enclosure is imposed.[35] However, sometime later, he concedes to the requirement of enclosure by Rome, its aim being to avoid anything that could threaten the Sisters' vow of chastity and, by consequence, its potential in directing their energies for the mission assigned to them by God for their time and place.

Theologian and Scripture Scholar, Sandra Schneiders, reflects on this point. While she argues for the distinctiveness of consecrated celibacy or the vow of chastity among the vows of poverty and obedience for those called to consecrated life, she is clear that it is not an end in itself. Rather, set in the context of religious life she notes that:

> When the affective concentration of consecrated celibacy, voluntary ... community, and shared ministry combine in a comprehensive life-form, it is a remarkably powerful social and spiritual phenomenon that can be both very attractive to idealistic persons seeking meaning in their personal lives and can offer a highly effective context in which to make a difference in this world through service to others.[36]

Toward Ecumenism and Inter-faith Dialogue

While the teaching of the Immaculate Conception of Mary continues to be problematic for some Christian denominations, it is wonderful to note the development of a greater understanding concerning this and other Marian matters in the document, 'Mary: Grace and Hope in Christ' (2004), the fruits of the Anglican-Roman Catholic International Commission (ARCIC). This states that both traditions accept that, 'God's grace calls for and enables human response ... [and] in the Annunciation story, the angel calls Mary the Lord's "favoured one" (Gk, *kecharitmen*, a perfect participle meaning 'one who has been and remains endowed with grace') in a way that implies a prior sanctification by divine grace with a view to her calling'.[37] The remaining difference between the traditions lies in naming the precise point at which Mary's prior sanctification begins. Catholic theology, East and West, holds that it begins with her conception, while Anglican theology holds that its point of beginning cannot be known with certainty.

The Protogospel can also serve as a joyful point of dialogue and celebration with those of the Muslim faith and Islamic tradition.[38] In the Qur'an is found an account of Mary's birth and dwelling in the sanctuary of the Temple under the guardianship of Zechariah, the priest (Sura 3:33–37). Also recorded there is an account of the annunciation by the angel Gabriel to Mary, that she will be with child, though no man will touch her, and an account of the birth of her son, Jesus (Suras 3:47; 19:16–25).

Conclusion

What can be gained by returning to the Protogospel of James?

First, this theological narrative complements any study of Mary and of Marian feasts. 'While [the Protogospel] cannot claim the seal of divine inspiration ... in some way ... [it] helped the first generations of Christians to intuit the truth of certain mysteries whose dogmatic formulations would later become more and more clear in the light of divine revelation', namely the dogma of the Immaculate Conception and the dogma of the Perpetual Virginity of Mary.[39] It can inspire the liturgies of the Feasts of Joachim and Anna (26 July), the Birthday of Mary (8 September), as well as that of the Presentation of Mary (21 November) and the Nativity of Jesus (25 December).[40] It is the source of religious traditions and devotions, for example, that Mary's parents were Joachim and Anna, that Joseph was a carpenter, that Jesus was born in a cave and that the manger he was laid in was normally used for cattle (PJ 1–2; 9:2; 22).[41] Moreover, we can enrich our theological understanding by drawing on the writings of the Eastern Fathers and iconographers in relation to the aforementioned feasts. We can source copies of the books of prayer or beautiful icons of the East to nurture the deeply contemplative dimension of Marian spirituality.

Secondly, tracing the pattern of spirituality encoded in the Protogospel provides a very helpful framework with which to review the life and mission of Nano Nagle and the early Presentation Sisters, and of all subsequent generations who are inspired by her today. It can help us notice an unmet need today; to petition God and others for help in responding to the need; and to suffer the long waiting and testing phases that may come our way before the need is met. Moreover, the spirituality that arises from reflection on the Presentation of Mary also provides a window into the enormously rich treasury of spiritual writings on Mary of the Eastern Orthodox Church.

Thirdly, the theological treasures yielded up by a careful study of the text can inform any understanding of two of the dogmas of the Church, namely the Immaculate Conception and the Perpetual Virginity of Mary. With Mary as our model, all Christians are called to exercise theological virginity or virginity of heart in relation to God – though none of us can exercise it to the same degree as she did (Mk 3:31–35 pars.). However, for those discerning a call and those already called to consecrated life, the exercise of returning to the tradition of the Presentation of Mary invites reflection on the potency that the combination of theological virginity and physiological virginity or sexual abstinence can have in facilitating the reign of God.

Finally, contemplating the Presentation of Mary in the Temple can provide fruitful ground for reflection and discussion on Mary, mother of Jesus, in terms of inter-religious dialogue, especially with the Eastern Orthodox Church and Protestantism; as well as for inter-faith dialogue with Islam. To conclude, we might say that contemplated variously in word, art, prayer or liturgy – or selected as a study text for inter-religious or inter-faith dialogue – the account of Mary's presentation in the Temple can serve as a powerful reminder that service to others, in whatever form, finds its origin and end in the contemplation of God. Nano Nagle knew the fruitfulness of this correlation – prayer and service. In the words of historian T. J. Walsh, 'In the quiet of her [Nano's] chamber, prayer and meditation dispelled the shadows and gave her a surer insight into her apostolate of childhood and the poor'.[42]

Endnotes

1. Hereafter, the Protogospel of James may be abbreviated to PJ.
2. Beverly Roberts Gaventa, *Mary: Glimpses of the Mother of Jesus* (Columbia: University of South Carolina Press, 1995), 105.
3. Thomas O'Loughlin, 'The Protogospel of James and the Modern Roman Rite: A Case Study in the Structure of Liturgical Memory' (Anaohora 3.2, 2009), 57–80.
4. T.J. Walsh, *Nano Nagle and the Presentation Sisters* (Dublin: M. H. Gill and Son, 1959), 139.
5. Nano Nagle to Miss Mulally, AL 31 January 1783, par 3, in Walsh, *Nano Nagle*, 366.
6. All quotations from Scripture are taken from the *New American Bible* version unless otherwise indicated.
7. Roberts Gaventa, *Mary*, 106.
8. Bertrand Buby, *Mary of Galilee: The Marian Heritage of the Early Church*. Vol. 3 (New York: Alba House, 1997) 34, 36. O'Loughlin notes that Anna, mother of Mary of Nazareth, is 'still found in popular cult today as – intercessor for those seeking husbands, and of the childless seeking to conceive. See, 'Structure of Liturgical Memory'.
9. St Athanasius in 367 CE writes, "In these [27 writings] alone the teaching of godliness is proclaimed. No one may add to them, and nothing may be taken away from them." (39th Festal Letter). The New Testament Canon was finally fixed at the Council of Trent, 1546.
10. John Baggley, *Festival Icons for the Christian Year* (London: Mowbray, 2000), 18.
11. Walsh, *Nano Nagle*, 140.
12. Roberts Gaventa, *Mary*, 119.
13. All quotations from the Protogospel of James are taken from Bertrand Buby's translation found in *Mary of Galilee: The Marian Heritage of the Early Church*.Vol. III (New York, Alba House, 1997), 37–52.
14. O'Loughlin notes evidence of the celebration of Mary's conception from the eighth century: 'It was the interest in this annual major feast which prompted theological speculation that eventually resulted in the notion of Mary's conception being unique. Liturgy was the generator of doctrine, rather than being the manifestation of some doctrinal 'fact' or belief'. See, 'Structure of Liturgical Memory', 68.
15. In Hebrew theological numerology the number 'three' means 'perfect'. Its use here indicates that the chronological (*chronos*) time Mary was brought to the Temple coincided with God's intended *kairos* time for her. 'Twelve' in Judaism is symbolic of all the tribes of Israel. It the early Christian community, it symbolized 'universal' or 'all peoples'.
16. Buby, *Mary of Galilee*, 49; see also, O'Loughlin, *The Protogospel of James*, 72–3.
17. The Protogospel signs off with a comment about the authorship by a certain James whose exact identity remains elusive to scholars (see Mk 6:3 pars).
18. O'Loughlin outlines the ways in which scenes from the PJ appear to be dependent on or parallel to scenes recorded in the Infancy Narratives of the Gospels of Matthew and Luke. He also notes where certain scholars have traced 'echoes' of the Gospel of John in the PJ. See 'The *Protoevangelium Iacobi* and the Status of the Canonical Gospels in the Mid-Second Century' (Felix curiositas. *Studies in Latin Literature and Textual Criticism from Antiquity to the Twentieth Century. In Honour of Rita Beyers*, Edited by G.Guldentops, C.Laes and G.Partoens (*Instrvmenta Patristica et Mediaevalia*, 72), Turnhout, 2017, 1–12), 8–9.

19. Roberts Gaventa, *Mary*, 111.
20. Roberts Gaventa, *Mary*, 107.
21. Walsh, *Nano Nagle*, 79.
22. Walsh, *Nano Nagle*, 52.
23. Leonid Ouspensky and Vladimir Lossky, *The Meaning of Icons*. Trans. G.E.H. Palmer and E. Kadloubovsky (NewYork: St Vladimir's Seminary Press, 1999), 153.
24. Roberts Gaventa, *Mary*, 120.
25. See *Lumen Gentium*, art. 56, in 'The Dogmatic Constitution on the Church', solemnly promulgated by Pope Paul VI on the Feast of the Presentation of Mary, 21 November 1964. See http://www.vatican.va/archive/hist_councils/ii_vatican_council/documents/vat-ii_const_19641121_lumen-gentium_en.html (viewed 28 Nov 2016).
26. Michael O'Carroll, 'Gregory of Nazianzus, Saint', 160. In *Theotokos: An Encyclopaedia of the Blessed Virgin Mary* (Eugene, OR: Wipf and Stock, 1982), 160.
27. Luigi Gambero, *Mary and the Fathers of the Church: The Blessed Virgin Mary in Patristic Thought*. Trans. Thomas Buffer (San Francisco: Ignatius Press, 1999), 163.
28. For a review of the evolution of the theological tradition in relation to the doctrine of the Immaculate Conception, see O'Loughlin, *The Protogospel of James*, 67–71.
29. Roberts Gaventa, 102. Mt 1:23, uses the Greek term, parthenos, 'virgin', found in Isa. 7:14 LXX [Septuagint], rather than the Hebrew, 'almh, used in Isa. 7:14, MT [Masoretic Text].
30. Buby, *Mary of Galilee*, 48.
31. Buby, *Mary of Galilee*, 34; see also, O'Loughlin, *The Protogospel of James*, 73–4.
32. Buby, *Mary of Galilee*, 35.
33. Origen, Against Celsus, 1.2, see R.E. Brown, J.A. Fitzmyer, K.P. Donfried (eds), *Mary in the New Testament* (Philadelphia: Paulist Press, 1978), 254–5. See Amy-Jill Levine, with Maria Mayo Robbins, *A Feminist Companion to Mariology* (New York: T&T Clark International/Continuum, 2005), 170.
34. Walsh, *Nano Nagle*, 134.
35. S. F. Pettit notes that, 'Dr. Francis Moylan, [was] a prelate beloved by his people for his immense labors in the cause of charity and education …'. See *The City of Cork 1700–1900* (Cork: Studio Publications, 1977), 66.
36. Sandra M. Schneiders, *Selling All: Commitment, Consecrated Celibacy, and Community in Catholic Religious Life* (NY: Paulist Press, 2006), 151.
37. ARCIC, arts. 5, 16.
38. This is the case in Pakistan (formerly part of India until 1947), where Presentation Sisters have a presence since 1894.
39. Gambero, *Mary and the Fathers of the Church*, 41
40. O'Loughlin outlines how the PJ is *the* foundational text for these Feastdays. See O'Loughlin, *The Protogospel of James*, 59–73.
41. Buby, *Mary of Galilee*, 50.
42. Walsh, *Nano Nagle*, 51.

Presented in the Temple of God's Glory

Mary L. Coloe PBVM

On 24 June 1776, Nano Nagle, along with three companions – Mary Fouhy, Elizabeth Burke and Mary Ann Collins – professed her vows and began a new religious congregation that had as its primary aim to bring education to poor Catholic children.[1] Nano named this new group the 'Sisters of the Charitable Instruction of the Sacred Heart of Jesus'.[2] Following her death, this name was changed, at the request of her Sisters, to the 'Sisters of the Presentation of the Blessed Virgin Mary'.[3]

In recent years, as religious congregations have reflected on their founding charism and taken on new ministries, the image of the compassionate Heart of Jesus has been a source of inspiration and a link back to Nano's original vision. I, and others also, have questioned whether Dr Moylan and Fr Lawrence Callanan, OFM, made the right decision in facilitating the change of the title of the Congregation. In this chapter, I will begin by examining some evidence from the Annals of South Presentation Convent, Cork, that may help our understanding of the decision; then I will explore how the new title is iconic of a rich spirituality for Presentation life and ministry in the twenty-first century.

The Feast of the Presentation of Mary

The early Annals of the Congregation record that the Feast of the Presentation of Mary in the Temple was the date chosen by Nano in 1782, to receive two young women into the novitiate, Miss Connell and Miss Anastasia Tobin. On this same day, Miss Oliffe was received.[4] These were the only women to begin their novitiate during Nano's lifetime, and her choice of this day for this ceremony, indicates that it had a special place in her spirituality. Following Nano's death her fledgling Congregation again chose this day to receive another young woman, Margaret Lane, into the Novitiate.[5]

The South Presentation Annals record that the decision to change the title to 'some more appropriate name' was requested by the Sisters

(September 1791). They 'repeatedly solicited Rev. Mgr Callanan'. The Annalist writes:

> [Father Callanan] ... had ever known Miss Nagle, the venerable Foundress, to have had a particular and marked devotion to the festival of the Presentation of our Blessed Lady; and, that he would not, therefore, feel any hesitation in giving it the name of the 'Presentation Order'.[6]

However, while there was a change of title, it seems that the Sisters retained a great devotion to the Sacred Heart, for the Annalist continues:

> From this time, the Congregation assumed this glorious title – they, however, only changed their appellation, because they were and are, and ever will continue to be, in spirit and in truth, 'Sisters united, closely united, in word and work, by, and in, the Sacred Heart of Jesus.' Live, Jesus, for ever!!![7]

The choice of the Feast of the Presentation as the day when young women entered the Novitiate, suggests that Nano saw in this feast an expression of Mary's total self-giving to God with which Nano identified. What is it about this feast that led Nano to have 'a particular and marked devotion,' to it, according to Fr Callanan?

The Temple as God's Dwelling Place

The Collect of this Feast speaks of Mary as the *dwelling place* of the Holy Spirit and prays, 'that we, like her, may be presented in the Temple of God's glory.' This ancient prayer from the Liturgy may give us a means of interpreting Nano's devotion, and also provide new insight into how to be Presentation today.

The Feast of the Presentation celebrates a meeting point, when Mary, the new Temple and *dwelling place*, of the Holy Spirit, is presented to the former Temple of Israel. Israel's Temple, represented by the High Priest, recognises and welcomes the New Temple, Mary. The Protogospel of James records that the High Priest 'set her down upon the third step of the altar, and the Lord God sent grace upon her; and she danced with her feet, and all the house of Israel loved her.'[8] The Eastern Church, with its rich theology of the Spirit, celebrates this feast as the moment of Divine exchange between the Old and New Covenants. In the Western Liturgy this same thing is celebrated in the feast of the Presentation of Jesus. On this day the Gospel of Luke is read, where Simeon, as prophet of the Hebrew Covenant proclaims, 'Now Lord you can let your servant go in peace, according to your word'. The former dispensation may graciously depart for the new has come. The Jerusalem Temple is no longer needed as the dwelling place of God's glory; there is a new indwelling of the Spirit, heralded first in Mary (celebrated in the Eastern feast of the Presentation of Mary), and then in Jesus (celebrated in the Western feast of the Presentation of Jesus). In both Feasts the Temple is central as it symbolises the presence of God dwelling in Israel's midst.[9]

Nano's Experience of Being in God's Presence

Nano, in the midst of a busy and exhausting ministry out in the lanes of Cork, also spent much time in prayer. Following her death, the Sisters discovered that Nano had ulcerated knees and they recalled her discomfort during her long hours of daily prayer, 'from five in the morning until nine,' and then in the evening. These times of prayer were extended during her Christmas retreat and 'on Holy Thursday nights, which she spent on her knees in [the] presence of the Blessed Sacrament until morning'.[10]

We do not have extant any of Nano's own writings where we would know her own motivation for these practices, but perhaps we can gain some insight from another historical fact – the choice of the name 'Sister Mary St John of God'. This sixteenth-century Saint established hospitals for the poor. Legend has it that one day as John washed and kissed the feet of a beggar from the streets he found them marked with the wounds of Christ and heard a voice saying, 'John, to Me is done all that you do for the poor in My Name … Mine are the feet that you wash'.[11]

From these two facts about Nano's life we can infer that she encountered God in both the solitude of her prayer and in her passionate love of the poor. Her passion pulses through her letters as she writes, 'my schools will never bring me to heaven, as I only take delight and pleasure in them.'[12] Nano also writes of her work spreading from Cork to other countries leading to her declaration, 'If I could be of any service in saving souls in any part of the globe, I would willingly do all in my power.'[13] From a small, rudimentary chapel in Cork, Nano's heart reached out to encompass the world, yet in all this missionary zeal, Nano knew that this work would be impossible except for God. Her letters speak of difficulties and failures alongside constant affirmations of God's providence: 'The Almighty is all sufficient';[14] 'Providence has ordered all for the best';[15] 'The Almighty has been pleased to make it turn out to our advantage';[16] 'By degrees, with the assistance of God we may do a great deal;'[17] 'It's all in the power of the Almighty';[18] and 'The Almighty makes use of the weakest means to bring about his works'.[19] Nano's hours of solitary prayer brought her to know a God in whom she could have utter trust, and a God who impelled her to go out to the winding lanes of Cork. Contrary to her first impulse, she was not called to live a monastic life. For her contemplation and ministry beyond the confines of monastic enclosure are both the essence of her vocation. For this reason, Sandra Schneiders lists Nano among the 'pioneers of apostolic religious life long before it was officially approved in 1900'.[20]

Called to prayer and action, to solitude and crowded lanes – this apparent paradox is seen in the life of Jesus, who spent time in prayer (Mk 1:35) and knew days of busy engagement with people (Mk 1:21–34; 6:30–1). It is also a paradox associated with the Temple. In what follows, I explore the implications of the current Collect Prayer of the Presentation of Mary (21 November), 'that we may be presented in the Temple of God's glory,' and how this can open up for us a rich Temple Spirituality that is particularly relevant in a more ecologically-conscious age. More than ever, the world needs people willing to be Temple people.

The Temple/Heart of God in the World

Temple spirituality can complement a heart spirituality and further draw out the richness of Nano's spirituality, now expressed through the spirituality of Presentation Sisters and all who follow in her footsteps today. As individuals, a temple spirituality calls for contemplation. Recent papers on the contemplative nature of Religious Life have shown that contemplation is not restricted to monastic enclosure – 'all are called to contemplation'.[21] Contemplation has been described as taking 'a long, loving look at reality'. Such contemplative activity can move people into Spirit-directed action in the world. Here is where temple and heart spirituality coincide. The contemplative attitude is linked with the heart. As Teresita Weind writes, 'From the heart we grow into a connectedness marked by compassion and kindness, selflessness and unconditional love'.[22]

The link between heart and temple was expressed symbolically most powerfully when the first temple of Israel, built by Solomon, was dedicated. Solomon was aware that no building could ever contain God's presence, but he prayed, 'that your eyes may be open night and day towards this house' (1 Kgs 8:29). In response God declared, 'I have heard your prayer and your supplication; I have consecrated this house which you have built; *my eyes and my heart* will be there for all time' (1 Kgs 9:3). The Temple of Israel represents the loving gaze and compassionate heart of God in *this* world. The heart of God is meant to be a power-house/temple of God's healing and life-giving activity *for* the world.

Temple and Cosmos

Israel's Temple always had a cosmic dimension. According to Jewish mythology, all the waters of the Earth have their origins in the heavens, and flow down to touch Earth at the place where the Temple stands. For this reason Jerusalem is called the Earth's navel (Ezek 38:12) since this is the meeting place of Heaven and Earth. The Temple rests upon the fissure above the great abyss, which is the source of the creative waters (Genesis 2:8).[23] After the flood, the rock of Noah's altar sealed up the waters of the abyss and Noah's altar became the foundation stone of a new creation. Jewish traditions link the altar of Noah with the foundation stone in the Holy of Holies supporting the Ark of the Covenant.[24] According to this theologized mythology, the Temple lies upon the wellspring of Earth, the centre and source of creation:

> The waters under the Earth were all gathered beneath the temple, they believed, and it was necessary to ensure that sufficient was released to ensure fertility, but not so much as to overwhelm the world with a flood.[25]

This cosmic mythology lies behind the strange story of waters flowing from the Temple in Ezekiel 47. In Ezekiel's vision, the Temple is the source of life, healing and fertility for the New Israel. Water flows from under the sanctuary to cleanse and fructify the whole land (47:1–12), recalling the creation myths of Canaan and Israel where waters well up from the cosmic rivers of paradise to provide life (Gen 2:6, 10–14).[26] Even the waters of the Dead Sea are brought to life and the trees growing beside this Temple water are miraculously life-giving: 'Their leaves will not wither nor their fruit fail, but they will bear fresh fruit every month ... Their fruit will be for food and their leaves for healing' (Ezek 47:12). God's Temple is to be a source of nourishment and healing for the world.

The very structure of the Temple represented God's act of creation. When all the elements of the Tabernacle within the Temple were completed the narrator records, 'Thus all the work of the tabernacle of the tent of meeting was finished ... And Moses saw all the work and behold, they had done it ... and Moses blessed them' (Ex 39:32, 43). These words echo the first account of creation, 'Thus the heavens and the earth were finished ... And God saw all that had been made and behold, it was very good ... So God blessed the seventh day' (Gen 2:1; 1:31; 2:3). We read in Exodus 40 that the Tabernacle was then erected in seven stages replicating the seven days of creation.[27] Margaret Barker quotes an early Midrash which states, 'The tabernacle is equal to the creation of the world' (Midrash Tanhuma 11.2).[28] In this symbolising tradition, the Holy of Holies corresponds with the first day of creation, the separating of light from darkness. The Temple veil corresponds with the second day when the firmament is made. This veil was made by weaving coloured wool into white linen (Exod 26:31), and these four colours represented the four elements from which Earth was made: red for fire, blue representing the air, purple representing water and the white linen, Earth. According to the Mishnah, the veil was woven by young women (m. *Middoth* 4.7).[29] The veil thus represents the entire created world.

In the ancient Middle East, the Temple of a deity was frequently depicted with elaborate images associating the Temple with a world-garden. The palace of a King was surrounded by lush gardens,[30] and this world view led to the association of the Garden of Eden and the Temple in much Jewish thought.[31] In Eden, God was present 'walking (hlk: hitpa''el) in the garden in the cool of the evening' (Gen 3:8). This same verbal form is used to describe God's presence with Israel 'walking about in a tent and a tabernacle' (2 Sam 6–7; also Lev 26:12; Deut 23:14).[32] The Temple was elaborately decorated with carvings of trees, flowers, and animals to depict the world of nature: cedars, cypress, gourds, olivewood, palm trees, pomegranates, oxen, lions, and a great laver of water symbolising the primal Sea. Just as Kings in the Ancient East established their palaces surrounded by gardens, so God's Temple was to be God's garden.[33]

Living a Temple Spirituality

The above brief reflections on the significance of the Feast of the Presentation for Nano and her small community and how this Feast also resonates with the 'heart' imagery of Nano's original title, offer all Presentation people – Sisters, Associates, friends and colleagues – a new opportunity to claim and reclaim a spirituality for today. Such a Temple spirituality will have three elements:

> Temple/Presentation people will be deeply contemplative. They will know that the Temple is to be the eyes and heart of God in the world (1 Kgs 9:3). They will look at their own reality through the lens of God's loving gaze and compassionate heart and this will necessarily call them to act. As people alive with the indwelling presence of God, they will be the bearers of 'good news to the poor and liberation to the oppressed' (Lk 4:18). A powerful vignette from the early years of the Congregation illustrate this. The Annals of South Presentation record Nano walking the dark lanes ...

after a well spent day, returning thro' the darkness of the night, dripping with rain, mingled in the bustling crowd, moving thoughtfully along by the faint glimmering of a wretched lantern, withholding from herself in this manner, the necessaries of life, that she may administer its comforts to others.[34]

> Temple/Presentation people will be sources of nurturing and healing (Ezek 47:12), moving into the most arid and needy situations to bring life. God is one who 'sees the affliction of my people; who hears their cry; who knows their suffering; and comes to deliver them' (Ex 3:7–8). Within the Temple of Israel great care was taken to blend the holy anointing oils (Exod 30:22–33). The priestly ministry today by virtue of Christian baptism is now extended by Presentation people through the quality of their nurturing and healing presence to others with whom they minister.

> Temple/Presentation people will be committed to care of the earth (Mk 16:15, *kosmos*). As Temple people, they cannot but have an ecological consciousness, alert to the world within and around as a sacrament of God's presence. The whole cosmos is now the dwelling place, the *oikos* of God's Spirit.[35] John writes, 'The Word became flesh and dwelt (literally *tabernacled*) among us' (Jn 1:14). Matter is now imbued with Divinity and the active agent of this is the indwelling Spirit. So the world is rightly called the Temple or Dwelling Place of God (Rev 21:1–8).

The vision of new creation reflected in the Gospels of Mark and John and the Book of Revelation is captured in Presentation/Temple spirituality and the spirituality of Nano Nagle. Nano, the lantern-carrier, worked to achieve the vision of 'good news to the poor' in her age, and our task is no less worthy. Temple people would seem to be essential in our time. The world cries out for people who can look at reality from a contemplative stance and see how to act collaboratively for justice for people and planet so that creation is birthing and not dying. Given the growing ecological consciousness in the world, Presentation/Temple spirituality is most relevant. The world, our *oikos*, needs to become more and more visibly a place where God's Spirit is at home.

Endnotes

1. M. M. de Pazzi Leahy, 'Transcript of the Annals of South Presentation Convent, Cork. 1771–1989'; hereinafter 'Annals'. Entry for January 24 1776.
2. Annals, 1776, January 25.
3. T. J. Walsh, *Nano Nagle and the Presentation Sisters* (Dublin: M. H. Gill and Son, 1959), 179, 396.
4. Annals, 1782, November 21.
5. Annals, 1789, November 21.
6. Annals, 1791, September 3.
7. ibid.
8. See Chapter 9 above.
9. Mary L. Coloe, *God Dwells with Us: Temple Symbolism in the Fourth Gospel* (Collegeville: Liturgical Press, 2001), Chapter 3.
10. Annals, 1777 (this entry appears immediately before June 24 1777).
11. Raphael Consedine, *Listening Journey: A Study of the Spirit and Ideals of Nano Nagle and the Presentation Sisters* (Melbourne: Presentation Sisters Victoria, 1983), 87.
12. Nano Nagle to Miss Fitzsimons, AL 17 July 1769, par 8, in Walsh, *Nano Nagle*, 346.
13. Nano Nagle to Miss Fitzsimons, AL 17 July 1769, par 11, in Walsh, *Nano Nagle*, 347.
14. Nano Nagle to Miss Fitzsimons, AL 17 July 1769, par 12, in Walsh, *Nano Nagle*, 347.
15. Nano Nagle to Miss Fitzsimons, AL 13 May 1770, par 1, in Walsh, *Nano Nagle*, 351.
16. Nano Nagle to Miss Fitzsimons, AL 28 September 1770, par 2, in Walsh, *Nano Nagle*, 354.
17. Nano Nagle to Miss Fitzsimons, AL 28 September 1770, par 4, in Walsh, *Nano Nagle*, 355.
18. Nano Nagle to Miss Fitzsimons, AL 17 December 1770, par 1, in Walsh, *Nano Nagle*, 355.
19. Nano Nagle to Miss Mulally, AL 29 September 1776, par 1, in Walsh, *Nano Nagle*, 357.
20. Sandra Schneiders, *Prophets in Their Own Country: Women Religious Bearing Witness to the Gospel in a Troubled Church* (Maryknoll, NY: Orbis, 2011), 31–2.
21. Schneiders, *Prophets in Their Own Country*, 98.
22. This quote is from a talk by Teresita Weind, given at the LCWR National Assembly in 1991.
23. See Frédéric Manns, *Le symbole eau-esprit dans le Judaïsme ancien*, vol. 19, SBFA 19 (Jerusalem: Franciscan Printing Press, 1983), 285. ADDIN ADDIN
24. F Manns, *L'évangile de Jean à la lumière du Judaïsme*, SBFA, 33 (Jerusalem: Franciscan Printing Press, 1991), 135.
25. Margaret Barker, *The Gate of Heaven: The History and Symbolism of the Temple in Jerusalem* (London: SPCK, 1991), 18.
26. For a discussion on the Temple as a source of fertility for the Earth see Barker, *The Gate of Heaven*, 75–82.
27. Seven times the phrase occurs, 'as the Lord had commanded Moses' (Exod 40:19, 21, 23, 25, 27, 29, 32). This phrase marks the placing of: the Holy of Holies, the Veil, the table for the bread, the golden lampstand, the altar of incense and anointing oil, the altar of burnt offerings, and finally the laver for the washing of the priests. When it was completed, the narrator states:

'Thus Moses finished the work.' (Exod 40:33; compare 'And on the seventh day God finished the work (Gen 2:2).
28. Margaret Barker, *Temple Theology: An Introduction* (London: SPCK, 2004), 17.
29. The *Protoevangelium* records a legend that Mary was one of the young women chosen to weave the Temple veil: Let us make a veil for the temple of the Lord. And the priest said: Choose for me by lot who shall spin the gold, and the white, and the fine linen, and the silk, and the blue, and the scarlet, and the true purple (Exod 25:4) And the true purple and the scarlet fell to the lot of Mary, and she took them, and went away to her house.
30. Lawrence Stager describes the lush gardens built by Nebuchadnezzar in Babylon, Queen Hatshepsut's gardens in Egypt, those of the Assyrian king Ashurnasirpal II in Assur, Sargon II and Sennacherib in Nineveh; see Lawrence E. Stager, 'Jerusalem as Eden,' *Biblical Archaeology Review* 26 (2000): 36–47. Mariusz Rosik also describes the significance of the garden for burial sites for kings in the Ancient Middle East; see, Mariusz Rosik, 'Discovering the Secrets of God's Gardens. Resurrection as New Creation (Gen 2:4b–3:24; Jn 20:1–18),' in *Liber Annus Lviii*, ed. Massimo Pazzini (Jerusalem: Studium Biblicum Fransiscanum, 2009), 82–3.
31. Howard N. Wallace, 'Garden of God (Place)', in *The Anchor Yale Bible Dictionary*, ed. David N. Freedman, Vol 2 (New York: Doubleday, 1992), 906. Also Howard N. Wallace, *Eden, Garden of (Place)*, idem. 282.
32. Gregory K. Beale, *The Temple and the Church's Mission: A Biblical Theology of the Dwelling Place of God*, New Studies in Biblical Theology 17 (Downers Grove: InterVarsity, 2004), 66.
33. The Gospel of John draws upon this cosmic-garden imagery in its presentation of the Passion narrative which takes place within a garden (John 18:1; 19:41), with the cross 'in the middle' as a 'tree of life' that was 'in the middle' of the Garden of Eden. With wonderful irony the Risen Jesus is first revealed to Mary Magdalene as the Divine Gardener. For more on this Johannine symbolism see, Mary Coloe (ed.) *Creation Is Groaning: Biblical and Theological Perspectives* (Collegeville: Liturgical Press, 2013), 71–90.
34. Annals, Introductory pages. Also cited in Walsh, *Nano Nagle*, 115–16.
35. The word ecology comes from the Greek word for house – *oikos*. The most frequent name for the Temple in the Old Testament was the House of God – the *oikos tou Theou*.

'God in our Midst':
A Theology of Indwelling

Anne M. O'Leary PBVM

A great theological richness can be found when we drink deeply from the well of both Scripture and Tradition in relation to Mary of Nazareth (b. c. 10 BCE). One of the benefits of returning to the source of the tradition of the Presentation of Mary as recorded in the Protogospel of James is that it can prompt us to study and reflect on the unfolding story of God's indwelling in creation and with humanity as recorded in the canonical Scriptures. This chapter will begin by tracing the unfolding story of God's indwelling with humanity and in the cosmos from the Judaeo-Christian tradition. Then, a framework for examining the spirituality and charism of Nano Nagle will be offered. As a conclusion, a way in which this framework can be used for personal and communal reflection today will be proposed.

The Indwelling of God in the Judaeo-Christian Tradition

Sacred World: The Cosmos as God's Dwelling Place

The beliefs of the ancient Israelites about God's presence at the beginning of time can be discerned, in part, from the two creation accounts found at the beginning of the Book of Genesis (1:1–3:24). Before the creation of the cosmos, the ancients understood that God dwelt in the Garden of Eden. The garden was God's sanctuary. With the creation of new spaces – the heavens and the earth – God expanded the boundaries of God's dwelling place. With the creation of human persons, God's presence 'was to be extended throughout the whole earth by his image bearers, as they themselves represented and reflected his glorious presence and attributes'.[1] With the cosmos and the world as God's dwelling place the vocation of 'the image-bearers' emerged. They are 'to fill the whole earth with God's glory'.[2]

That the ancients worshipped the Creator God in the cosmos and in creation is reflected in several of the Psalms: 'O Lord, our Lord, how awesome is your name through all the earth! You have set your majesty above the heavens!' (Ps 8:2).[3] However, the ancients did not see the vocation to give glory to God as being confined to them; it was the vocation of the whole of creation – animals and plants, vegetable and mineral, liquid matter and solid stones – to give God praise in the temple of God's creation. This appreciation is also reflected in some of the Psalms (Ps 150), and perhaps most beautifully in the Book of Daniel:

> Mountains and hills, bless the Lord;
> praise and exalt him above all forever;
> Everything growing from the earth, bless the Lord …
> You springs, bless the Lord …
> Seas and rivers, bless the Lord …
> You dolphins and all water creatures, bless the Lord …
> All you birds of the air, bless the Lord (Dan 3:75–80)

Sacred Places and Spaces: The Ark of the Covenant, The Temple of Jerusalem, and the 'New Heart' as God's Dwelling Places

The ancients, including the patriarchs – Abraham, Isaac and Jacob, continued to experience the God who dwelt outdoors. One night when Jacob slept under the stars, he had a vision of angels ascending and descending the stairway that links heaven and earth. After this vision, he set a stone to mark the place of his spiritual experience and he named it, *Bethel*, which in Hebrew means 'house' or 'dwelling place of God' (Gen 28:10). A sanctuary was set up there and it remained a place of worship and devotion for the Israelites for centuries after.

Moses, Israel's greatest prophet, had an experience of God as a burning bush on Mount Sinai (Ex 3, 19). Upon receiving the Ten Commandments, he was instructed to have a safe-deposit made worthy of God's message. A golden box was fashioned large enough to contain the two tablets of stone on which God had written the commandments with his finger (Dt 9:10). The two arching angels that adorned it symbolized the angels of God whom the Israelites believed were, in fact, guarding the sacred stones of the covenant because the intensity of God's presence was contained in them. The people carried this mobile tabernacle with them as they journeyed to the, as yet, unknown Promised Land in order 'that God's glorious presence would continue to dwell among them during their wilderness wanderings (Ex 25:8)'.[4] They set it under the shelter of a booth or tent by night and the priests who carried it by day kept guard over it. When they reached Gibeon, north of Jerusalem, the Ark was set in a tent and remained there until David, the king, brought it to the city.

God commissioned King David to build a house or temple of stone for him in Jerusalem. David made the preparations for it but it was his son, Solomon, who oversaw the building project. Solomon's temple was destroyed by the Babylonians and a remnant of the people of Jerusalem was taken into exile to Babylon. The Psalmist records the Israelites' grief and desolation at this turn of events: 'We sat mourning and weeping when we remembered Zion, and on the poplars of that land, hung up our harps' (Ps 137:1).

Later, through his prophet, Ezekiel, God reassured the people of Israel that he knew of their plight and, in spite of their past infidelities to him, he sought to restore them: 'I [God] will sprinkle clean water upon you to cleanse you from all your impurities, and from all your idols I will cleanse you. *I will give you a new heart and place a new spirit within you*, taking from your bodies your stony hearts and giving you natural hearts' (Ezek 36:25–27). Ezekiel testifies to a major shift in theological vision. He provides the earliest scriptural reference to the heart as a dwelling place or tabernacle of God's Spirit. It is the first intuition that the Temple of stone in Jerusalem would in time be replaced by a temple of flesh, Jesus Christ.

Sacred Woman: Mary's Womb as God's Dwelling Place

The belief of some of the later first century CE Israelites that Divinity came to dwell in the womb of Mary of Nazareth can be clearly discerned in the New Testament writings and in the earliest apocryphal gospel, the Protogospel of James (c. 140 CE). Mary's womb became the temporary tabernacle for God's glory: 'And the Word became fleshand made his dwelling ['tabernacled'] among us, and we saw his glory' (Jn 1:14). In historical time, 'God came into our midst' as an infant and he was named Jesus (b. 4 BCE). Later, the Ecumenical Council at Ephesus (431 CE), would describe Mary as the God-Bearer (*Theotókos*), the one who bore in her flesh the Word of God.

Jesus: The Temple of God Incarnate

When Jesus was eight days old, Mary and her husband, Joseph, brought him to the Temple of Jerusalem for the ritual of circumcision and presented him to the Lord as prescribed by the Law of Moses. Their presentation of Jesus in the Temple mirrors the presentation of his mother by her parents, Joachim and Anna. When he was twelve years old he chose to remain in the Temple after the Feast of Passover where he sat and discussed religious matters with the teachers of the Law. All who heard him were astounded at his understanding and his answers. His parents, who had begun to journey home to Nazareth unaware that he was not with them, returned to look for him. When they found him, his mother inquired of him about his actions. His response is telling: 'Why were you looking for me? Did you not know that I must be in my Father's house?' (Lk 2:49–50).

On a first reading, one might presume that Jesus is zealous to be a priest among priests at the temple. However, later, Jesus speaks of destroying the Temple and then rebuilding it (Jn 2:19). If the Temple of Jerusalem is destroyed, there is no need for the priestly institution. Therefore, his need to be in his Father's house must refer to some other place.

A closer reading of the Gospels indicates something extraordinary, that the 'some other place' is, in fact, him. Jesus has replaced the Temple of Jerusalem as the dwelling place of God. The Temple of stone is no longer the essential locus of worship. He is. Jesus explains to the Samaritan woman: '"Believe me, woman, the hour is coming when you will worship the Father neither on this mountain nor in Jerusalem." The woman said to him, "I know that the Messiah is coming, the one called the Anointed; when he comes, he will tell us everything." Jesus said to her, "I AM he, the one who is speaking with you"' (Jn 4:21, 25–6).

Sacred Lives: The Person and Community as God's Dwelling Place

Before Jesus took leave of his disciples he promised them that the community of believers would become the new Temple or dwelling place of God. He assured them that 'where two or three are gathered together in my name, there am I [God] in the midst of them' (Mt 18: 20). Paul reminds the disciples in Ephesus of this promise: 'All believers, Gentiles or Jews, constitute this Temple and thus have access to the living God. Every structure knit together in him grows into a holy temple in the Lord; and you too, in him, are being built into a dwelling place of God in the Spirit' (Eph 2:14, 20). He also explains this theological reality to the Corinthians: 'Do you not realize that you are a temple of God with the Spirit of God living in you? If anybody should destroy the temple of God, God will destroy that person, because God's temple is holy and you are that temple' (1 Cor 3:16–17).

It is awesome to think that the same Divinity that appeared to Moses, that dwelt in the Ark of the Covenant, that dwelt in the Holy of Holies at Jerusalem and dwelt in the womb of Mary of Nazareth, and in the flesh of her son, now dwells in all those who believe that Jesus is Lord.

Sacred World: The Cosmos as God's Dwelling Place
The Gospel of Matthew reminds us that the salvation or healing wrought by Jesus Christ's life, death and resurrection, extends to the ends of the earth (Mt 28:19); and the Gospel of Mark, that salvation is for 'the whole of creation', the entire cosmos (*kosmos*, Mk 16:15).

The mission of the Cosmic Christ is our mission today. This mission becomes more urgent whenever we hear the cry of 'creation is groaning in labor pains' (Rom 8:22) because of the neglect or abuses of humanity – for example, whenever we find that because of greed there is not even enough cold water to drink in order to survive (Mt 10:42) or to moisten the parched land that provides the earthly bread of life. The mission becomes more urgent whenever and wherever we find that the temple of creation is being destroyed. Paul reminds us that all of creation 'awaits with eager expectation the revelation' that has been given to us, the children of God' (Rom 8:22, 19; cf. Rev 21:1–4).

In more recent times, echoing Sacred Scripture and earlier ecclesial documents, Pope Francis' in his encyclical, *Laudato Si': On Care for our Common Home* (2015) gives a clarion cry to all who have ears to listen:

> I urgently appeal, then, for a new dialogue about how we are shaping the future of our planet. We need a conversation which includes everyone, since the environmental challenge we are undergoing, and its human roots, concern and affect us all. The worldwide ecological movement has already made considerable progress and led to the establishment of numerous organizations committed to raising awareness of these challenges. Regrettably, many efforts to seek concrete solutions to the environmental crisis have proved ineffective, not only because of powerful opposition but also because of a more general lack of interest. (Art 14)[5]

Moreover, he counsels: 'If we are truly concerned to develop an ecology capable of remedying the damage we have done, no branch of the sciences and no form of wisdom can be left out, and that includes religion and the language particular to it'. (Art 63)[6]

The Indwelling of God and the Spirituality of Nano Nagle

In the first section of this chapter, we traced the unfolding story of God's dwelling with humanity and in the cosmos from the Judaeo-Christian tradition. This section will outline a framework for fruitfully examining the spirituality and charism of Nano Nagle by examining these twin aspects under the following five headings:

› The Temple of the World and Cosmos: Nano's Theology
› The Temple of Everyday Life: Nano's Christology
› The Temple Within: Nano's Mariology
› The Dishonouring of the Temple: Nano and the Paschal Mystery
› Rebuilding the Temple: Nano's Missiology

The Temple of the World and Cosmos: Nano's Theology

In reflecting upon the Temple of the World and the Cosmos in sacred Scripture, we are drawn to reflect upon God as Creator and Master Designer of all things past, present and future. In the context of exploring the spirituality and charism of Nano Nagle, it invites us to ponder the question: 'Who is God for Nano?'

Nano's primary image of God was, I would suggest, that of the *All-mighty*, the *All-powerful*, the great Caretaker of the future. Her letters reflect what she knew well from her lived experience that 'the Almighty is all-sufficient …'.[7] Her stance appears to be one of absolute trust in God. Her choice of spiritual readings provides further evidence of this spirit of trustfulness. One of the few spiritual reading books of Nano's that has survived is a book by Nicolas Barré (1621–1686), the founder of the Infant Jesus Sisters, entitled, *Lettres Spirituelles*. One of the dominant themes of this book is the notion of total abandonment to the providence of God. Her spirit of faithful trust is also reflected in the fact that there is no evidence that she saw God as One to be feared. We are told in the First Letter of John, that 'perfect love drives out fear' (1 Jn 4:18). For Nano, her ever-deepening love for God enabled her to go where others feared to tread, to be where others feared to be, and to do what others feared to do. Even in the most challenging circumstances she believed that, 'We must think that the Almighty permits everything for the best. You'll see with His assistance everything promises well'.[8]

Nano's letters, like her life, reflect the deep respectful awe with which she approached the Almighty God who is in and over all things, who plans for our tomorrow things unimagined by us today.

The Temple of Everyday Life: Nano's Christology

In reflecting on the sacred places and spaces of God's dwelling in the Old Testament or Hebrew Bible – namely, the Ark of the Covenant, the Temple of Jerusalem, and the 'new heart' envisioned by Ezekiel – we are drawn to reflect on the Divinity who showed the depth of his love by coming among us and walking the human journey from the cradle to the cross. In the context of exploring the spirituality and charism of Nano Nagle, we are invited to ponder the question: 'Who is Jesus Christ for Nano?'

A study of the chronicles of Nano's life and her letters makes very clear that her spirituality was very Christocentric. Her primary image of Jesus Christ was, I would suggest, that of the Love Incarnate. This was reflected in a myriad of ways in her life, not least in the title she gave her Congregation, 'Sisters of Charitable Instruction of the Sacred Heart of Jesus'; in her choosing to formally begin the Congregation on the eve of the great Feast of the Incarnation (1775); and, subsequently, her provision of bread for the poor of Cork on this Festival, in imitation of the Divine-Provider/Providence who had fed the thousands when he multiplied five barley loaves and two fish (Mk 6:34–44 pars).

Nano's concern was not just for the provision of food for hungry bodies, as exemplified in her feeding fifty beggars on Christmas Day, but for the provision of food for hungry souls. She took great delight in preparing the children at her schools to receive their First Holy Communion, and in her first seven schools (two for boys, five for girls) in Cork, the Sacrament of the Eucharist was provided for the children every day.

Nano's letters show her ever-deepening love for Jesus Christ whom she knew as Love Incarnate, as Divine Provider/Providence, and as the Bread of Life. She mirrored in her city-rounds what she had come to know from her chapel-contemplation of her people's cry, 'Give us this day our daily bread' (Mt 6:11); she became love incarnate—a provider for those who were most hungry in body, mind, or soul.

The Temple Within: Nano's Mariology

In reflecting on the Presentation of Mary in the Temple from the Protogospel of James, and on the great mystery of her womb becoming the temporary Temple of God from the New Testament, we are drawn to reflection upon Mary whose 'Yes' to God's invitation facilitated God's dwelling in flesh in human history. An exploration of the spirituality and charism of Nano Nagle, invites us to ponder the question: 'Who is Mary for Nano?'

We get only brief glimpses into Nano's Marian spirituality from her letters. However, what we do find is very instructive. Her primary image of Mary was, I would suggest, that of Patron and Protector of all that she was about in mission and ministry. When planning to move from her small cabin to the newly erected convent at three in the morning because of political disturbances at the time, she orchestrates it to happen on the eve of the Feast of Our Blessed Lady, the Feast of Mount Carmel (16 July 1780). The reason she provides gives us a window in to her character as well as her spirituality: 'We removed [on the] 15 [July], so were there on the festival of our Blessed Lady, under whose protection we are. I hope she will preserve us from our visible and invisible enemies and make this house prosper and others of the same Charitable Institution in time'.[9]

Chapter nine reflected on her devotion to the Feast of the Presentation of Mary, and her choice of 21 November 1782 as the occasion to receive a Novice, Miss Oliffe, into the Congregation. The reflection of the Jesuit homilist, Fr Nicholas Barron, at the Eucharist on that occasion provides further insight into the Marian spirituality that Nano and her early Sisters would have appreciated. He writes:

> We on this day commemorate the Sacred Mystery, when the tender and divine Virgin Mary presented herself in the temple before him to be informed of his will; her humility and obedience so far won his heart, as to make choice of her for his spouse and the mother of Jesus. Can we doubt her powerful intercession? *Can the mother of Jesus reject the prayers of the Sisters of the Sacred Heart of Jesus? Can Jesus himself reject the prayer of his mother and his Sisters?*

This suggests that Nano and the Sisters understood the special role accorded to Mary as intercessor (*mediatrix*) between earth and heaven for their needs, as she was for the needs of those at the wedding at Cana (Jn 2:1–12).

That desire for the patronage of Mary is indicated by the Sisters immediate and enthusiastic adoption of the new title for the Congregation, 'Sisters of the Presentation of the Blessed Virgin Mary', when recommended as an alternative by Fr Callanan OFM (1781). He knew that it was one of Nano's favourite Marian feasts. The Annalist at South Presentation Convent calls it 'a glorious' title.

The desire for the protection of Mary for the mission and ministry of the early community is reflected in the fact that soon after her foundation, Nano sought to get copies of the *Office of Our Blessed Lady* 'from abroad' (mainland Europe) to be used in daily prayer by the Sisters as she could not access these in Ireland. This was the Office used especially by members of uncloistered Societies at this time. Its relative shortness meant that the Sisters could have more time for the apostolate. In fact, Bishop Moylan, in his correspondence with Rome toward gaining official Church recognition, recommends that 'the Sisters were not [to be] bound to recite the Divine Office as such, but rather the *Little Office of Our Lady*, since practically their whole time was to be spent in instructing the poor'.[10]

Nano's devotion to Mary is practical. She regards her spiritual mother as her Patron, Protector and Intercessor. She is drawn to this woman who was once Patron to a promise that seemed impossible – that God would dwell in her womb; who was once Protector of an Infant Child when Herod sought to murder him (Mt 2:12–15), and of an adult son whom some thought to be out of his mind (Mk 3:21); and who was once intercessor on behalf of those who were in danger of being dishonored because of lack of the stuff of hospitality (Jn 2:4).

The Dishonouring of The Temple: Nano and the Paschal Mystery

In reflecting on Jesus as the Temple of God Incarnate, we are drawn to reflect upon the way the Temple of His Body was dishonored by those who remained blind to his identity and mission. His body was broken, his soul was tormented. Yet his suffering was part of God's plan for salvation. In the context of exploring the spirituality and charism of Nano Nagle, we are invited to reflect on another dimension of Nano's Christology, her devotion to the Paschal Mystery.

Nano's devotion to the Passion of Jesus was reflected in a myriad of ways in her life, both in her words and in her deeds. In a letter to Teresa Mulally, after sharing how she coped with the delicate matter of coming to an agreement with the Ursuline Sisters that they would not accept any Novices that had previously joined her fledgling Society (as such an incidence did occur), she concludes: 'It's a good sign of our future success that we should meet with crosses in the beginning'.[11]

It was customary for Nano to read the entire Passion to the children in the schools during Holy Week each year. This simple act is noteworthy because Bible reading was not the practice of Roman Catholics in those days, being considered, since the Reformation, to be a peculiarly Protestant habit. However, perhaps the most telling glimpse into her love of the Suffering Christ is the record of the hours she spent on her knees, oblivious to the sores that kneeling caused her.

In sum, Nano's life reflects her entering ever more deeply into the Paschal Mystery. It reflects an ever-deepening understanding of the intimate solidarity between the Suffering Christ and those who were dishonored around her in the community of Cork; and an ever-deepening understanding of the intimate solidarity between the Passion of Christ and her passion for Christ.

Rebuilding the Temple: Nano's Missiology
In reflecting upon the topics of the 'Temple of Community' and the 'Temple of Creation and the Cosmos' in sacred Scripture, we are drawn to reflect upon the mission of the building up of the Church, the Body of Christ; and, Earth, the planetary home of humanity and every created thing. In the context of exploring the charism and spirituality of Nano Nagle, we are invited to ponder the mission aspect of Nano's life which is part of her great legacy to us today.

From the outset, Nano had a sense that her mission was part of God's mission for the world. Were she in the business of seeking fame or fortune, she would not have entered a convent in France, nor, we suspect, would she have left it when beckoned to respond to the mission to the poor in Ireland. She presents her motivation to Eleanor Fitzsimons thus: 'Nothing would have made me come home but the decision of the clergy-man that I should run a great risk of salvation if I did not follow the inspiration'.[12] She senses that her salvation is at risk if she does not follow the inspiration, the breath of God that kept prompting her to radically alter the plan for her life that she had previously been so sure about.

While Nano's vision was to be of service to the poor of Cork, it is clear from the outset that it was not confined to Cork. In the first extant letter we have from her, she concludes her reflections to her confidante, Eleanor Fitzsimons, on her mission by saying: 'If I could be of any service in saving souls in any part of the globe, I would willingly do all in my power'.[13] One year later she reveals that she has put her vision into action. Some boys whom she instructed in her schools are being sent as missionaries for evangelization to the opposite end of the globe, the West Indies. Nano writes: 'They are well instructed, and as the true faith is decaying very much there by reason of them that leave this country knowing nothing of their religion, (this) made them lay this scheme, which I hope may have the desired effect'.[14]

In speaking of her custom of preparing children for the sacrament of penance at First Confession, Nano acknowledges the cost involved and she acknowledges her willingness to pay it. She writes: I 'being obliged to speak for upwards of four hours and my chest not being as strong as it had been – I spat blood; which I took good care to conceal for fear of being prevented from instructing the poor. It has not the least bad effect now'.[15] While the degree of self-neglect and secrecy from her companions is far from virtuous and not to be imitated, reflecting on the whole of her life, we find ample testimony that Nano knew only too well that the mission of rebuilding the dignity and lives of others costs, and sometimes, costs greatly – physically, mentally, emotionally and spiritually.

Nano's letters, like her life, reflect an ever-deepening awareness of the origin and end of the mission that had been entrusted to her by God. It would seem as though no kind of project for good was outside her imaginings; no kind of place was outside her anticipation; and no amount of energy was outside her generous giving.

Conclusion

The chapter began by tracing the unfolding story of God's dwelling with humanity and in the cosmos in the Judaeo-Christian tradition. This in turn provided a framework for examining the spirituality and charism of Nano Nagle. I would like to conclude by suggesting that we can use the framework of Temple Theology not only as a way of examining the spirituality and charism of Nano Nagle but also as a way of reflecting upon our journey in faith today.

We can reflect on our personal or communal experience of God using what can be termed 'the Five Presentation Mysteries': first, contemplate an experience of finding and praising God in the temple of creation; second, contemplate an experience of finding and loving Jesus Christ in the temple of our everyday life; third, recall an experience of contemplating the presence of God's Spirit in the temple within, as Mary did;[16] fourth, contemplate an experience of how the temple of creation, the temple of our everyday life, or the temple of our inner being has been or is being dishonored by us; and, finally, contemplate an experience of participating in the mission of rebuilding one or more of these 'temples' – the temple of creation, the temple of our community or workplace, the temple that is within us. In this way, a person or community can, like Nano, grow in mindfulness of, and responsiveness to, the ever-present and immanent reality of God in our midst.

Endnotes
1. G.K. Beale, *The Temple and the Church's Mission: A Biblical Theology of the Dwelling Place of God*. New Studies in Biblical Thought 17 (Downers Grove, IL: InterVarsity Press, 2004), 83.
2. Beale, *The Temple*, 86.
3. All quotations from Scripture are taken from the New American Bible version unless otherwise indicated.
4. Beale, *The Temple*, 107.
5. See http://w2.vatican.va/content/francesco/en/encyclicals/documents/papa-francesco_20150524_enciclica-laudato-si.html (29.11.2016)
6. ibid.
7. Nano Nagle to Miss Fitzsimons, AL 17 July 1769, par 12, in T. J. Walsh, *Nano Nagle and the Presentation Sisters* (Dublin: M. H. Gill and Son, 1959), 347.
8. Nano Nagle to Miss Fitzsimons, AL 13 May 1770, par 3, in Walsh, *Nano Nagle*, 351.
9. Nano Nagle to Miss Mulally, AL 29 July 1780, par 2, in Walsh, *Nano Nagle*, 364.
10. Cited in Mary Pius O'Farrell, *Nano Nagle: Woman of the Gospel*, (Cork: Cork Publishing, 1996), 203.
11. Nano Nagle to Miss Mulally, AL 17 March 1779, par 2, in Walsh, *Nano Nagle*, 362.
12. Nano Nagle to Miss Fitzsimons, AL 17 July 1769, par 3, in Walsh, *Nano Nagle*, 345.
13. Nano Nagle to Miss Fitzsimons, AL 17 July 1769, par 11, in Walsh, *Nano Nagle*, 347.
14. Nano Nagle to Miss Fitzsimons, AL early in 1770, par 2, in Walsh, *Nano Nagle*, 347.
15. Nano Nagle to Miss Fitzsimons, AL 17 July 1769, par 8, in Walsh, *Nano Nagle*, 346.
16. About, Mary, the Contemplative, João Braz De Aviz and José Rodríguez Carballo note: 'Unspeakable happiness and an unfathomable enigma, she becomes the temple of silence without which the seed of the Word will not germinate, nor the astonishment over God and his wonders blossom. She is a place where are heard the vibrations of the Word, and the voice of the Spirit as a gentle breeze. See, *Contemplate: Year of Consecrated Life* (Congregation for Institutes of Consecrated Life and Societies of Apostolic Life, Rome: Catholic Truth Society, 2016), 91.

Church – 'Home and School of Communion' – Enriched by Presentation Charism

Anne M. Codd PBVM

> To make the Church the home and the school of communion: that is the great challenge facing us in the millennium which is now beginning, if we wish to be faithful to God's plan and respond to the world's deepest yearnings.
> – John Paul II, *At the Beginning of the New Millennium*, 2001

It is by now widely recognised that the theological concept of communion provides an important key to the core vision of Vatican II. It offers us a way to understand and experience ourselves as *Ekklesia*, that is, the assembly of those called to be God's people in and for the world in our time and place. In this chapter I will begin by offering a brief exploration of the background and the significance of 'communion' in present-day theology of Church, and I will, ultimately, endeavour to show how the evolving Presentation charism nourishes the life-mission of the *Ekklesia* as 'the home and school of communion'.

I will refer, in particular, to the work of the French Dominican, Jean-Marie R. Tillard, (d. 2000). Tillard believed ardently in the potential of 'communion ecclesiology', not only to support inter-denominational dialogue, but also to deepen unity in diversity within the Catholic community itself. Of special interest here is Tillard's understanding of the nature and value of religious life as a state of life within the Church understood as communion, as a gift among gifts within the community of all those baptised and thereby consecrated for mission. Tillard identified living 'evangelical freedom' as a defining characteristic of authentic religious life.

Nano gave her life, freely, for the spread of the gospel through word and witness. Education for liberation has from the beginning been the hallmark of Nano's charism as lived by those who have come after her. That she was called to found a religious congregation – a community of communities fostering freedom for mission – is entirely consistent with her life story when viewed from the perspective of history. By reflecting on Nano's charism through the lens of living evangelical freedom I hope to highlight the significant contribution which, I believe, the communities who live that charism around the world today are making to Church and society.

Since Vatican II the way of life of 'ministerial' religious has been emerging in the Church in ways that are sometimes ahead of current canonical provision (e.g. in terms of lifestyle). However, law follows life, and movements which arise in response to the exigencies of Church and society do need to be shaped by appropriate regulation for fruitful mission. Tensions which arise in this process are unavoidable. With Nano it was so from the beginning. Through my brief exploration I hope to encourage all who share Nano's charism today to sustain with courage a relationship of communion within the Church, lived in a spirit of dialogue. In this way may we, as the whole ecclesial community, not only pray daily 'thy kingdom come' but also progress that coming in fidelity to our several and diverse vocations.

Theology of Church as Communion
Background

After the Council of Trent (1545–1563) the Catholic Church understood and presented itself predominantly as a 'perfect society', *societas perfecta*.[1] As M-J le Guillou observes,

> the notion of society ... led to a static conception of the Church as a fully-formed juridical institution, standing outside time, and resulted in the practical disappearance of the whole dynamic vision of the Church as the instrument of a plan of universal and cosmic dimensions.[2]

However, during the first half of the twentieth century, a wave of newness was making itself felt in several areas of Catholic theology including biblical scholarship and the study of the early Church. At the same time, in a war-torn world questions were being asked of established institutions, of religious traditions in general and of Christianity in particular. It was in this context that Pope John XXIII called the Second Vatican Council (1962–1965). Writing in 1989, Walter Kasper observed:

... one of the guiding ideas of the last council – perhaps the guiding idea – was ... communio – communion. By taking this as a leitmotif, the council succeeded in uncovering one of the deepest questions of the time, refining it in the light of the gospel, and answering it in a way that took it beyond a purely human questioning and seeking.³

Since its emergence in the work of J.A. Mohler (d. 1838), communion ecclesiology has held in a dynamic unity both the transcendence of God, which we can experience as the action of God's Spirit in our lives, and human freedom, by which we choose to respond to God's invitation in Christ. Communion ecclesiology understands the relationships which unite us as Church to be enabled by divine activity, and to be living expressions of Trinitarian love.

Ecclesiology of Communion in Vatican II

The Second Vatican Council made a ground-breaking contribution to how the Church now understands herself and her mission in the world. This understanding rests on belief in the enduring invitation which God, as divine community of three-in-one, extends to humanity and all creation. This invitation is to find fulfilment in sharing the unending, unbounded love of the Trinity. Participation in the divine life manifests itself in the created world as justice, love and peace ... a state of being which we call the kingdom of God, and which was inaugurated by Jesus Christ. The Church of God is the community of those who, through the Spirit, believe in Jesus as Son of God and Saviour of the world, and who witness to their belief by fostering the coming of the Kingdom.

The theological concept of 'communion' is used to express our relationship with the divine three and with one another within the all-embracing circle of their love. Kasper distils the three fundamental aspects of this communion in the documents of Vatican II as follows: (1) the basis of all communion is the familial relationship with God to which all are invited, created as we are in the image and likeness of God; (2) this communion has been realised in a unique way in history through Jesus Christ who, he says, is 'at the heart of all communion between God and human beings', and (3) it is the Holy Spirit, dwelling in the Church and in the lives of believers who forms the Church into a 'unity of communion with God and among its own members'.⁴

Yves Congar (d. 1995), identified a distinct role for the Holy Spirit in sustaining the Church's life *and* also its structure, though the latter he saw always to be in need of reform. Congar espoused the vision of communion and championed dialogue as its mode of engagement, not only as the means of reform but as the key to unity within the Church as communio-institution, and between churches. His fellow Dominican, Jean-Marie Tillard echoed his emphasis on the unity which does not destroy diversity as essential to Christian being:

> Communion (which is not divided) and singularity (which is not absorbed) sketch together the nature of the created being 'in the image of and resembling' a God whose Trinitarian nature is proclaimed by Christian faith.[5]

Tillard's commitment to communion ecclesiology also underpins his sense of the Church 'in many places', the local as embodiment of the universal. This Church 'multiplies itself without being divided … its extension does not change its essence'.[6]

The evolution of Vatican II's *Constitution on the Church in the Modern World* reflects the important work of Karl Rahner (d. 1984) in his insistence that the new sciences – physical, human and social – be called on to enlighten the Church's understanding of her mission in the world. Henri de Lubac (d. 1991), also emphasised that the Church – at once visible and invisible, local and universal – is in-the-world on mission, and is called to engage in the significant conversations of its time. While sacramental life and liturgical practice are essential in the life-mission of the Church, de Lubac insisted that for authentic Christian mission they be embodied in the work of charity and justice. Edward Schillebeeckx, too, emphasised the Church's relatedness to the mystery of God through Christ *and* its connectedness to the human community through the Spirit. The Church is neither an exclusively spiritual reality nor a solely sociological phenomenon, and communion ecclesiology holds its two-fold character in holistic unity.

Communion in the Church Now

The aspiration of a hospitable, inclusive Church – much sought after today in pastoral programmes of listening, reflecting and planning – is legitimate, but it is also challenging. We cannot claim the divine invitation to communion as a privilege for ourselves alone. The Church as a 'home and school of communion' is gifted as such for the whole of humanity, in all its cultural and religious diversity. Pope Francis insists:

> God attracts us by taking into account the complex interweaving of personal relationships entailed in the life of a human

community. This people, which God has chosen and called, is the Church. Jesus did not tell the apostles to form an exclusive and elite group. He said: 'Go and make disciples of all nations' (Mt 28:19).[7]

Religious Life in the Church Understood as Communion
Dilemmas in Post-Vatican II Context

When Vatican II endorsed and developed as Church teaching the twin themes from contemporary, renewed Catholic theology, (1) the universal call to holiness and (2) the missionary call of all the baptised, some commonly-held assumptions regarding the vocation of vowed 'religious' came under serious scrutiny. Definition of this way of life as renunciation of what is good in favour of better was no longer justifiable. At the same time, the ecclesiological vision of the Church as community of disciples, sign and sacrament of communion with God and with one another, highlighted the calling of all in the Church to their co-responsibility for its service to God's mission in the world. For the initiated, the dignity and value of 'lay' life was brought into sharp focus. For those already vowed as members of religious communities, there were questions to be addressed. Many revisited earlier decisions with new freedom, reading their experience in new light, and negotiated their departure from the 'religious state' with no sense of a concomitant reneging on Christian faith or commitment.

In 'Western' contexts the dramatic drop in the numbers of those joining religious congregations in the period following Vatican II is easily enough ascribed to the economic advancement and rising secularisation of these societies, and trends in the Presentation Congregation are certainly a case in point. It must also be recognised that, even as these congregations held, in obedience to the call of the Council, their special General Chapters of renewal and adaptation, the resultant changes to life-style and in many cases to the focus and location of ministry, led to a lowering of previous levels of cohesiveness and even of visibility of members in their immediate social and community settings. We may add to this a noticeable decline in the confidence of congregations to invite new members into the often turbulent milieu of community life, and indeed the difficulty of discerning authentic and sustainable 'vocations' to the vowed life as it was evolving, and we get some sense of the dilemmas which faced leaders and members alike.

Re-locating Religious Life in the Post-Vatican II Church

Tillard was one theologian of note who addressed the dilemmas outlined above directly, from the earliest days following the Council. Tillard is well known for his vision of a 'Church of Churches', based on a profound appreciation of the authenticity, the deep implications and the potential of the ecclesiology of communion. I have long been attracted to Tillard's self-declared intention to place himself 'beyond polemics'.[8] This stance is also evident in his search for a rationale for religious life in the post-Vatican II Catholic context. Tillard worked diligently, like his Dominican confrere, Congar, to further ecumenical dialogue.

Tillard exposed the limitations of viewing Church as followership of Jesus (including the 'radical' followership by those who 'left all') in his temporal deeds and words of charity and mercy. In this regard, Tillard notes the tendency of some religious congregations to locate their spirituality too firmly within the *imitation* of the early disciples.[9] But, as Tillard observes, the Christian era in which the Church resides begins with the resurrection of Christ and the gift of the Spirit:

> There is no reality which is precisely Christian outside of the tension between continuity and break which characterises the event of the Death–Resurrection. Outside of the opening up of the eschatological period during the temporal age, there is no *Ekklesia*.[10]

Essential to the Church of God are the Spirit, apostolic witness centred on the Lord Jesus Christ, and communion as unity with God and within the human multitude in all its diversity. In the Christian era we *participate* in the mystery of communion. Any perusal of the Presentation Congregations' accounts of their self-reflection for well over a decade now will show a keen awareness of this mystery.

It is within the understanding of *Ekklesia* as communion that Tillard addresses questions regarding the identity and purpose of religious life. Of course I realise that his exploration began over four decades ago. I would argue, however that its location (1) within the ecclesiology of communion which has been repeatedly validated as a critically important interpretative key to the Council, and (2) within the post-conciliar era which, in the wider context of Church history is still current, renders it foundational. Moreover, I find two further good reasons to revisit Tillard's important work: there are in my experience enduring tendencies, on the one hand, towards the elitism which presents or perceives religious life as a somehow more radical option for the kingdom of God than that which is asked of all the baptised and, on the other hand, towards an interpretation of the vowed life as somehow 'prophetic' to the point of being an alternative to the Church perceived only as institution.

Reading *Perfectae Caritatis*[11] in the context of the entire vision and thrust of Vatican II, Tillard presents an ecclesiologically-integrated rationale for religious life. As already indicated, he proposes as the defining characteristics of all ecclesial being its awareness that it is sustained by the Spirit, its apostolic witness, and its communion. To live as disciples in full accord with these essential norms, Tillard argues, requires of all a radical 'evangelical' freedom to seek first the kingdom of God. In religious life he sees not only the principle of this evangelical freedom as a guide, but also a concretising of its practice in the details of how the life is constituted and, at its best, structured. It is this motif of evangelical freedom which I am proposing as a core, organising principle for exploring Presentation charism in ongoing relation to the Church's mission.

The ministerial religious life (as instanced in the Presentation Congregation), a life which facilitates evangelical freedom for mission in real and practical ways, is a gift to the entire ecclesial community. It is a means whereby the gospel comes alive in a particular way, in the name of and to the benefit of all. Tillard warns in the strongest terms against viewing religious life as, in any way, reducing the demands of the gospel to 'a concentrate for the elite [or] an anthology of the most sublime selected texts, the other pages being left for those who dare not aim for the peaks'.[12] At the same time, against any temptation to identify religious life in terms of its derivatives, to confuse some specific elements, for example the vows, with the primary element i.e. the Gospel, Tillard asserts: 'The religious life that sought to divide the Gospel into separate portions would be a strange one indeed!'[13] Rather, following *Perfectae Caritatis*, Tillard recognises that 'its specific characteristics have no other purpose than to enable [people] to live [the] wholeness of the Gospel in a particular mode'. This understanding of religious life as a particular rather than a more perfect form of gospel living leads naturally to another important principle, articulated by Tillard and essential to our conversations right up to the present day: the complementarity of diverse vocations in the Church.[15] All the states of life through which baptised members of the Church are called to live their fundamental commitment to discipleship will be essential to God's kingdom-mission expressed in communion while we journey from Pentecost to Parousia.

Religious Congregations in the Church as a Hierarchically-Ordered Communion

It is not only at a personal or community level that practical evangelical freedom is a distinguishing mark of religious life. Institutionally, also, religious congregations are a clear indication that the Spirit blows freely (cf Jn 3:8). The founding inspirations of religious congregations lie mainly (though not exclusively) outside of the hierarchical organs of Church leadership. Founders and members of religious congregations are gifted with a freedom to identify need and to move in response to that need. This often brings them to the margins of the Church and/or of society. In some cases, they undertake direct service; at other times they labour to raise awareness of ecclesial, human and, especially today, ecological dilemmas, in the name of the Gospel, guided by the values of the Kingdom, the vision and radicality of all-embracing communion.

When quantum physics revolutionised human thinking in the early twentieth century, the teaching Church was slow to recognise the far-reaching implications of what was happening. At the present time, an ongoing, rapid expansion of knowledge – for example, the 'new cosmology' which is expanding the horizons of our consciousness as well as our resources for interpreting faith traditions and spiritual awareness; the realisation that human agency is indeed a major cause of climate change; the explosion of communication technologies; all this and more in addition to the perpetuation of massive human suffering through injustice, war and disaster – provides challenging landscapes for prophetic reflection and action. We must believe that the Spirit is alive and active in our time. Those free in fact as well as in spirit must be attentive to where the Spirit calls, notwithstanding their limitations and in some cases diminishment.

Where the Spirit moves, the Church is called. Mutual and complementary relations are essential between the responsibility of magisterial authority and the prophetic thrust within the Church, including that of religious congregations. It is not helpful, nor even defensible, to assume irreconcilable dichotomies. Throughout his long service as theologian and episcopos, Kasper has consistently observed that no person or section of the community of faith may lay claim with any legitimacy to a monopoly on the Spirit. Throughout history, tensions have been unavoidable, challenging but potentially creative when pursued in mutual critique and discernment, through dialogue. Tillard engages the dialectic between the ethic of responsibility and the ethic of conviction, borrowed from Weber and developed by Paul Ricoeur, to summarise the situation:

Whereas leaders of the hierarchy are obliged (by reason of the mission received from the Spirit) to keep to the difficult paths of the ethic of responsibility, without which the Church would be in danger of succumbing to chaos, the religious have to give prominence to ... the importance of conviction.[16]

Presentation Charism and the Church's Mission
Many chapters in this book both reflect and advance a rich understanding of the unfolding in time as well as the missionary significance of the life, work and charism of Nano Nagle. Here, I can only trace the main contours of Nano's project, together with the influences which moved and sustained her, insofar as they can be ascertained. My purpose is to view them in terms of evangelical freedom as I have explored it above. On this basis I will propose that it is, in hindsight, entirely credible as a work of the Spirit that Nano (eventually) founded a religious congregation which would continue to serve God's kingdom according to that same inspiration.

From the earliest accounts of Nano's life we are introduced to a child, born into a strongly Catholic family in a position of some privilege, who was able through her gifts of nature and of grace to savour the freedom which was hers in the pleasant surrounds of her home in Ballygriffin. Being well-connected, her family was able in due course to provide for Nano an opportunity for education and for entry with the comparative freedom of their class into the French society of her day. Whatever her private reflections on the lack of freedom of her peers in the hedge-school while still in Ireland, we know that she did take note of the contrast between the liberty and luxury of her life in Paris and the choice made by poor people (whom she observed) to be already present for early morning Mass before the Church doors opened. Back in Dublin, she was challenged by the freedom of her sister Ann to be generous with the poor. As time passed, Nano too made brave choices. She sought freedom to pray in the seclusion of a far-away convent where the poor of her own country would be out of sight. There she struggled for freedom to follow a pressing but indistinct urge to return to Ireland.

In due course Nano moved, with extraordinary courage and conviction, though of necessity by stealth, to provide the beginnings of liberation for the impoverished, disenfranchised Catholics of Cork city, through education for their children by day and visitation of their family elders in their hovels of homes by night. In this she was guided by her emblematic lantern and her burning desire, represented by the imagery of the Sacred Heart, to light their way to freedom. Fired by her contemplation of the divine, gratuitous love, she dedicated herself totally to teaching the children the basics of Catholic faith and rudiments of knowledge through which they could rise in freedom from their deprivation.

For the continuation of her work Nano saw the value of introducing a religious congregation to Cork, and she freely devoted her means to this project. When her purpose was not being fulfilled, she finally, courageously, single-mindedly, and practically bereft of funds, gathered the nucleus of a new Congregation of women who would share her passion for the liberation of the poor through knowledge of the faith and education for life.

And so, the Presentation Congregation was born. From the free gift of one woman of herself, to God and to people enslaved not only economically but also socially, culturally and politically, came a family of women called to be freed by the Gospel to freedom for the gospel, not only in principle but in practice, throughout the five continents.

In our time, there are striking resonances between the spirituality of being in communion, which has emerged from deep and wide reflection on the core identity of the Congregation, and the communion ecclesiology which expresses the essence of Church. The extension of Presentation ministries into direct action in areas of extreme poverty, as well as global and local partnerships for development, brings the *Ekklesia* itself to life in free and creative ways, in ever-widening circles of human endeavour.

Nano's dialogue with the Church authorities of her day is well documented. She was at once clear in her conviction, and respectful in her dealings. If Presentation communities are faithful to Nano's charism in our own day, they will sometimes also struggle for shared understanding and common purpose within the one mission of God. The tenacity of Nano has indeed been a source of inspiration for many brave women through two centuries and more. The spirituality of being in communion holds intensive strength the seeming opposition of freedom and regulation.

The charism of the Presentation Congregation, marked by a strong quality of practical evangelical freedom, and serving the freedom of the children of God through education for liberation resonates clearly with God's mission, as served in and by the *Ekklesia*. May the Spirit who gives all good gifts spur all who share the Presentation charism to enrich the Church in its communion with God and humanity, in a harmony of shared destiny with all creation.

Endnotes

1. The term is used in the sense that it is 'subordinate to no other and lacks nothing required for its own institutional completeness'. Avery Dulles, *Models of the Church* (New York: Doubleday, 1974), 31. Dulles points out the origin of the concept of *societas perfecta* in the ecclesiology of Robert Bellarmine. Rahner characterises the *societas perfecta* as 'an organization founded by Christ, with its offices and ministries, hierarchically structured and jurisdictionally empowered', 'Theology of the Parish', in Hugo Rahner (ed.), *The Parish: from Theology to Practice* (Westminster, Maryland: Newman Press, 1958), 26.
2. Karl Rahner (ed.), *Encyclopedia of Theology, a Concise Sacramentum Mundi*, (London: Burns and Oates, 1975), s.v. Church.
3. Walter Kasper, *Theology and Church* (London: SCM Press, 1989), 150.
4. Kasper, *Theology and Church*, 152.
5. Jean-Marie R. Tillard, *Church of Churches, The Ecclesiology of Communion* (Collegeville, Minnesota: The Liturgical Press, 1987), 18.
6. Tillard, *Church of Churches*, 14.
7. Pope Francis, *Evangelii Gaudium*, (Rome: Libreria Editrice Vaticana, 2013), Art. 113.
8. Tillard, *Church of Churches*, 4 (footnote 4).
9. In this same sense, vowed celibacy cannot be justified solely in terms of imitation of Jesus.
10. Tillard, *Church of Churches*, 5.
11. The Decree of Vatican II on the Adaptation and Renewal of Religious Life.
12. Jean-Marie Tillard, *A Gospel Path, the religious life* (Brussels: Lumen vitae, 1978), 93.
13. Tillard, *A Gospel Path*, 94.
14. Tillard, *A Gospel Path*, 95.
15. The process of rewriting the Constitutions of the Union of Presentation Sisters (2010–2012) provided that Congregation with a graced opportunity to study this principle through extensive research, reflection and conversation.
16. Tillard, *A Gospel Path*, 109.

Part Four

Evolving Charism

Presentation Charism in a Latino Context

Gloria Inés Loya PBVM

Your Word is a lantern for my feet, a light for my path.
(Psalm 119:105)

Linterna es a mis pies tú palabra y lumbrera a mi camino.
(Salmo 119:105)

Pope Francis has called the Christian faithful (*Christifidelis*), which includes the laity, bishops, priests and the religious, to become missionary disciples who live and proclaim the joy of the Gospel in our time.[1]

> The Gospel, radiant with the glory of Christ's cross and resurrection, constantly invites us to rejoice ... 'Rejoice' is the angel's greeting to Mary (Lk 1:28).
>
> Mary's visit to Elizabeth makes John leap for joy in his mother's womb (Lk 1:41). In her Song of Praise, Mary proclaims: 'My spirit rejoices in God my Saviour' (Lk 1:47).[2]

The tercentenary of the birth of Nano Nagle is an historical moment to reflect on God's joyful gift (charism) bestowed upon Nano Nagle, the Sisters of the Presentation, and on the Church. By reflecting on the charism from within the context of Latino/a and Hispanic culture we will discover new hope for mission. Pope Francis points to saints such as Spanish-born St John of the Cross, St Teresa of Avila, and Mexican-born Juan Diego (b. 1474) – the first Roman Catholic indigenous saint of the Americas – who in their mission uncovered the timeless wisdom as well as the newness and freshness of the Word.[3] This is also what Nano Nagle did as she carried the light of her lantern and the light of the Gospel into the darkness, desolation, and discrimination endured by the People of God in Ireland under the Penal Laws. Because the world still needs the Gospel and Nano's lantern light, it is timely to remember Pope Francis' challenge 'to go beyond the comfortable spaces, places and territories towards ... new socio-cultural settings ... wherever the need for the light and the life of the Risen Christ is greatest'.[4] Nano's charism gives light to the journey towards an evangelization that includes prophetic intercultural dialogue.

In the eighteenth century the people of Ireland were kept in poverty, ignorance and in a limited expression of their Roman Catholic faith. Nano Nagle's cousin, the great orator, Edmund Burke (1729–1797), describes the Penal Code that oppressed the Gaelic People in 1747:

> It was a machine of wise and elaborate contrivance and as well fitted for the oppression, impoverishment and degradation of a people and the debasement in them of human nature itself, as ever proceeded from the perverted ingenuity of man.[5]

Nano, through faith in the Sacred Heart of Jesus and through foresight and wisdom, sowed the seed for a new model of ministerial religious life based on the Gospel. She responded to the crying needs of the poor and oppressed Catholics of Ireland. Historian, Mary Pius O'Farrell summarizes it thus:

> Nano Nagle's plan was original; it only took time to expand. From the day when she first gathered poor children together in Cork, she acted in defiance of many penal statutes. Poverty, ignorance, moral abuse and social injustice formed the battleground of Nano and her followers ... she adopted a prudent and low profile, while being as courageous as she dared ... She began to restore personal dignity and worth to the poor.[6]

Nano Nagle received her spiritual gift of loving compassion from the Holy Spirit for the benefit of the Church and for furthering the reign of God in the world. In his Letters to the early communities (1 Cor 12), St Paul writes about such gifts as this. While there are distinct and diverse gifts, all are united as they flow from God's grace. All gifts (charismata) are manifested in diverse forms of service (*diakonia*). There are diverse cultures and ethnicities to be served in the Church and all people are united as one in the Body of Christ (1 Cor 12:12). St Paul develops his image of the Body of Christ (1

Cor 12:1–31) and writes more profoundly (1 Cor 13:1–13) regarding the unity within the diversity of gifts saying that they become even more important and effective when they are informed by love (*agape*). Nano's unrelenting response to God's call became manifest in her loving compassion for the poorest and most vulnerable.

In the mission and ministry of Presentation women today Nano's charism continues to evolve.[7] This paper will explore two significant aspects of this evolving charism in the context of Latino/a culture. This exploration is framed as follows: first, Latino/a culture and spirituality;[8] and then, selected Presentation narratives. Finally, concluding remarks in the form of considerations for religious life will be presented.

Latino/A Culture and Spirituality

While there are many Latino cultures, the focus here will be specifically on the *méxicano* culture as locus of the human experience of divine revelation.[9] By 'culture' is meant the language, symbols, rites/rituals, religiosity/devotion, history, communication, relationships, narratives and webs of meaning within a group of people. No culture is perfect, neither is any culture worthless.

It can be learned from history that one cannot proclaim the love of God authentically if one does not respect the people. In the New Testament, Peter and Paul respected the Gentile cultures so that the mission of Jesus could grow to the ends of the earth (Acts 15). The Italian-born Jesuit missionary to China, Matteo Ricci (1552–1610), realized that if Christianity were to enter deeply into China, there had to be respect for the elements of truth in the Chinese culture. In 1659, the Church stated that it would be foolish to attempt to import Italy, France or Spain into China.[10] Another Italian-born Jesuit, Robert de Nobili (1577–1656), learned from the wise men of India of the deep spiritual traditions that were indigenous to the peoples of the sub-continent. Sadly, however, not all Christian missionaries valued the indigenous cultures where they went. Latino/a culture also suffered through some missionary endeavours, however benevolently intended.

The Mayas were the earliest peoples of *Mesoamérica*. They lived in a spiritual and religious cosmic universe from which they learned moral reasoning and the ethical life.[11] All of creation was accepted as a blessing from the deities. Unlike the Europeans of the sixteenth century, the peoples of this time and place did not separate the sacred world from the profane world. In the Mayan creation stories, *The*

Popol Vuh, an account of the evolution of the universe is described within the religious and symbolic cosmos of the ancient Mayas:

> *Este es el principio de las antiguas historias del Quiche donde se referirá, declarará y manifestará lo claro y lo escondido del Creador y Formador, que es Madre y Padre de todo.*
> (This is the origin of the ancient histories of the world which refers to all that is declared and manifested about the clear/visible and hidden/invisible regarding the Creator and Formator, who is Mother and Father of the Universe.)

> *Habiendose echado las lineas y paralelas del cielo y de la tierra, se dio fin perfecto a todo, dividiendo en paralelos y climas. Todo puesto en orden quedo cuadrado repartido en cuatro partes como si con una cuerda se hubiera todo medido, formando cuatro esquenas y cuatro lados.*[12]
> (Having drawn the parallel lines and the limits of the heavens and of the earth, all was perfectly created, dividing the various areas [seasons] of the climates. All was placed in the order of four, dividing the four corners of the earth as though all was measured perfectly forming four sides.) [east, west, north, south]

For the ancient Mayas, God had both feminine and masculine qualities as Mother and Father of Creation. Earth was the fertile mother who gave birth to the soil which is the foundation of life.[13] A mystical relationship existed between humans and mother earth because from the earth came the growing and harvesting of the maize. The heavens expressed the transcendence and the vastness of their sacred cosmos.[14] Because life was intimately linked to the Creator it was lived daily by strict rules and responsibility in community. As well as earth, the ancient Mayas also appreciated the elements of fire, water and wind.

After the decline of the Mayan empire in the fifteenth century, came the Aztecs. They lived in the city of Teoteuacan, Mexico City. *The Colloquies* are recorded narrations between the Aztec wise men and the new Iberians/Spanish arrivals. In 1519, Hernán Cortéz and the Iberians invaded Mexico. The Aztec wise men initiated the first intercultural dialogue between the spiritual indigenous cosmic world and the Christian European world.

> Our Lords, our very esteemed Lords; great hardships have you endured to reach this land. Here before you, we ignorant

people contemplate you. And now, what are we to say? What should we cause your ears to hear? Perchance, is there any meaning to us? Only very common people we are. Perhaps we are to be taken to our ruin, to our destruction. But where are we to go now? We are ordinary people, we are subject to death and destruction; we are mortal; allow us then to die, let us perish now, since our gods are already dead.

For our ancestors before us, who lived upon the earth, were unaccustomed to speak thus (as you do). From them we inherited our way of life which is truth.

Spanish-born Franciscan friar, Fray Bernardino de Sahagún (1499–1590), an ethnographer, created *The Florentine Codex*[16] (also known as the *Historia General de las Cosas de la Nueva España*).[17] Fray Bernardino respected and honoured the Aztec language and culture and his work contributes to our present understanding of this rich civilization.

In Mexico, two historical and cultural worlds met in a profoundly complex and violent clash between the Iberian and the indigenous peoples. What emerged from this long process was a merging of languages, cultures, religious, ethical and moral traditions into what is called the *mestizaje*.[18] Latinos/as of the Caribbean prefer the concept *mulatez* as it relates more accurately to countries such as Puerto Rico, Cuba, and the Dominican Republic because their people evolved from African as well as Spanish roots. This clash of cultures became a crucible that held the darkness of conquest with the power of divine grace revealed within the very people who are mestizos and mulattos. Theologian, Virgil Elizondo (1935–2015) describes this clash of cultures as a 'birth' of a new mestizo and mulatto people in the Americas. In pain and loss, through the contradiction of the Cross, mestizo and mulatto cultures were transformed into something new without losing their unique origins.[19] For Elizondo, *mestizaje* does not name an object but a process by which a culture has to die in order to survive. But in order to survive, a culture has to be transformed, the awareness of which is essential to understanding contemporary cultures and their dynamic interplay.[20]

In 1531, a new presence of grace and of the beautiful evolved through the liberating proclamation and theophany from the Hill of Tepeyac in which María de Guadalupe calls Juan Diego. She is a *mestiza* with characteristics of the indigenous and of the Iberians in her language (*Náhuatl* and Spanish) and in her human features. She invites Juan Diego to become her disciple, and though he is reluctant, she slowly discerns with him as he embraces his call to carry out her message to create a new church in the new world. The Word is proclaimed and planted in the Americas through her initiative. Reflecting on the tradition, theologian Virgil Elizondo captures the spirit of the Madonna thus: 'I have a living desire that there be a temple built, so that in it I can show and give forth all my love, compassion, help and defense, because I am your loving mother; to you, to all who love me, call upon me, and trust in me. I will hear their lamentations and will remedy all of their miseries, pain and sufferings'.[21]

Mexican author, Antonio Valeriano (c. 1521–1605), penned the earliest extant narrative, *The Nican Mopohua* about the apparition at Guadalupe.[22] Here, the great wonder is narrated regarding the appearance of the Holy Virgin Mary Mother of God, Our Venerable Queen. There in Tepeyace, is the one who is named Our Lady of Guadalupe. Cardinal Rivera Carrera of Mexico has written that the canonization of Juan Diego reminds us of how the Church lifts up to sainthood only real historical people, not simply myths and symbols.[23] Our Lady of Guadalupe is the central figure of Latino/a faith, history and liturgy because she presents her Son and Christianity to peoples of the Americas. The Feast of Our Lady of Guadalupe is celebrated wherever there are Latinos/as. The drama of rejection, loss, liberation and utter joy continues to be celebrated through flower, song (*flor y canto*), and dance in the community.

Latino/a immigrants to the US can endure obstacles such as discrimination, poverty and deportation. Those who remain there are able to continue their education and become professionals who serve the community. Those of all cultures who choose ministry must be prepared and educated in the challenge of evangelization and inculturation. Respect for and dialogue with cultures are prerequisites for Christian ministry.

In his apostolic exhortation entitled, *On Evangelization in the Modern World* (*Evangelii Nuntiandi*, 1975), Pope Paul VI sums up evangelization as something that must speak to every aspect of human life. Evangelization must be aimed at illuminating and transforming men (and women) as they are: 'What matters is to evangelize human culture and cultures ... always taking the person as one's starting point and always coming back to the relationships of people among themselves and with God'.[24] Contextualization, therefore, is not something on the fringes of the theological enterprise; it is a theological imperative. Culture and world events become the very source of the theological enterprise. Both poles – human experience and the Christian tradition, are to be read together dialectically.[25]

The Latino/a and Hispanic culture is celebrated throughout the Americas today in rituals in homes, in the streets and in the Church with fervor, colour, music, dance and deep prayer. The people's faith expressions contribute to a unique popular religiosity/devotion. This communal expression of faith contributes richly to the lives of the people and challenges the cynicism found in a secular, post-modern world that upholds radical individualism above all else.

Nano Nagle's vision was expansive and inclusive. She wrote: 'If I could be of any service in saving souls in any part of the globe, I would willingly do all in my power'.[26] Missionary Presentation Sisters and students have shared the richness (and limitations) of their cultures of origin, even as they respectfully, by and large, embraced the rich cultural heritage of their host communities.

Presentation Narratives

The term Latino/a is used to describe the more than fifty million people living in the US with cultural roots in the Latin American Countries. This is the youngest and fastest-growing cultural group in the US. The ministerial experience of Presentation women living the charism within the Latino/a community throughout the US is rich and is grace-filled.[27] In 2013 I interviewed several Sisters and one Associate regarding their experience in Latino/a ministry. Two of these narratives – extracts of which I give below – speak for themselves as they show that the charism is alive and well.[28]

Narrative 1

In East Los Angeles, California, I met parents who were punished for speaking Spanish in school when they were young. We tried to teach Spanish so that they would see the importance of their language. There were many gangs in the area and we tried to do what Nano did: to be present with the people such as when someone was shot. Through the ministry of education we taught Christian values.

In 2006 three of us Presentation Sisters initiated a new program called, El Proyecto de las Rosas, *(The Project of the Roses) in a small rural town in Central California. We believed that this is what Nano did as she reached out to the poor. The Latino/a culture and its people are also rich in a unique spirituality based on what is called popular piety. In each situation of my ministry with Latinos, their faith has been a tremendous example and inspiration to me.* (Pati)

Narrative 2
I am from Jalostotlitlán, México. *My family came to the US and later I joined them in California. During my first five years living here I was in shock. In México I was working and living comfortably. I realized what little knowledge I had about not only the language, but also about US culture and the way of life. So many things were different for me in the customs, the manner in which people did things. I even felt uncomfortable in the liturgy. I lived in misery for five years until I began to study English and later theology at the university. Little by little I began to understand.*

For me Nano's lantern is like my banner. As children in our pueblito *we didn't have light or electricity in our house. My father used to light the oil lantern. When he lit it, it meant it was time to pray the rosary together; it meant it was time to have fun and to enjoy family life together; and also it meant it was time to have dinner. Before I learned of Nano's mission I would see the painting of Nano in the convent and she was carrying the lantern. This reminded me of my childhood. I remember when the lantern was lit in our home, it was time to pray, to enjoy each other's company and to share a meal.*

I am supported in my small community of Presentation Associates, the Guadalupe Community. We do as I did in my childhood. It is a beautiful gift: we pray together; we enjoy one another; we share our struggles; and we celebrate with a meal. It makes me feel that I, as a Méxicana, *am also part of Nano's heritage both in this small community, and in the Presentation Family. The Presentation of Mary reminds me of my love for the Virgin Mary. I continue my love for the* Virgencita *in this community.*[29]
(Lupita)

Lupita's family was from *Los Altos de Jalisco*, a region in the eastern part of Mexico, as was my mother's family, the Quezadas. During the 1920s the people were persecuted by the government and the churches were closed. Nevertheless, our families continued our Catholic faith by hiding the priests and religious and celebrating the Eucharist in their homes, even in the face of death. *Viva Cristo Rey!* My father's family, the Loyas, came to the US after her grandfather was killed in the Mexican revolution. The Church embraces such narratives as they hold truth and reveal the Gospel of suffering and of resurrection.

Conclusion

What might the accounts of Latino/a culture and spirituality and Presentation narratives provided above offer to a reflection on the evolving charism of Religious Life as expressed by the Presentation Sisters? What is original and grace-filled in the intermixing (*mestizaje*) of the evolving charism of Nano, as reflected in the lives of Presentation Sisters, and Latino/a culture and spirituality is that the paradox of the Cross of Jesus, witnessed by his mother, is at the root of both.

This face of this paradox is often reflected in the many new and unprecedented challenges of our time.[30] The Gospel-inspired evolving charism of Nano, founder of the Presentation Sisters, continues to be a core life-source in a world of fragmentation and chaos, where narrow historical understandings limit constructive or creative responses. Presentation communities that sustain an openness to intercultural dialogue with the poor and immigrants will encounter transformation. Such openness reflects the purpose of the charism of religious life in general of which Sandra Schneiders writes: 'The single-hearted quest for God is the mystical or unitive heart of Religious Life ... this dimension is nurtured and experienced in its most concentrated form in contemplative prayer ... Religious come together with others ... bound only by shared faith in and total self-gift to Christ for the sake of the world.'[31]

The Presentation way of life, like culture itself, is an organic life-form that is undergoing a transformation.[32] J.R.R. Tolkien provides some insight into this. Tolkien metaphorically describes in *The Hobbit*, how the character, Bilbo Baggins, does not want to journey further after the treacherous Misty Mountains:

> '*Must we go any further?*' asked Bilbo ...
> 'Yes! ... Over *the Edge of the Wild on the borders of the unknown*'.[33]

Bilbo had a magic ring to make his journey. We do not need a magic ring. We have Nano's charism, and the Gospel to discern and to light the pathway through the unknown.

Endnotes

1. Pope Francis, *Apostolic Exhortation, Evangelii Gaudium, of the Holy Father Francis to the Bishops, Clergy, consecrated Persons and the Faithful on the Proclamation of the Gospel in Today's World* (Rome: Vatican Press, 2013),
2. Pope Francis, *Evangelii Gaudium*, 5.
3. Pope Francis, *Evangelii Gaudium*, 11
4. Pope Francis, *Evangelii Gaudium*, 30.
5. Sr Mary Pius O'Farrell, *Nano Nagle, Woman of the Gospel* (Cork: Cork Publishing, 1996), 15–16.
6. O'Farrell, *Nano Nagle, Woman of the Gospel*, 21.
7. O'Farrell, *Nano Nagle, Woman of the Gospel*, 89–90.
8. James E. Hug (ed.), *Tracing the Spirit, Communities, Social Action, and Theological Reflection* (New York: Paulist Press, 1983) is a classic resource. Robert L. Kinast, 'Theological Reflection in Ministry Preparation' in *Tracing the Spirit*, 83–99. Robert J. Schreiter, *Constructing Local Theologies* (Maryknoll, New York: Orbis Books, 1985).
9. Stephen B. Bevans, 'The Anthropological Model' in *Models of Contextual Theology*, 56. Aylward Shorter, *Evangelization and Culture* (New York: Geoffrey Chapman, 1994).
10. Hubert Jedin and John Patrick Dolan (eds), *History of the Church: The Church in an Age of Absolutism and Enlightenment* (Vol 6) (New York: Crossroad, 1981), 286.
11. See G. I. Loya, *The Mexican American Woman in California: Pathways Towards a Pastoral Project*, Doctor of Ministry Project (Berkeley: Pacific School of Religion, Graduate Theological Union, 1996), 44–6.
12. Albertina Saravía (ed.), *The Popul Vuh* (México: Editorial Porrua, 1971), 1.The English translation is mine.
13. ibid.
14. Saravia, *The Popul Vuh*, 2.
15. Miguel Leon Portilla, *Aztec Thought and Culture, a Study of the Ancient Nahuatl Mind* (Norman, Oklahoma: University of Oklahoma Press, 1963), 62–7.
16. This codex consisted of a twelve-volume intercultural dictionary exploring the connection between the Aztez and European cultures.
17. Robert Ricard, 'Ethnographic and Linguistic Training of the Missionaries,' ch. 2 in *The Spiritual Conquest of México* (Berkeley, CA: University of California Press, 1982), 39–60.
18. Virgil Elizondo, *Mestizaje, la Dialectica del Nacimiento Cultural y el Evangelio* (San Antonio, TX: Méxican AmericanCultural Center), 9.
19. ibid.
20. Jacques Audinet, 'A Mestizo Theology' in Timothy Matovina (ed.), *Beyond Borders: Writings of Virgilio Elizondo and Friends* (Maryknoll, NY: Orbis Books, 2000), 143–9.
21. Virgil Elizondo, *La Morenita, Evangelizer of the Americas* (Mo: Liguori Press, 1981), 76.
22. Xavier Noguez, *Documentos Guadalupanos, Un estudio sobre las Fuentes de información tempranas en torno a las mariofanias en el Tepeyac* (México: El colegio Mexiquense, A.C., Fondo de Cultura Económica, 1993), 19. My translation.
23. Norberto Carden Rivera Carrera, *Juan Diego, El Aguila que Habla* (México: Plaza & Janes, 2002), 16.

24. Pope Paul VI, *Evangelii Nuntiandi, On Evangelization in the Modern World* (Washington, D.C.: US Catholic Conference, 1975), 16–17.See Stephen B. Bevans, *Models of Contextual Theology, Faith and Cultures, Revised and Expanded Edition* (Maryknoll, New York: Orbis Books, 2013), 15–16.Francis Xavier (1506–1552) was the missionary to Asia who learned to discover strengths and virtues in the cultures. In James Martin (ed.), *Give us this Day, Daily Prayer for Today's Catholic* (Collegeville, MN: Liturgical Press, 2013), 40.
25. Pope Paul VI, *Evangelii Nuntiandi*, 32.
26. Nano Nagle to Miss Fitzsimons AL 29 April 1770, par 11, in T. J. Walsh, *Nano Nagle and the Presentation Sisters* (Dublin: M. H. Gill and Son, 1959), 347.
27. Timothy Matovina, 'Remapping American Catholicism' in *Latino Catholicism, Transformation in America's Largest Church* (Princeton NJ: Princeton University Press, 2012), 1–41.
28. I am grateful to each who participated. Although we cannot include all interviews here, they are available in a separate document.
29. Blessed Miguel Pro SJ (1891–1927) was one of the martyrs: 'We ought to speak, shout out against injustices, with confidence and without fear.We proclaim the principles of the Church, the reign of love, without forgetting that it is also a reign of justice' in Martin (ed.), *Give us this Day*, 221. A most comprehensive work in three volumes: Jean Meyer, *#1 La Cristiada, Guerra de los Cristeros* (México: Siglo Veintiuno Editores, séptima edición, 1985), 174–5.
30. Paul Lakeland, *Postmodernity: Christian Identity in a Fragmented Age* (Minneapolis, MN: Fortress Press, 1997).
31. Sandra M. Schneiders, *Buying the Field: Religious Life in a New Millennium* (New York: Paulist Press, 2013), 96–8.
32. Sandra M. Schneiders, 'Religious Life as an Organic Lifeform: Getting It Together' in *Finding the Treasure, Locating Catholic Religious Life in a New Ecclesial and Cultural Context* (New York: Paulist Press), 54–66.
33. J.R.R. Tolkien, *The Hobbit or There and Back Again* (Harper Collins: Britain, 1995), 98–9.

Stewardship and the Charism of Nano Nagle

Anne M. O'Leary PBVM

This chapter examines the topic of stewardship and the charism of Nano Nagle (1718–1784), founder of the religious congregation that came to be known as the Sisters of the Presentation of the Blessed Virgin Mary (hereafter, Presentation Sisters). To this end, we use an early description of bursarship as the hermeneutic or lens to frame the examination.

The following is a description of the office of bursar or treasurer, taken from the first approved Constitutions of the Presentation Sisters. The Office of the Depositary or Bursar (1809):[1]

> - The Bursar, the second in rank among the Discretes, shall be a person acquainted with *management* of household business; a prudent, and careful *economist*, and *qualified by her courteousness and affability to conciliate the respect and good will of the whole*, with whom she may have occasion to contract business.
>
> - She is to *receive and keep the money* of the Convent, and pay all *the disbursements*, which are always to be made according to the directions of the Mother Superior. She shall keep *a faithful and exact account in writing* of the receipts and expenditures, which she shall lay every week before the Mother Superior, in preference of the Discretes, to be *audited and signed* by her. (Italics mine.)

Through this lens, we come to know a charism within the charism of Nano Nagle, of her gifts and skills in the areas of administration, management, finance and organizational development.

Context and Call

From the Christian perspective, we see that in every historical age, God calls persons and groups, and raises them up to respond to the unmet needs of the time. When Nano Nagle was a teenager she was introduced to society life in Paris and, later, she joined the society life of Dublin upon her return to that city to be with her mother, Ann, and her sister, Ann – after the death of her father, Garret (c. 1746). The Nagle women, like others of their means and status, enjoyed a very genteel lifestyle and moved in the upper echelons of society.

For the majority of the people in eighteenth-century Ireland, life was not so genteel. In fact, it was very harsh and oppressive. The harshness manifested itself in two main ways – in violence and economic poverty, both the offspring of ignorance and oppression. This harshness is graphically reflected in Dean Dominic Murphy's *Memoirs of Miss Nagle*. He cites a journal of the day called *Cork Remembrancer* which recorded striking extracts from the local newspapers about the dark reality of life in Cork in the 1760s and 1770s. During these decades Nano opened several school and was busy with overseeing the building of a convent for the Ursuline Sisters whom she sponsored to come to Cork from Paris where they were trained as religious. One such extract reads: 'Dec. 3, 1769.— Rioting had become so common in this city, that it was not safe for anyone to stand at his doorway without a weapon of defence.'[2]

A second entry on March 8 1772 provides an even more stark vision of how things were in Cork city:

> One of the sentinels at South Gate was knocked down by the three desperadoes, who (were it not for the noise of passengers approaching) would have thrown him over the bridge. The evening of the same day … was concluded in a most pious and devout manner, by the warlike sons and daughters of Fairlane and Blackpool, who met in a long field near Fair-hill, and fought with one another till night came on. The females were armed plentifully with stones; and the male inhabitants, according to Cherokee custom, with tomahawks of a new construction; which were about four feet long, and so dexterously contrived (having a hook and spear at the end) that any who missed grappling, were sure to stab with the sharp point.[3]

Murphy provides the following critique of the *status quo* of the day:

> The very magistrate who could look with passive indifference, on such scenes as these extracts describe, could yet assemble a

few years later and deliberate on the necessity of extinguishing the germ of the Ursuline and Presentation orders, which proposed to educate the people. And it was the same thing throughout the length and breadth of the land.[4]

It is salutary to think that the flame of hope that Nano lit in Cork could so easily have been extinguished.

The harshness that people endured economically is described by T.J. Walsh in *Nano Nagle and the Presentation Sisters* with a graphic image of the reality of the poor in that century thus: 'The homes of the poor were for the most part mud-walled cabins, roofed with thatch, airless and insanitary dwellings. In such surroundings beggary and social dejection abounded.'[5] Such poverty was also experienced in rural Ireland. Walsh notes:

> The wretchedness of the tenantry which moved Nano Nagle in her home at Ballygriffin was universal in the Cork countryside. George Berkeley (1684–1753), the philosopher-bishop of Cloyne, described the destitution in vivid terms: 'The house of an Irish peasant is a cave of poverty; within you see a pot and a little straw; without, a heap of children tumbling on a dung-hill. In every road the ragged ensigns of poverty are displayed; you often meet caravans of poor, whole families in a drove, without clothes to cover, or bread to feed them.'[6]

At this time in Ireland, 'It was illegal for Catholics to acquire property by purchase, gift, mortgage, or inheritance'.[7] Not only could they not acquire land, it was almost impossible for them to keep it. Walsh writes, 'The fourteen percent of profitable lands still in Catholic ownership in 1703 was reduced to five percent in 1776.'[8] Moreover, there is evidence that the Nagle family struggled to retain ownership of their lands as in 1727–1728, 'Garret Nagle … Nano's father sold lands contiguous to Ballygriffin to a Protestant, named Mr Peter Graham.'[9] If Mr Nagle had not sold some of his land to mollify the requirements of the Penal Laws, he risked losing everything.

For the majority of the people, this was a time in Ireland not only of economic poverty but spiritual poverty, intellectual poverty, moral poverty, social poverty, poverty of self-esteem and self-determination – a time of every kind of poverty imaginable. This is the context in which Nano, as a young woman, received her inner calling. We know in hindsight that she had the potential to respond in faith to God's leading at every step of the journey (cf. Ps 119:105).

The Nagle Family: Bridging the Two Irelands

What grew in Nano in relation to living the mission of Jesus, did not fall like apples off the trees in the orchards of Ballygriffin. It must have been seeded and nurtured in her home because from what has been recorded in relation to her siblings indicates that they also reflect life-long dedication to the service of the poor, needy and disenfranchised.[10] We get a glimpse of the charity of the Nagle family from a letter that a certain Fr James Roche, parish priest of Ballygriffin, writes to Nano's brother, David, in which he expresses his deep gratitude to David for the relief he gave 'to the orphans of poor Halloran.'

> For that and all your charitable actions, I wish you the kingdom of heaven. And I beg you that one [Mr] Carty be turned off your land for giving scandal. The potato-harvest is disappointing and I fear famine. I have repaired my cabin since I last saw you. I would starve but for the house and land you have given me.[11]

What a tribute to David! Even as he was blessed to enjoy a comfortable life in Bath, England, he did not forget his place of origin or his childhood neighbours. The spirit of giving without counting the cost is further reflected in the short life of Nano's sister, Ann, as we know from the account of her disposing of silk, intended for a gown, to relieve a distressed family.[12] Nano's reflection on this incident marks a critical dawning in her life, orienting her unflinchingly toward the poor and away from the high society life she had known.

Phase I: Early Network of Schools (1749–66)

Inspired by her sister, Ann, Nano set about responding to the needs of the poor. She chose to do so in her native Cork. Nano's gift of discretion and her practice of the virtue of prudence in forwarding her vision are evident from the outset. In a letter to the first Ursuline novice, Ms Eleanor Fitzsimons, Nano, ever the Discrete, writes:

> When I arrived [in Cork from Dublin] I kept my design a profound secret, as I knew, if it were spoken of, I should meet with opposition on every side, particularly from my immediate family as in all appearance they would suffer from it. My confessor was the only person I told of it; and as I could not appear in the affair, I sent my maid to get a good mistress and

to take in thirty poor girls. When this little school was settled
I used to steal there in the morning – my brother thought I
was at the chapel.[13]

The establishment of seven schools across Cork city – five for girls and two for boys – must have taken quite a bit of networking not to mention discreet inquiries, given the severity of the times that were in it. Under threat of imprisonment or life-long exile as a convict, Nano, surreptitiously, had to find safe spaces, secure a number of helpers, as well as connect with the underground priests about celebrating Mass in her schools, and much more.[14]

Given that 'Cork had surpassed other ports in England and Ireland in the export of salted provisions,'[15] it is not surprising that Nano's global vision first became a reality when some boys whom she had instructed went as missionaries to the West Indies. To accomplish this, Nano also had to engage discreetly with the shipping merchants of Cork to secure passage for her boys. The need was the evangelization of the Irish who worked as labourers on the ships that travelled between Cork and the West Indies; as well as the Irish who were taken there as slaves in the seventeenth century and who knew little or nothing of their faith. The response was to send young Irish boys who had been instructed in the faith at Nano's schools. At this time, there was much trade between Cork and the West Indies; Nano's uncle, Joseph, had property there too.[16] It is likely that both of these factors – the trade between Cork and the West Indies and the Nagle connection with it – contributed to her choice of the West Indies for the extension of the work she had begun in Cork.[17]

Phase 2: The Ursuline Project
Evidence of Nano, the Manager, can be detected from the time when she began the work of making her vision of a foundation of Ursuline Sisters (hereafter, Ursulines) a reality. She was in a strong financial position after the death of her uncle, Joseph Nagle, in 1757. He was an attorney-at-law and 'regarded as a leader of the Catholic laity in Cork,'[18] and, not surprisingly, 'the most disliked by Protestants of any Catholic in the Kingdom.'[19]

The first building project Nano managed was the building of a small cottage (or cabin) on the side of a street in Cork city called Cove Lane. It would become her home. This type of dwelling would not betray any suggestion of a residence associated with Catholic gentry or, later, religious nuns. It contained just three rooms and a garret or loft area. For the Ursuline project, Nano sought a more discreet site at the rear of this cottage on which to build.

To this end, in 1769, now aged 51, Nano leased land behind her cottage on Cove Lane from Isabella Harper, widow, whose late husband, John Harper, had leased it from David Nagle. It was left to Nano's brother David by their uncle Joseph Nagle. With the expiry of the Harper lease [c. 1770] the land reverted to David Nagle. David released his sister, Nano, from the terms of her lease of the property. It is his name that appears on the lease of the site of the Ursuline convent.[20] That said, the lot or trianglular shaped property that became the property of the Ursulines, and later Presentation Sisters, was but 'a small spot saved out of a very large estate' that has been owned by Nano's uncle, Joseph Nagle.[21] Most of it had already been lost to the then colonial government under the Penal Laws. Nano managed the entire building project of the Ursuline Convent from beginning to end. She managed its development, engaging with architects, builders, masons, lumber providers, carpenters, furnishers, all those whose crafts and skills go into the construction and furnishing of large buildings. Later, she oversaw the erection of additional buildings to serve as schools and accommodation for students or pensioners, as boarders were then called.

Let us now turn to Nano's financial acumen. She invested heavily in the East India Company. This indicates that she was clearly aware of international opportunities to invest. Nano instructed Mr George Waters, an Irish banker in Paris, to invest and supervise her shares in the East India Company, a merchant trading company of London. It was founded in 1600 to pursue trade with East India but in time pursued much more trade with other parts of India and China. With a large building project underway, Nano must have been very anxious when in 1769 she discovered that 'the interest paid by the East India Company had fallen to one-half of its former value.'[22] She became even more vexed as this turn of fortune prevented her from investing more at that time in the Ursuline foundation.

From a fragmentary document discovered in the Ursuline convent in Blackrock in the 1980s we find that Nano had made up her mind to sell her shares in the East India Company and invest with a different broker in Eton in England.[23] She did not manage to do so – probably because her banker in Paris, Mr Waters, did not advise her. He rarely communicated with her. A year later, she discovered that she would have lost more had she changed to a different company. It was providential that she chose, albeit reluctantly, to leave things as they were.

To accomplish and sustain the Ursuline project, Nano also deposited funds with Mr George Waters in Paris to meet the expenses of the novices who were in training there while she was busy with her first major building project in Ireland.[24] Moreover, Nano writes to the leader of the group, Eleanor Fitzsimons, regarding the other novices: 'If it could be permitted them to have anybody to teach them anything you thought would be hereafter an advantage for the house [mission], don't spare any expense.'[25]

On 18 September 1771, the Ursuline Sisters took formal possession of their convent.[26] Moreover, in the *Positio Super Virtutibus: The Life and Activity of the Servant of God, Nano Nagle*, it is written: 'On the same day, a Deed of Agreement was signed by Mother Margaret Kelly on behalf of the Ursulines and by Nano Nagle on her own behalf. Under the terms of the agreement, Nano Nagle would endow the convent to the sum of £2,000.'[27] In return, she was acknowledged as foundress of the Ursuline convent and entitled to certain 'spiritual favours.'[28]

Phase 3: Nano's Society

The unexpected adoption of the practice of enclosure by the four Ursuline Sisters, newly arrived in Cork from Paris, meant that they could not venture out to Nano's schools scattered across the city. In spite of this turn of events, Nano's vision and resolve remained steadfast. She saw that a further complementary response was needed. Nano would begin a religious society of her own whose members would continue her mission of education and care of the vulnerable right across the city.

The erection of the convent and school for the Ursuline Sisters, along with the community's maintenance, had cost Nano a considerable sum of money – estimated at four or five hundred pounds. Fortunately, she still possessed sufficient funds to commence another building project. Nano obtained a further lease of a plot of ground in 1771 from a widow, named Mrs Ann Robbins. It was less than a hundred yards from her little home on Cove Lane.[29] In the Spring of 1775, Nano managed to set in motion the work of construction on the second convent. This building project took almost two years to complete. Its completion took longer than expected because of a further building project that the Ursulines had underway. One day, in his efforts to prevent the building of this convent, Bishop Francis Moylan (1735–1815) went to find Nano.

He threatened to have, what was erected of the building, destroyed, and ordered her to commence her work at the other end of the City ... She mildly bowed ... only saying that if he was pleased to drive her hence, she would never pursue her intended object in Cork; but, would retire to some other part of Ireland, where she would meet no opposition, and more encouragement, to effect her purposes on behalf of those whom she always carried in her heart, the Poor.[30]

Even before Nano and three companions moved in, the new convent was used for classes for children. This new home was given a symbolic blessing on Christmas Day 1777 through the presence of fifty beggarly children whom Nano had invited to dinner and served.[31] Once in residence, Nano, ever the conciliator, negotiated a further arrangement with the Ursuline Sisters. She would give them the solid albeit small cottage she and her companions had been living in at Cove Lane, if they would give her back two smaller cottages that she had earlier given to them and which they were using for classrooms. Nano's new-found interest in these two smaller cabins was due to the fact that they were very proximate to her new convent. She also asked to take back from the Ursulines half the land at the back of the small cabins. Nano decided to build a solid dividing wall between the two communities and hire a garden architect (possibly William Grosvenor) to design a pretty walled garden for the Ursulines – since they were observing enclosure.[32] In a letter to Teresa Mulally, Nano writes: 'I have made a pretty garden, and inclos'd all the ground back of the house, which has cost a great deal making the walls, we cou'd not do well without it, some place to walk in as nobody, we receive will go out only to Chaple, and to the schools ... '[33]

The Ursulines were not getting the walled garden for nothing. Here, we see how well Nano was able to drive a hard bargain. For the pleasure of the walled garden, Nano 'laid claim to the doors and timber not wanted after the upper floor was made into one room' in the Ursuline Convent to create a classroom.[34] It seemed that Nano worked on the principle: 'Waste not, want not.' Moreover, the Ursuline Ladies, as they were initially called, 'were to pay 20 shillings a year for the garden and since she [Nano] agreed to give up what they owed her for the furniture they bought for the pensioners [boarders], they were to give her [Nano] a pension of £5 per year for life, a matter which was to be written down in their books.[35] Moreover, 'If hereafter there was danger of a lawsuit about the agreement, the [Ursuline] ladies were to pay £12 per year for the rent of the house fronting the street [that is, Nano's cabin in

Cove Lane which they probably used for lay helpers] and also to pay her or her heirs the money she paid out in the building on their ground.'[36] Nano Nagle was nothing if not thorough in her financial dealings, making provision for today while planning for tomorrow. Her transactions in relation to money, property, goods and labour clearly reflect a fruitful merging of courage, prudence and justice.

Having built a cottage, the Ursuline Convent and school extensions, a convent for her newly-founded religious congregation, the Sacred Heart convent, and an expensive dividing wall, one might think that Nano had finished with building projects. Not so, however. In her account books for the years 1781–82, we see Nano, the Accountant, at work. They reveal some of the streams of revenue that Nano had, including dowries, and they show Nano not only as accountant, but as auditor.

After completing the wall project (c. 1781) Nano set to building the house she had told Teresa Mulally (who would become her companion in mission in Dublin) about: the asylum [or alms house] for aged and destitute women. The fact that she had to apply to the charity of the public (probably pious ladies) as she was not able to build this house at her own expense, indicated that in her later years the return on her investments in England, France and Ireland were poor. This is confirmed by the fact that she turned to begging to support her schools, ministry of hospitality and almsgiving. The South Presentation Annalist records a story about Nano's habit of begging in her later years, and how she had herself been mistaken for a beggar when she sat in a shop all day waiting for the owner to return.[37]

What a journey! From society-lady and philanthropist to founder-turned-business woman, to sister-turned-beggar. Moreover, having built the alms house Nano set her sights on the erection of a house for prostitutes. She did not live to see that part of her vision fulfilled, but her desire to build a house for the ladies of the night tells us that these, too, were among those whom she befriended and ministered to during her lantern-lit rounds of the city, again not unlike her patron beggar-hospitaller, St John of God (who visited brothels of Granada every Friday in honour of the passion of Jesus).

Phase 4: Preparation for Succession

Before she died, Nano prepared her companions for succession as much by her deeds as by her last words, 'Love one another as you have hitherto done ... and spend yourselves for the poor.'[38] Nano dictated a very comprehensive Will from her death bed on the day before she died.

Immediately after the foundress's death, her solicitor, Mr Thomas Roche visited the convent and removed the contents of her desk – a small trunk, an iron chest and a large red chest that contained personal and family papers. What is more, Mr Roche kept the key for more than two years. Walsh's assessment is that,

> The inexperience of the Sisters in business affairs and the belief that Roche acted with the authority of David and Joseph Nagle calmed any misgivings as to the propriety of his actions. Several times Mother Angela Collins requested Roche to prove the foundress's will [registered] in law but invariably he found excuses for the delay. He paid several of the minor legacies from ready funds and made cash available to Mother Angela to meet the more urgent needs.[39]

During that time, Mrs Gould, Mr Roche's daughter, did the accounts for the Presentation Sisters. The alarm was raised when Mother Angela Collins, Nano's successor, noted several mistakes in Mrs Gould's accounts. She began to investigate and found a whole range of mistakes including multiple payments for the same activity or overcharging for another. To a mason named Mr William Flaherty, a payment of £140.9s.3d was paid out, at least £38.13.6 of which 'he declared on oath that he had already received from herself [Nano].'[40] In fact, he felt that he was owed even less and said that 'it was in small sums she paid it to him according as it answered her convenience.'[41]

In a letter dated 12 June 1800, in desperation, Mother Angela Collins gave Nano's brother Joseph a full and detailed audit of the discrepancies in the accounts she received from Mrs Gould. From Joseph's response to her, the realities of the position become clear. Roche had appropriated and dissipated the considerable estate of Nano Nagle. Mother Angela Collins and the Presentation Sisters were penniless. But Mother Angela's motives were not solely directed to her immediate concerns, the prevention of starvation. Rather, she writes, in the same letter a postscript:

> PS: I have often thought that the Poor sustained a great loss, in not having the affairs settled long since, as her having willed all the residue of her property to this House, and [had] the [matter] been settled it may have enabled us to receive more subjects, consequently to Instruct more Poor Children many

of whom we are obliged to refuse, so numerous are they in this City, and I do think she must have expected the residue would be considerable, or she would never have charged us with giving fifty pounds out of it, in Charitys which she particularised to me.[42]

Joseph Nagle, in reply, regretted that the Ladies of both Convents were in such dire circumstances. He secured £800 for the Ursuline community and a further £2,150 which he owed to Nano, but which she requested him in her will to pay to her Sisters.[43] This latter loan was paid by his nephew-in-law, Charles Chichester of Devon, in 1806 to Nano's Order. Later, Nano's brother would secure for both religious Congregations further substantial amounts. After such darkness, the dawn had come. The prospect of having to choose between starvation or disbanding was finally put to rest. The struggle of the early Sisters mirrors the struggle of the people. Their trust in Providence, mirrors Nano's. In gratitude to Joseph and to draw a clear line under the difficult times they had been through, the Presentation Sisters together with the Ursulines issued a joint response to Nano's brother, c. 1812. It is interesting to note that the wisdom of making a joint response with other religious Congregations about matters of mutual concern goes back a long way. Joseph Nagle died in 1813.

Conclusion
Nano's mission did not achieve its ultimate goal with the education of poor children and the care of the vulnerable and those in need. Her vision was the (trans)formation of each person in Christ, and of society as a whole, through service in a spirit of compassion. Hand in hand with her growth in generous service was her growth as a mystic and prophet. What is mysticism, one might ask? What is true prophecy? Theologian Dorothee Sölle's response to the former is helpful: 'As the experience of oneness with God, mysticism is the radical substantiation of the dignity of a human being.'[44] Prophecy, we know from the Hebrew and Christian Scriptures, can be described as the experience of the passionate fire of God, which cries out when the dignity of anyone or anything is being diminished or destroyed (cf Ex 2:11–3:22; Acts 9:1–19). When both work in tandem, as in the life of Nano, what unfolds can well be described as the 'mysticism of service.'[45]

This chapter is intended to demonstrate a charism within Nano's charism, namely, the wise management and creative use of resources for the further development of the mission. Religious congregations such as the Presentation Sisters must continue to nurture this charism for stewardship among their members and co-workers, and especially among those with responsibilities in or related to this area. This is best done through appropriate and ongoing formation and training.

On 2 August 2014, the Congregation for Institutes for Consecrated Life and Societies of Apostolic Life in Rome issued a Circular Letter entitled, *Guidelines for the Administration of the Assets in Institutes of Consecrated Life and Societies of Apostolic Life*. It provides a timely reminder in relation to stewardship and the charism of religious congregations such as the Presentation Sisters today:

> Fidelity to the founding charism and to the subsequent spiritual heritage of the Institute, is, together with the demand of the Gospel, the first evaluative criteria for the decisions and actions that take place at every level because 'the nature of the charism directs their energies, sustains their fidelity and directs the apostolic work of all toward one mission.'[46]

In the light of the above, it is not surprising to read this commitment in the Constitutions of the Presentation Sisters (approved by Rome on 28 August 2014), a commitment that could well be adopted by anyone who is privileged to be able to make choices in relation to financial and material resources:

> We hold in trust our resources, finances, and properties in solidarity with the whole community of life. We recognise our responsibility to live sustainably and to call forth the full potential of our resources for the furthering of life and mission.[47]

Endnotes

1. *Rules and Constitutions of the Institute of the Religious Sisterhood of the Presentation of the Ever Blessed Virgin*. (Cork: James Haly King's Arms Exchange, 1809), 52.
2. Dominick Murphy, *Memoirs of Nano Nagle and the Ursuline and Presentation Orders in Ireland* (Cork: Joseph Roche, 1845), 18.
3. Murphy, *Memoirs*, 19.
4. Murphy, *Memoirs*, 20. For other extracts from the Cork Remembrancer, see William Hutch, *Nano Nagle: Her Life, Her Labours, and Their Fruits* (Dublin: McGlashan and Gill, 1875), 28-32.
5. T. J. Walsh, *Nano Nagle and the Presentation Sisters* (Dublin: M. H. Gill and Son, 1959), 19.
6. Bishop Berkeley (1685-1753), Bishop of Cloyne's exhortation to the Roman Catholic clergy of Ireland, entitled: 'A Word to the Wise' cited in Walsh, *Nano Nagle*, 7, n. 16.
7. Walsh, *Nano Nagle*, 2.
8. Walsh, *Nano Nagle*, 3.
9. Walsh, *Nano Nagle*, 37.
10. Nano's generous spirit was inherited from both her mother's side of the family, the Mathews, from near Thurles, Co Tipperary, as well as her father's side, the Nagles of Ballygriffin, Co Cork. Below, an excerpt which includes a reference to a close relative of Nano's. Posted by the Office of Public Work (OPW) on an information plaque erected in 2014 at the entrance to The Loop Trail named *Cosán Féilim*, beside the present Church of St Lawrence O'Toole at Inch, Thurles, Co Tipperary, it reads: 'This Church replaced the earlier penal times chapel located just 300 metres along the trail. A date-stone inscribed with the words, 'Roger Fogarty 1760' was brought from the earlier building and is to be seen in the walls of this Church beside the 1806 date-stone. The earlier building was a stone-walled chapel built in 1759-60 by Fr Roger Fogarty, parish priest from about 1726 to 1776, with financial assistance from Thomas Mathew of Annfield'.
11. Mary Pius O'Farrell, *Nano Nagle: Woman of the Gospel* (Cork: Cork Publishing Limited, 1996), 43.
12. Letter of Sr Clare Callaghan to Bishop Coppinger, Cloyne, c. 1800-1804, cited in Walsh, *Nano Nagle*, 381-2. (Story given in full elsewhere in this volume.)
13. Letter from Nano Nagle to Miss Fitzsimons, 17 July 1769, cited in Walsh, *Nano Nagle*, 345.
14. For a summary of the harsh 1709 Penal Laws aimed at the obliteration of education of Catholics in Ireland, see Hutch, *Nano Nagle*, 18-19.
15. Walsh, *Nano Nagle*, 17.
16. ibid.
17. For a fragment of a Letter from Montserrat which refers to Nano Nagle, her uncle, Joseph, and £12,000, see O'Farrell, *Breaking Morn*, 54-55. Historian S. F. Pettit writes: 'Cork made its fortune and won its fame through the multifarious activities centred on the Butter Market at the foot of Shandon. There the prestigious Committee of Merchants directed the whole business of collecting the butter from the farmer ... and carted down to the quays to be shipped to Liverpool, Lisbon, Hamburg, Amsterdam and the new lands of the West Indies and of Carolina and Georgia'. See *The City of Cork 1700—1900* (Cork: Studio Publications, 1977), 82.
18. Walsh, *Nano Nagle*, 28.
19. Letter from Nano to Miss Fitzsimons, 17 July 1769, cited in Walsh, *Nano Nagle*, 345.

20. *Cause of Beatification and Canonization of the Servant of God, Nano Nagle (1718–1784). Positio Super Virtutibus. The Life and Activity of the Servant of God* (Rome, 1994), 287.
21. *Servant of God*, 288.
22. *Servant of God*, 272.
23. *Servant of God*, 297.
24. *Servant of God*, 271.
25. Letter from Nano Nagle to Miss Fitzsimons, 13 May 1770, cited in Walsh, *Nano Nagle*, 352.
26. Walsh, *Nano Nagle*, 81. See Hutch, *Nano Nagle*, 64–5.
27. *Servant of God*, 286.
28. ibid.
29. For Letters related to this and some other leases taken out by Nano Nagle, see Mary Pius O'Farrell, *Breaking of Morn: Nano Nagle (1718–1784) & Francis Moylan (1735–1815): A Book of Documents* (Cork: Cork Publishing Limited, 2001), 56, 60.
30. Walsh, *Nano Nagle*, 95.
31. Interestingly, the custom of entertaining fifty beggars on Christmas Day was continued by the Sisters at South Presentation until 1887. We can only speculate as to why it was discontinued, or why it was not adopted by many other Presentation communities.
32. *Servant of God*, 271.
33. Letter from Nano Nagle to Miss Mulally, AL 31 January 1783, par 5, in Walsh, *Nano Nagle*, 367. The spellings are as written by Nano.
34. *Servant of God*, 287.
35. ibid.
36. ibid.
37. First Annals of South Presentation Convent, Cork (Full story told elsewhere in this volume).
38. O'Farrell, *Woman of the Gospel*, 173; Hutch, Nano Nagle, 90.
39. Walsh, *Nano Nagle*, 143.
40. *Servant of God*, 461.
41. ibid.
42. Walsh, *Nano Nagle*, 143.
43. See Hutch, *Nano Nagle*, 94.
44. Dorothee Sölle, *The Silent Cry: Mysticism and Resistance* (Minneapolis: Fortress Press, 2001), 43.
45. Joseph de Guibert, *The Jesuits*, 55, cited in Chapter 5: 'Nano Nagle: Embracing Solitude in Colonized Ireland', in Bernadette Flanagan, *Embracing Solitude: Women and New Monasticism* (Eugene, OR: Cascade Books, 2014), 109.
46. John Paul II, Apostolic Exhortation *Vita Consecrata* (25 March 1996, 36) cited in the Circular Letter from the Congregation for Institutes for Consecrated Life and Societies of Apostolic Life, *Guidelines for the Administration of the Assets in Institutes of Consecrated Life and Societies of Apostolic Life* (Vatican: Libreria Editrice Vaticana, 2 August 2014, 1–23), 7. See http://cdn.cmglobal.org/en/files/2014/12/CIVCSVA_Circular_Letter_ENG.pdf (29.11.16)
47. Constitution 63 from the *Constitutions of the Union of Sisters of the Presentation of the Blessed Virgin Mary* (Monasterevin, Presentation Sisters, 2014), 38. See also Donald Senior, *The Gift of Administration: New Testament Foundations for the Vocation of Administrative Service* (Collegeville: Liturgical Press, 2015), 106–109.

Missionaries on the Prairie

Margaret H. Preston

Recent scholarship regarding the work of women religious and the creation of the social service system of the United States suggests that their role was much more complex than that for which they have been given credit. While their work in the development of education is well known, their presence in the evolution of US healthcare has recently begun to receive deeper discussion.[1] In *Unlikely Entrepreneurs: Catholic Sisters and the Hospital Marketplace* Barbra Mann Wall shows how women religious were integral to ensuring that the Catholic Church was a significant presence in the *business* of US healthcare. For example, by the early twentieth century, the Catholic Church was running, 'five-hundred-and eighty-one Catholic acute and specialty hospitals in the United States, mainly under the auspices of sisters', while into the twenty-first century, Catholic hospitals remain the 'largest single group of the nation's not-for-profit hospitals …'.[2] Thus, while scholars have long recognized these women as teachers, nurses and philanthropists, they must also give them credit for their role as business entrepreneurs who understood that if the bills were not paid, the mission could not be sustained. This chapter will show the evolving charism of Nano Nagle – how, through hard work and clear business savvy, the Sisters of the Presentation of the Blessed Virgin Mary of Aberdeen, South Dakota, understood these principles and established a medical mission that, to the present, serves the healthcare needs of the population of America's Northern Great Plains.[3]

In 1880, a small group of Presentation Sisters, led by M. Mary John Hughes, departed on their long journey across the Atlantic from Queenstown [now Cobh].[4] They believed they were called to teach the native children of America's Great Plains.[5] M. John Hughes would go on to establish convents in Fargo, North Dakota[6] and Aberdeen, South Dakota. It is doubtful that she could have ever envisioned that one of the convents she established would not only incorporate the Presentation Order's traditional call to teach the poor, but would also respond to the region's crucial need for medical care.

After landing in New York, the women made the uncomfortable journey to the nation's Midwest to arrive in Wheeler, South Dakota, where they founded their new convent and St Ann's Mission school.⁷ The winter of 1880 was one of the harshest on record and during the spring of 1881, the rains so overwhelmed the prairie that the 'James River became a giant lake stretching across the breadth ... of South Dakota'; the floods caused the women's home to become uninhabitable.⁸ The Sisters had to move and they found opportunity in Fargo, North Dakota where a local priest requested that they establish a school for immigrant children. Thus, leading her band north to Fargo, Hughes helped to establish St Joseph's Convent and Academy in 1882.⁹ Then, just a few years later in 1886, at the request of the local Bishop, M. Mary John Hughes, with Sr Aloysius Chriswell and Sr Joseph Butler, opened the doors of a second Presentation convent and school in Aberdeen, South Dakota.¹⁰

In 1894, Sr Joseph Butler assumed the position of Mother Superior, and the convent was under her authority when, in 1900, Aberdeen was struck with a diphtheria epidemic. Despite the fact that the women had no medical training, Sr Joseph set up a temporary infirmary in part of the convent to care for the sick. Within a year, she would go on to establish St Luke's Hospital in Aberdeen. Its success was soon recognized and others sent requests for the Order's help. In 1906, M. Joseph Butler oversaw the establishment of St Joseph's Hospital in Mitchell, South Dakota. In 1910, the Presentation Order agreed to run a hospital in Miles City, Montana.¹¹ This was the same year that M. Joseph Butler received an appeal from Sioux Falls' Bishop Thomas O'Gorman, to help build and administer a fourth hospital in Sioux Falls, South Dakota. In December of 1911, McKennan Hospital, named after the benefactress who left the seed money for the hospital, opened its doors.¹²

M. Joseph Butler completed her term of office as mother superior in 1915. In addition to the four hospitals, each with a nursing school, she helped to establish nine parish schools. Butler died at the age of 75 in 1935. In 1988, the *Argus Leader* reflected on M. Joseph Butler's work in South Dakota in an article titled 'Sister's Good Deeds Made State Smarter, Healthier'. The newspaper recognized her fifty years in religious life and her vision to transform education and health care in South Dakota.¹³

Into the early twentieth century, as the Presentation hospitals steadily strengthened their standing, the Order's records offer us a glimpse of a third woman whose business savvy allowed her to lead the Order through the Great Depression and World War II, helping the convent come out of both crises fiscally stronger than it entered. On 1 May 1888, Margaret McCarthy was born in Bandon, County Cork. At the age of 19, Margaret met M. Joseph Butler who had returned to Ireland on a recruiting trip. M. Joseph Butler, also from Bandon, came home to encourage women like Margaret to join her in America. Taking the name Sr Raphael, she entered the Aberdeen novitiate in 1908.

Within a few years, Sr Raphael trained as a nurse and was working in St Luke's Hospital. She immediately showed talent in administration and, from 1913 to 1921, she worked in St Luke's Superintendent's office. In 1921, she took the position of superior-administrator of St Joseph's Hospital in Mitchell, South Dakota.[14] In 1927, she became superior-administrator of McKennan Hospital, the Presentation's largest centre for health-care provision.

McKennan was the hospital for which, in 1925, Sr Raphael suggested that the Presentation Order seek a low-interest rate loan from Massachusetts Mutual Life Insurance Company. There was, however, a catch. Mass Mutual stated that it would only offer the loan if the Presentation Order took full control of the hospital and accepted the loan's risk. McKennan Hospital was established by the bequest from Helen McKennan, and although the Presentation Order ran the hospital, it was under the administration of a lay board. Helen McKennan, who died in 1906, left $25,000 in the care of three trustees. Yet the hospital cost over $100,000 to build, and was still struggling financially. By 1925, the Presentation Order, like many Catholic Orders throughout the United States, had established a solid financial track record. Thus, on 5 May 1925, Presentation Sisters Incorporated took full responsibility for McKennan Hospital and promptly negotiated a loan for $235,000.

In 1932, the Presentation Order elected the forty-four-year-old Sr Raphael to be Mother Superior which made her, in effect, CEO of this faith-based organization that had one-hundred-and-ninety-two sisters and ran four hospitals and seventeen schools throughout eastern South Dakota and western Minnesota. In looking at some of Sr Raphael's extant letters, we see a woman who understood the financial complexity of the Order's businesses. In 1934, she wrote to the Vice-President of Massachusetts Mutual stating that she was sending $10,000 toward McKennan hospital's loan and this despite 'the drought and the grasshoppers ... and the inability of so many of our customers to pay their obligations to us [due to] financial difficulties'. Nevertheless, Sister Raphael spoke proudly of being able to continue to meet her financial obligations.[15] Two years later, and clearly on top of things, she wrote to the Cashier of Mass Mutual on 23 April, regarding the loan stating: 'I notice you have charged me for accrued interest ... this is entirely contrary to our agreement with your home office ... according to their figures we were to pay

$2,700 per month until 1 July 1936, at which time all the interest due ... would be fully paid up'. She went on to state that 'we have complied with the arrangement in every way and are amazed' that Massachusetts Mutual would imply that there was an unpaid balance of $236.32.[16] That same year, Sr Raphael asked to have the interest rate on her loan maintained at 4.5 per cent and not raised to 5.5 per cent: 'Our situation in South Dakota this year is the worst in our history. There is absolutely no feed of any kind left ... I can see little hope of any income during the coming year.' She noted in the letter that she was very grateful for all of Mass Mutual's support and 'as proof of our good faith we hope to be able to pay in the neighborhood of $15,000 ...' toward the loan's principal.[17] As the 1930s come to an end, she regularly sent Mass Mutual money.

Sister Raphael continued to show audacious business instincts. In 1940, she recognized that Aberdeen's St Luke's Hospital needed another building, but she could not afford to build one. Thus, despite much advice to the contrary, she was confident that she could find a company to safely move Aberdeen's vacated four-storey Lincoln Hospital building ten blocks. Sr Raphael researched and found The Crowe Brothers Company of Chicago and contracted them to move the five thousand ton building. Over the next five months, the building slowly made its way through Aberdeen and in November of 1940, it became part of St Luke's Hospital.[18]

As the United States entered World War II, Sr Raphael continued to seek to strengthen the Order's financial position. In 1942, she applied for a new loan for her various businesses; this time with Northwestern Mutual Life Insurance Company. Neil Gleason, who represented the convent's interests, expressed his support for her application despite some missing documentation and stated, 'that if it were not for my faith in the Presentation Sisters, their excellent institutions and your leadership, I would be rather reluctant to pass upon these statements as submitted.'[19] Sr Raphael responded with an apology for the missing papers and argued that the Order was a good risk despite many challenges. She wrote: 'We live in a farming country and these bills are paid depending upon crop condition ...'. Moreover, she stated that while the hospitals made every effort to collect funds, 'so much drought and poor crops' had challenged people's ability to pay. On 15 December 1942, Mr Gleason confirmed the positive outcome of the application and requested that she, 'as president of the respective corporations', sign the papers for the three loans at 3.25 per cent interest rate. These loans were $190,000 on Presentation Academy of Aberdeen, $98,000 on St Joseph's Hospital in Mitchell and $180,000 on Presentation Sisters Incorporated for

McKennan Hospital in Sioux Falls – a total of $468,000, which was the equivalent of borrowing nearly $20 million dollars in 2012.[20]

Sr Raphael immediately began repayment, and over the next two years she was able to make 'substantial' installments. So impressive were her payments that in 1944, Mr Gleason wrote to inform her that Northwestern was challenged by her plan to significantly reduce the principal on the Presentation Academy loan. He suggested that, instead, Northwestern Mutual 'might be more favorably impressed if some portion of the sum could be applied on the Mitchell and Sioux Falls loans' since reducing the Aberdeen loan would result in a considerable loss to the company. He noted that Northwestern had provided this low interest rate to many Catholic hospitals and these same organizations were paying back greater sums than those on which Northwestern had counted. As a result, Northwestern Mutual could not continue to accept such large repayment without penalty. Mr Gleason wrote, 'the situation has become acute and they cannot ignore the interests of policyholders ....' He revealed that while Northwestern took responsibility for not anticipating borrowers' substantially increased incomes, 'they cannot ignore their responsibilities'. As a result, Northwestern would begin to administer a 2 per cent service charge on excess payments.[21] This does not seem to have deterred Sr Raphael and in a letter from Mr Gleason in June of 1945, he confirmed that she would make payments of $13,000 on the Aberdeen loan, $18,000 on McKennan's and $1,000 on St Joseph's – all with a 'premium of 2 per cent'. Nevertheless, he expressed happiness at the reduction in indebtedness because this would make it 'possible to undertake some of the other projects which you have been planning'.[22]

In 1945, as the war came to an end, Sr Raphael made her most significant decision for the economic health of the Presentation Order: she purchased one hundred acres in Aberdeen to eventually house a new convent. In 1946, her term as Mother Superior ended and by this time the religious order now numbered two-hundred-and-twenty-one, owned over $2.3 million in land and property, ran four hospitals, one orphanage, a junior college and had sisters teaching in schools throughout eastern South Dakota and western Minnesota.[23] Far from retiring, she now spearheaded the task of fund-raising for and of constructing the $2 million dollar structure to house both the convent and Presentation Junior College.

M. Raphael McCarthy died on 3 July 1966. Six years earlier, on her golden jubilee, South Dakota Senator Karl Mundt had placed into the United States Congressional record a recognition of M. Raphael which offered a review of her life and noted that both her 'keen business sense' as well as her 'moral efforts' greatly benefited South Dakota.[24] Finally, until a corneal transplant in 1961 (age seventy-three), M. Raphael McCarthy was legally blind. Sr Sabina Joyce recalled that when a local businessman who worked with Sr Raphael was told of her successful corneal transplant he stated, 'We could never put anything over on her when she couldn't see'. Sioux Falls' Bishop Brady described her condition more graciously in 1951 when he noted: 'God has not blessed her with much sight in her eyes, but has given her the vision of a prophetess in her soul'.[25]

In the years after World War II, healthcare faced impressive challenges as the science of care became more complex and the demands upon healthcare businesses increased. Care was no longer provided in the home; the hospital had become preeminent to health. In addition, the business of medicine was increasingly complex and providers such as the Presentation Order sought to respond.

One business advantage that Aberdeen's Presentation Sisters had recognized was that they could achieve greater economies of scale by combining all hospital purchases. They reasoned that, for example, if all four of their hospitals bought bed sheets from the same supplier ... their supplier might offer them a lower price. Thus, PACE (Presentation Affiliated Cooperative Effort) was born and the Presentation Order centralized purchasing for all four hospitals. Impressively, PACE was one of the first successful group purchasing organizations in the United States. During its first two decades, PACE membership increased to thirty-five hospitals and included some two hundred other businesses for which PACE made purchases. By 1977, PACE officially incorporated, having grown to serve hospitals, clinics, surgical centers, long term care facilities, and schools in South Dakota, Iowa, Nebraska, Minnesota and North Dakota.[26]

The changes to healthcare were not the only challenge that the Presentation Sisters had to face in the turbulent decades after World War II. These years also delivered a revolution in the lives of those who had dedicated themselves to serving the Church and society. In 1962, the Second Ecumenical Council of the Vatican (Vatican II) began and while it had an impressive impact on Catholics generally, religious orders were dramatically affected. Inspired by Vatican II, female religious orders underwent serious renewal. This led to some internal divisions within orders. While there were those who sought to maintain traditional ways of life, others embraced the 'loosening' of religious rules and regulations. Ultimately these challenges caused many women to leave the religious life.[27] At the same time, greater educational and professional opportunities for all women diminished the numbers that chose to enter the convent. These changes impacted on Catholic hospitals, which had to increasingly rely on lay nurses and administrators.

Reacting to this changing landscape, the Presentation Sisters sought to centralize their efforts beyond PACE. In 1978, they established Presentation Health Systems (PHS) 'to combine the strengths of their individual institutions'.[28] This new organization sought to further share costs among Presentation hospitals including 'legal affairs, personnel management, employee benefits administration, bill collection and risk management'.[29] This worked well, but the 1980s brought a host of complex legislation and that further increased the demands upon all US healthcare systems.

As the challenges grew, the Presentation Sisters continued to look for more opportunities to strengthen their businesses. One option was to partner with another South Dakota-based religious order that was also in the business of healthcare. The Benedictine Sisters, who arrived in Yankton in 1874, opened the Hospital of the Sacred Heart in 1896.[30] By the 1990s, both the Presentation and Benedictine Sisters had come to understand that greater collaboration was important if their businesses were to survive.[31] Pushed by the Catholic Health Association of the United States that was calling for broader collaboration by Catholic hospitals, the women of both orders began to discuss the possibility of uniting their work. Nevertheless, this change would not be easy. John Porter, president and CEO of Presentation Health Systems, described it as a 'lengthy intellectual and emotional process'.[32] Serious and thoughtful discussion of how these two religious orders would join forces to strengthen their provision of healthcare began in 1996.

The challenge was that while both Orders were, of course, Roman Catholic, they had very different cultures with very different histories. As Sr Kate Crowley OSB reflected, the women needed to learn about each other's cultures before trying to unite their businesses. To begin the process, they established a leadership council made up of representatives from both Orders. This cohort was to regularly meet to discuss the feasibility of uniting forces. Next, four women, two from each Order, formed a planning task force. After two years of discussion and discernment, the Presentation Sisters of Aberdeen and the Benedictine Sisters of Yankton entered into an agreement to co-sponsor what would now be called Avera Health. In the summer of 2001, Robert Voglewede, senior vice-president for Avera Health, interviewed the four aforementioned women: Sr Mary Denis Collins and Sr Lynn Marie Welbig of the Presentation Order and Sr Mildred Busch and Sr Kate Crowley of the Benedictine Order. Sr Welbig reflected on how their efforts were more than just establishing a mere partnership: 'We created a new entity. It is like a union ... a marriage. It is a new thing with a new personality ... [we are] going to go forward with a monastic and an apostolic identity. I think that is just a very rich concept.'[33]

The challenges, including a sense of loss, were still at the surface when the name change was announced in 1998. 'We have mixed feelings', noted Sr Joyce Meyer, President of the Aberdeen Sisters of the Presentation of the Blessed Virgin Mary, 'about the Presentation name disappearing from the health system'. Nevertheless, she went on to state that the new name was 'inclusive of all our partners that are part of [the] system'. In addition, Meyer noted how much the world of medicine had evolved. She stated that the name change 'reflects the mission of helping people stay healthy rather than just taking care of them when they're ill'.[34]

Over a decade has passed since the two religious orders united their ministries. Today, Avera Health is an organization with over thirteen thousand employees with revenues of over 1.5 billion dollars. Its mission statement reads: 'Avera is a health ministry rooted in the Gospel. Our mission is to make a positive impact in the lives and health of persons and communities by providing quality services guided by Christian values'. The largest private employer in the state of South Dakota, Avera Health also has hospitals and clinics in Minnesota, Iowa, Nebraska and North Dakota.[35] Responding to the demands of the marketplace, the Presentation Order continues to lead collaboratively a medical ministry it began over one hundred years ago when a few women founded a business that has ever since provided care to their neighbours.

Endnotes

1. Among them see Margaret M. McGuinness, *Called to Serve: A History of Nuns in America* (New York: New York University Press, 2013) and Anne M. Butler, *Across God's Frontiers: Catholic Sisters in the American West 1850–1920* (Chapel Hill: University of North Carolina Press, 2012).
2. Barbra Mann Wall, *Unlikely Entrepreneurs: Catholic Sisters and the Hospital Marketplace* (Columbus: Ohio State University Press, 2005), 3, 22 and 33–4.
3. The author would like to gratefully acknowledge that this research was facilitated by grants from the Research and Scholarly Activities Committee and the Jane and Charles Zaloudek Faculty Research Fellowship both of Augustana College, and the Cushwa Center for the Study of American Catholicism, University of Notre Dame. I am grateful for feedback from the late Dr Margaret Ó hÓgartaigh and the readers from the American Catholic Studies Seminar, Cushwa Center. Many thanks to archivist Sr Lois Ann Sargent and the women of the Presentation Convent of Aberdeen.
4. She was accompanied by her sibling, M. Agnes Hughes of Presentation Convent, Doneraile, and Sr Teresa Challoner, Presentation Convent, Manchester.
5. The Presentation Sisters first arrived in the United States in 1854 with five women establishing a convent in San Francisco, California followed by another four traveling to Dubuque, Iowa in 1875.
6. To clarify, the region was called the Dakota Territory until 1889 when they were separated into North and South and awarded statehood.
7. Susan Carol Peterson and Courtney Ann Vaughn-Roberson, *Women With Vision: The Presentation Sisters of South Dakota* (Urbana: University of Illinois Press, 1988), 60. See the Bureau of Catholic Indian Mission Records, Bureau General Correspondence, 1862–1884, Marquette University. (Henceforth BCIM Records).
8. David Laskin, *The Children's Blizzard* (New York: Harper, 2005), 45. The women also found that much of the population that they had come to teach had moved further west.
9. Margaret Mooney, *Doing What Needs to be Done: Sisters of the Presentation of the Blessed Virgin Mary, Fargo 1882–1997* (Fargo, ND: Access Midwest, 1997), 23 and 30.
10. Peterson and Vaughn-Roberson, *Women With Vision*, 65.
11. Peterson and Vaughn-Roberson, *Women With Vision*, 90 and 164–95. See also Kathleen McGreevy, *A Century of Care ... A Journey of Faith: Avera Queen of Peace Hospital 1906–2006* (Mitchell: Avera Queen of Peace Health Services, 2006) and Dolores Harrington, *A Woman's Will ... A Sister's Way: The McKennan Hospital Story* (Sioux Falls: n.p., 1961). Miles City sat on the Milwaukee Railroad line that ran through Aberdeen.
12. Margaret H. Preston, *A Journey of Faith a Destination of Excellence: Avera McKennan Hospital's First Century of Caring* (Sioux Falls: Avera McKennan Hospital, 2010).
13. 'Sister's Good Deeds Made State Smarter, Healthier' *Argus Leader* (May 1 1988), 5. The *Argus Leader* is the newspaper that serves Sioux Falls, SD.
14. Sr Pauline Quinn, 'Biographies of Mother Superiors: Mother Raphael McCarthy 1932–1946,' 2.
15. M. Raphael McCarthy to Mr W. A. Rawlings, Vice-President, Massachusetts Mutual Life Insurance Company, July 1 1934, Presentation Archives, McCarthy, Raphael 10.6 Box 1 F 5.

16. M. Raphael McCarthy to Mr William C. Olson, Cashier, Massachusetts Mutual Life Insurance Company, April 23 1936, Presentation Archives, McCarthy, Raphael 10. 6 Box 1 F 5.
17. M. Raphael McCarthy to Mr W. A. Rawlings, Vice-President, Massachusetts Mutual Life Insurance Company, July 7 1936; Presentation Archives, McCarthy, Raphael 10.6 Box 1 F 5.
18. Quinn, 'Mother Raphael McCarthy 1932–1946', 3.
19. Mr Neil J. Gleason, President, Neil J. Gleason & Co to Mother Raphael McCarthy, December 8 1942, Presentation Archives, McCarthy, Raphael 10.6 Box 1, F 3.
20. Mr Neil J. Gleason to M. Raphael McCarthy, December 8 and 15 1942. Equal to $19,700,000.00 using the nominal GDP per capita; see www.measuringworth.com.
21. Mr Neil J. Gleason to M. Raphael McCarthy, March 20 1944 in McCarthy, Raphael 10.6 Box 1 F 4. Thanks to Mr Rick Lundberg for clarification of accounting terminology.
22. Mr Neil J. Gleason to M. Raphael McCarthy, June 20 1945 in McCarthy, Raphael 10.6 Box 1 F 3.
23. Peterson and Roberson, *Women with Vision*, 108.
24. 'Congressional Record Proceedings and Debates of the 86th Congress, Second Session' Vol. 106, No. 30, Washington, D.C., Thursday, August 11 1960.
25. Sr Mary Thomas, 'Interview with Sisters Colman Coakley, Annrita Johnson, Sabina Joyce, Suzanne Cotter, and Bernadette Farrell,' (May 13 2008) and Quinn, 'Biographies of Mother Superiors: Mother Raphael McCarthy 1932–1946', 7. McCarthy had corneal scarring and cataracts. Mother Raphael McCarthy 10.6 Box 1, Folder 1 Presentation Archives.
26. Kathleen McGreevy (ed.), 'Setting the PACE ...' *All of Us* Vol. 14, No. 6 (November/December 1992), 9; Kathleen McGreevy, 'A History of Avera Health,' unpublished paper (August, 2001; updated by Clare Willrodt, June, 2009) and http://www.avera.org/avera/pace/index.aspx.
27. John J. Fialka, *Sisters: Catholic Sisters and the Making of America* (New York: St Martin's Griffin, 2004), 217.
28. McGreevy, 'A History of Avera Health', 8.
29. ibid.
30. Robert F. Karolevitz, *A Commitment to Care: The First 100 Years of Sacred Heart Hospital 1897–1997* (South Dakota: Pine Hill Press, 1997), 19–21 and http://www.yanktonbenedictines.org.
31. McGreevy, 'A History of Avera Health', 10.
32. John Porter, 'Becoming Avera Health' All of Us Vol. 20, 2 (April/May, 1998), 3.
33. Robert Voglewede, 'An Interview Regarding Co-sponsorship' (Summer, 2001).
34. Joyce Terveen, 'Presentation to be renamed Avera Health,' *Argus Leader* (March 12 1998).
35. http://www.avera.org.

Nano Nagle and Everyday Leadership

Bernadette Flanagan PBVM

You're not one you're a thousand
just light your lantern
since one live flame
is better than a thousand dead souls.

Rumi

The leadership trainer Margaret Wheatley observed recently that 'leadership has taken a great leap backwards to the familiar territory of command and control'.[1] When living in times of uncertainty and turmoil the human instinct can be to grab hold tighter. Nano Nagle's life provides a lesson in leadership for uncertain times; it reminds us of the paradox that it is best to relinquish control during times when the circumstances surrounding us are most out of control. But how can we learn to exercise effective leadership in a manner similar to how it was lived by Nano Nagle? How can each one of us be authentically attuned to growing discontent and dissatisfaction in our lives; the small voice of the Spirit calling, evoking, provoking? How can we find a perspective in life, which enables us to attend to our leadership calling in the context of our responsibility to co-create a better world? Below I will suggest that at the heart of Nano Nagle's everyday leadership were four virtues which have been explored by Tobin Hart: Presence, Heart, Wisdom and Creation.[2] Firstly, however, I wish to reflect on leadership in its own right.

Everyday leadership is situated in the everyday experience of people and finds its expression within the ordinariness of life. It is expressed around the world through diverse initiatives taken by people in roles such as health services provision, education, volunteering, and the founding of non-profit organizations. Jon L. Wergin, who is a professor on the Program in Leadership and Change at Antioch University in Los Angeles, refers to this type of leadership as 'Locally Situated Leadership'[3] or 'Leadership in Place'. The foundational conviction of 'leadership in place' is that leadership is not a position or appointment, but rather leadership is a capacity which each person can exercise in her own setting.

'Leadership in place' is part of a cluster of post-hierarchical notions of leadership. Other leadership styles in this cluster are 'transformational leadership',[4] which emphasizes making a connection with others to transform a situation of common concern, and 'servant leadership' – a phrase whose contemporary usage can be traced to Robert K. Greenleaf's book, *The Servant as Leader* – which focuses on leaders who aim to serve their organizations with a view to enabling all in the organization to become healthier, wiser, freer, more autonomous and more likely to become servants themselves.[5]

In these post-hierarchical models of leadership there is a shift in focus from the normative actions and distinctive traits of leaders to a focus on the core of the person who is exercising leadership. The shift in focus towards the core authenticity and inner world landscape of exceptional leaders has led to designating the nature of these new frameworks as 'contemplative leadership' paradigms.[6] Nancy Eggert, who has led the way in developing these paradigms has identified four key practices which underpin this type of leadership: Appreciation, Detachment, Creativity and Compassion. Amanda Sinclair has also offered four angles that come together to frame an interiority-focused picture of leadership.[7] She views the tasks of leadership as (1) moving beyond inherited patterns of leadership, (2) awakening to new, freer, and more meaningful ways of working, (3) cultivating a capacity to be with oneself and others in the vulnerability of the body and (4) deepening presence to self as leader through intentional practices of breathing. There are strong parallels between the Hart, Eggert and Sinclair frameworks as is evident in the table below:

Tobin Hart	Nancy Eggert	Amanda Sinclair
› Presence	› Appreciation	› Breath attentiveness
› Heart	› Compassion	› Body awareness
› Wisdom	› Detachment	› Freedom in personal history
› Creation	Creativity	› Resistance to outdated uses of power

So while, historically, the practices of contemplative living and the exercise of leadership have not been closely associated, there is a growing body of scholarship which integrates these discourses today.[8] This integration creates an opportunity to explore the four foundational spiritual practices of Nano Nagle which enabled her to exercise leadership with a global, longitudinal impact i.e. presence, compassion, wisdom and creativity.

Presence

Presence is a complex concept. The word 'presence' is derived from Latin *praesens*, which consists of the words *prae*, meaning 'in front', and *sens*, meaning 'being' i.e. the ability to live with awakened sensibilities to the unique beings who cross our paths / pass in front of us, in so many ways and places. An experience of the deep reality of the full and total presence of another to our human condition can be profoundly transformative. The Israelites in their Exodus journey were reassured and encouraged by the sense of Divine presence: Ex 33:14, 'My presence will go with you, and I will give you rest.' Today, nursing scholarship has given great attention to the therapeutic power of authentic nurse-presence when it is made available to patients. This scholarship views therapeutic presence as an inter-subjective encounter between a nurse and a patient in which the nurse encounters the patient as a unique human being in a unique situation and in which a nurse chooses to be fully attentive to that person.[9]

The cultivation of awakened personal presence can have profound outcomes. When an encounter is underpinned by an active, lived presence, its impact can be of exceptionally long duration; the encounter may even reverberate during the whole of a lifetime. It can result in a sense of connectedness with the person encountered, which is not dependent on any prior knowledge of the person. Becoming present to reality is energizing; when an encounter is suffused with presence, those involved may experience a physical, emotional and spiritual surge of energy, even in spite of whatever challenging circumstances may surround the encounter – poverty, hunger, grief, homelessness, etc. Feelings of isolation or abandonment may be overcome, even after the physical presence ceases. The experience of presence in an encounter can enhance self-esteem and empower an individual to find her voice.[10]

In the life of Nano Nagle, it is evident that the quality of presence which she brought to the daily encounters of her life was transformative. In a letter from Mother Clare Callaghan to Bishop Coppinger, which was written to clarify some details regarding the authentic version of Nano's biography, we learn that being in the country she (Nano) was afflicted to discover the ignorance of the poor, which she principally perceived in one of the servants of the house whom she had conversed with on some points of religion.'[11]

The concept of being 'afflicted' by the pain, suffering, destitution and ignorance that she encountered amongst the staff on the Nagle family estate, reflects the depth of presence which she brought to her conversations.

The writings of the Austrian psychiatrist and Holocaust survivor Viktor Frankl (1905–1997), are one of history's greatest testaments to the transformative power of the exercise of presence (rather than flinching) in the face of suffering and tragedy. In one particularly poignant passage of his book setting out his strategy for vitality in the face of the extreme horrors of Auschwitz, Frankl reminded his readers that the art of presence – the ability to inhabit the present – made all the difference between life and death, both spiritually and bodily:

> ... in robbing the present of its reality there lay a certain danger. It became easy to overlook the opportunities to make something positive of camp life, opportunities which really did exist. Regarding our 'provisional existence' as unreal was in itself an important factor in causing the prisoners to lose their hold on life; everything in a way became pointless. Such people forgot that often it is just such an exceptionally difficult external situation which gives man the opportunity to grow spiritually beyond himself.[12]

Similarly Nano Nagle recognized that it was precisely the circumstances that circumscribed the tortuous social reality of Ireland that required her presence. Though she side-stepped these realities through her early decision to join a religious community in Europe, ultimately her journey into her transformative social leadership commenced by becoming present to the mundane realities on her family's estate.

Heart/Compassion

In recent decades, neurophysiological research related to learning and education has focused predominantly on the brain. This emphasis on the brain is a logical extension of the ascendancy of rationalism since the seventeenth century. Until that time, however, *logos* and *mythos*, mind and heart, were seen, not as conflicting, but rather as complementary ways of making meaning of the world. Many of the world's ancient civilizations respected the heart for harboring an 'intelligence' that operated independently of the reasonable mind, while being in communication with it. A verse of the ancient Brihadaranyaka Upanishad says:

Self-luminous is the being who dwells within the lotus of the heart.[13]

In the Hebrew and Christian scriptures, the word 'heart' occurs more than one thousand times. It is a designation for the most authentic self. In Jeremiah 17:9–10 the heart is presented as that dimension of a person which may be a puzzle even to the individual, the inner questing, restless self whose deepest desires are sometimes only known to God. This perspective is often reflected in the customs, writings, art, spiritual practices, and even medical systems of ancient civilizations. Indeed, the view that the heart is a key centre of insight, emotion, intention, discernment, wisdom and spirit may be one of the strongest common themes across the world's major religions and spiritual traditions.[14]

In recent times a 'Science of the Heart' has been developed to provide a scientific explanation for how and why the heart affects mental clarity, creativity, emotional balance and personal effectiveness.[15] Some of the first modern psychophysiological researches to examine the interactions between the heart and brain took place in the 1960s and 1970s. Evidence was found which suggested that the heart was not simply following the brain's directions, but rather that there was a 'heart brain'. This concept would prove helpful in gaining insight into why one-half of heart disease cases are not explained by the standard risk factors – such as high cholesterol, smoking or sedentary lifestyle. It was also found that patients' emotional state and relationships in the period after myocardial infarction are as important as disease severity in determining how patients recover. The Institute of HeartMath has drawn public attention to this research so as to develop practical interventions that incorporate the understanding that the heart profoundly affects perception, awareness and intelligence.

Before the findings of contemporary heart science, spiritual teachers always understood the power of the heart in conversion. In a Greek Christian contemplative tradition – Hesychasm – reflective practices were developed that centered on different bodily sites and functions with respiration and heart rhythm being the most important. The practices were based on Christ's injunction in the Gospel of Matthew to pray in the inner room (the room of the heart).[16] In one of the most widely known texts from the Eastern Church, a pilgrim describes his practice this way: 'Later I began to practise the Jesus prayer in and out through the heart coordinated with the breathing … That means when I was inhaling I was looking with the mind's eye into the heart while I was thinking and saying "Lord Jesus Christ" and when I was exhaling, "have mercy on me"'.[17]

The practice of compassion, which characterized the endless initiatives taken by Nano Nagle to serve the poor, also emerged from the heart space. The community which she formally established on Christmas Eve, 1775, in Cork, Ireland, was named by her as 'the Institute of the Charitable Instruction of the Sacred Heart of Jesus.' Her intuitive connection with the heart as the space from which life is empowered and directed captures an ancient wisdom. She shares this intuition with the Jesuit mystic, Pierre Teilhard de Chardin: 'It is in the Sacred Heart that the conjunction of the Divine and the cosmic has taken place ... There lies the power that, from the beginning, has attracted me and conquered me ... All the later development of my interior life has been nothing other than the evolution of that seed.'[18] In emphasizing the heart space in the community which she established, Nano Nagle stressed the power of love to change the world; more than zeal, courage, perseverance, love is what impels her forward and so her parting words to her companions are, 'Love one another as you have hitherto done.' The energy of the heart, cultivated in love and compassion, will resource a leader with resilience in the face of an array of difficulties.

Wisdom

Some verses from the prophet Isaiah (50: 4–5) illustrate the lifestyle of a wise disciple: 'The Lord God has given me the tongue of the wise, that I may know how to sustain the weary one with a word. He awakens me morning by morning, he wakens my ear to listen as a disciple, the Lord God has opened my ear; and I have been attentive.' Proverb 12:18 illuminates this statement further: 'Reckless words pierce like a sword, but the tongue of the wise brings healing.' Avoiding 'reckless words' – words spoken without thought of their effect on others – is a core attitude of the wise leader. The thoughtless word can wound someone with the intensity of a knife attack. This type of wound not only saps the inner resources of the person who receives it, but it may also be disabling or even deeply destructive long after the speaker of the word has moved away. But wise words can also bring healing. These words are not 'reckless.' They are well thought out, weighed and considered: Nano Nagle had an experience early in her innovative enterprise of just how destructive an unwise word could be, so she kept secret her plans to open a school until such time as she felt she could bring her brother and sister-in-law round to the idea.[19]

As a wise woman, Nano knew when to talk and when to keep silent. It is one of the arts of leadership to know when to talk and when to keep silent, even if it might be difficult to do so. All leaders must choose their words carefully, picking the right time to speak, so that their words can have the best impact; this was a leadership skill which Nano Nagle had internalized, even at a time when leadership science was unknown.

Creativity

According to Tobin Hart, creativity involves the focusing of energy, the engagement of the circumstances of life, committing and moving forward despite odds and uncertainty. It is often assumed that the success of leaders in creative pursuits is predominantly the result of good luck or exceptional talent. Such a perception, however, is challenged by the narrative of Nano Nagle's life. Her creative legacy was born from long periods of insecurity and uncertainty. When her brothers, David and Joseph, both made their permanent residences in Bath in England (1762), she moved from the comfortable suburbs of Cork city, where she had for so long resided with David and Ann, to an inner-city cottage where she would spend the next thirteen years searching, praying, interceding, negotiating, struggling to incarnate the vision she held in her heart. She lived in a small cottage which was attached to one of her schools. It was on the side of the street and contained three rooms and an attic. Though the Ursulines constantly begged her to abandon her cottage, which was located at the gate of their convent, she resisted their invitations and nourished instead a creative, imaginative, innovative response to the call at work within her.

Nano Nagle's leadership was inspired by movements that she had heard of or encountered on the European continent. From 1774 to her death in 1784 Nano Nagle toiled to give expression to her spiritual vision – a community of women with the flexibility and depth of commitment to meet the most pressing needs in the society of their time. After being joined by three other women in 1775 – Elizabeth Burke, Mary Fouhy and Mary Ann Collins – one of her chief preoccupations during the final decade of her life was to create a definitive version of a Rule of Life for the group. She gave serious consideration to rules drawn up by three different French groups. The first group was a Franciscan Third Order whose members served in hospitals in France and the Netherlands. However, when Nano wrote about her impression of the Rule to Teresa Mulally, she noted that its fasting instructions would be too severe for working in Irish conditions. The second group whose rule was of interest to

Nano Nagle was the Hospitallers of St Thomas of Villanova, a group who were on the estate at Saint-Germain-en-Laye where her cousins lived. They had been founded in the seventeenth century in France by a friar of the Hermits of St Augustine, Ange le Prous. Nano was unable to obtain a copy of the Rule of this group for her perusal, because of an internal requirement that it be kept confidential to the group. Eventually, through her family circle she was able to obtain a description of its main elements, all of which she asserted to Teresa Mulally closely corresponded to the day-to-day living realities of her group. However, the solemn vows taken by the Sisters in the group would require the practice of enclosure, which service of her schools in Cork city could not accommodate. The third Rule that attracted Nano's attention was that of the Sisters of the Infant Jesus/*Dames de St Maur*, a group founded by Fr Nicolas Barré in France in 1662. There are no reflections by Nano Nagle on the rule of this group in her letters.

The issue of a definitive rule which would capture the inspiration which she had embodied over her lifetime was not resolved before she died. In the end the intangible spirit of her life superseded the written description of its direction, and this may be a noteworthy point for leaders today. In a study conducted by The Centre for Creative Leadership[20] (Greensboro, NC / Brussels, Singapore), it was found that the inability to engage change emerged as one of the primary causes for projects floundering. Time and time again, highly competent and successful individuals, persons with excellent education and strong skill sets get on the wrong path because they stubbornly refuse to adapt to the changing demands of the moment. The ability to take the untrodden path, creatively, and to imagine a future not yet born, without seeking to rush such a birth, were critical to the quality of lived leadership which is manifested in the life of Nano Nagle.

Endnotes

1. See http://www.margaretwheatley.com/articles.html.
2. T. Hart, *The Four Virtues* (New York: Atria / Simon & Schuster, 2014).
3. J.L. Wergin, *Leadership in Place: How Academic Professionals Can Find Their Leadership Voice* (San Francisco, CA: Jossey-Bass, 2007).
4. B. Bass and R. Riggio, *Transformational Leadership* (Mahwah, NJ: Lawrence Erlbaum, 2006).
5. R. Greenleaf, *Servant Leadership: A Journey into the Nature of Legitimate Power and Leadership* (Mahwah, NJ: Paulist Press, 1977), 13.
6. N. Eggert, *Contemplative Leadership for Entrepreneurial Organizations: Paradigms, Metaphors, and Wicked Problems* (Westport, CT: Quorum Books, 1998).
7. A. Sinclair, *Leadership for the Disillusioned: Moving Beyond Myths and Heroes to Leading That Liberates* (Crows Nest, NSW: Allen and Unwin, 2007).
8. L. Reave, 'Spiritual values and practices related to leadership effectiveness', *The Leadership Quarterly* 16 (2007), 655-87.
9. S.K. Chase, M.E. Doona, & L.A. Haggerty, 'Nursing Presence: An Existential Exploration of the Concept'. *Scholarly Inquiry for Nursing Practice: An International Journal* 11 (1997) 3-14 at 3.
10. J. Pettigrew, 'Intensive nursing care: The ministry of presence'. *Critical Care Nursing Clinics of North America*, 2/3 (1990), 503-8.
11. See, http://presentationsistersunion.org/_uploads/fckpg//Letters_of_Nano_Nagle.pdf, 26.
12. V. Frankl, *Man's Search for Meaning: An Introduction to Logotherapy* (Boston: Beacon Press, 2006), 71-2.
13. See C.P. Holmes, *The Heart Doctrine: Mystical Views of the Origin and Nature of Human Consciousness* (Kemptville, ON: Zero Point, 2010), 11.
14. L. Arguelles, R. McCarty, and R.A. Rees, 'The Heart in Holistic Education', *Encounter: Education for Meaning and Social Justice* 16/3 (2003), 13-21.
15. See http://www.heartmath.org
16. C. Consiglio, *Prayer in the Cave of the Heart: The Universal Call to Contemplation* (Collegeville, MN: Liturgical Press, 2009).
17. Author Unknown. *The Way of a Pilgrim*, translated from Russian by R. M. French. (San Francisco: Harper San Francisco, 1991), 11.
18. P. Teilhard de Chardin, *The Heart of the Matter*, Translated by René Hague. (San Diego: Harvest Books, 1978), 43.
19. Nano Nagle to Miss Fitzsimons, AL 17 July 1769, in Walsh, *Nano Nagle*, 344-7. (Story told in full elsewhere in this volume).
20. See http://www.ccl.org

The Song Must not Stop with Us: Investing in the Future of Presentation

Mary T. O'Brien PBVM

Reflecting on the life-story of Nano Nagle as well as on her writings, one notes with amazement the amount of time and energy she devoted to ensuring the future of the Congregation she founded. From her death bed she entrusted everything to her successor, Sr Angela Collins, advising her to be vigilant and kind, and to ensure 'the continuance of the good work, which she [Nano] herself was unworthy to see'.[1] Again and again in her Letters, while writing with immense confidence about the future growth of this mustard seed, this 'work of God', guaranteed to 'prosper after our death', it is interesting to discover that she never credited herself for her own contribution.[2] In fact she took some serious steps to ensure that the song given to her in trust for others would continue to be sung, not only in Cork but throughout the world; not only in eighteenth-century Penal Ireland, but into God's future. She did, in fact, do 'all in her power' in this, as in other endeavours.

In her Letters one gets an insight into what was on Nano's mind, the things that were of concern to her, even as the Presentation enterprise was in its infancy. Those concerns are remarkably close to the concerns that we have today in the Western world in the twenty-first century. In each of the sixteen Letters of hers which have been preserved there is mention of her genuine concern for a continuation of the 'work of God' just begun. She mentions prospective candidates for the Ursuline foundation and for Presentation. Writing to Eleanor Fitzsimons and Teresa Mulally, she is quite specific about proposed co-workers (candidates). Some are mentioned anonymously, others by name, like Kavanagh, Lawless, Nagle, Brady and others. She seems to have researched something of their suitability and their character references, their health records and personal qualities. She makes sure that nothing is spared in their training and education, and she expresses genuine concern about procuring suitable physical plant and living conditions for them, including 'a pretty garden'.[3] She prays and hopes that parents and family members will not oppose a young lady's vocation.[4] Money matters such as dowries and money shortfalls are mentioned in her letters to both Eleanor Fitzsimons and Teresa Mulally, always linked with her unswerving belief that 'the Almighty will do everything for the best'. In this, as in everything, Nano is a woman of faith, discerning and eminently practical, keenly aware of the need for continuity in what she was about and of what might be needed to ensure that continuity.

Some examples of her advice to Eleanor Fitzsimons may even be considered daring and inappropriate by today's standards: 'Never be discouraged from choosing any young lady you think proper.'[5] The point to be made here is that Nano, a person known for her natural timidity, so treasured the spiritual gift given to her that she literally spared no effort to ensure that it was shared with others in her lifetime and bequeathed as living energy to others after her death. That phrase so often repeated in her writings about 'doing all in my power' is relevant in this regard. There may well be a message here for the present generation about doing 'all in our power' to ensure that the Presentation song will not stop with us, while still trusting the outcome to the 'Will of the Almighty' as she did.

If we believe that we, members of the Presentation family – vowed members, friends of Presentation, Associates and Co-Journers – have been gifted in differing ways with sharing in that original divine shaft of spiritual energy which Nano received, and if we believe that we continue to sing her particular song in the Church and in the world, then certain things follow. The first of these is that we (as Congregation and as individually gifted vowed members or Associates) have a responsibility for 'doing all in our power' to ensure that the song does not stop with us. This means a lot more than praying for vocations, 'praying the Lord of the harvest', which, of course, we must not neglect. It means a lot more than appointing Directors of Vocation Ministry in our Provinces and leaving the task to designated persons, while others sit back lamenting, like Job, 'the days that are gone' and the impasse reached (Job 29:1–2). There is no going back to the 'good old days' when candidates in their late teens or early twenties were knocking at convent doors, and novitiate houses were filled to overflowing. We are in a new and changed place today. Life expectancy has increased dramatically; education is a lifelong process. Many people change careers several times during the course of their lives; most young people are educated to primary degree level and beyond. Vocational choices are often delayed until the early thirties or later. The pace of change is accelerating. It would be foolhardy and inappropriate to focus vocation ministry on teenagers or second-level students, although it is never too late or too early to sow seeds.

Within our communities in recent decades, especially in the Western world, vocation ministry has been something of a Cinderella. It certainly has not been given the priority it deserves. The reasons for this are diverse. Perhaps it was taken for granted that we had a divine right to continuity. Perhaps we misunderstood the universal call to holiness as a signal for signing out of the consecrated way of life. Perhaps we were preoccupied with urgent matters arising from diminishment and contraction, such as reorganisation of ministries, sale of property and care of the elderly – all valid concerns in their own right. Perhaps we listened to the voice of the world rather than the divine voice within. Perhaps we lost courage because of the publicity given to stories of child abuse by the few. Perhaps we resigned ourselves to a gradual dissolution and disappearance – inflicted this time by our own past successes and by the arrival of the welfare state. Perhaps we tied our identity to 'badges' (distinctive dress, horarium, and enclosure). We may even have linked identity with schools and hospitals and imposing buildings. Perhaps there are other factors.

For whatever reason, there is no denying that crisis point is near at hand, if it has not already arrived. But crisis begets opportunity. A wake-up call is in order, and Pope Francis has lost no time in sounding it. In his Apostolic Letter to Consecrated Persons at the beginning of the designated Year of Consecrated Life, he writes,

> Do not yield to the temptation to see things in terms of numbers and efficiency, and even less to trust in your own strength. In scanning the horizons of your lives and the present moment, be watchful and alert … I urge you not to join the ranks of the prophets of doom who proclaim the end or meaninglessness of the consecrated life in the Church in our day; rather, clothe yourselves in Jesus Christ and put on the armour of light – as Saint Paul urged (cf. Rom 13:11–14) – keeping awake and watchful. Let us constantly set out anew, with trust in the Lord … I am counting on you 'to wake up the world', since the distinctive sign of consecrated life is prophecy.[6]

Addressing Leaders of Religious Congregations earlier in Rome, he issues a challenge, which involves 'leaving the nest that encloses us to become emissaries' of the Good News.[7] That challenge is acutely relevant to the evolving Presentation charism as well as the future of most Apostolic Congregations in the Western world.

Ensuring the continuation of the Presentation song in the present climate may seem as challenging as for the exiled Israelites of old to 'sing the song of the Lord' in a strange land. Invited by their captors in Babylon to sing 'one of Israel's songs', they replied, 'O how could we sing the song of the Lord on alien soil ... ?'[8] Many Religious men and women today can identify with those exiles 'on alien soil'. Their song does not seem to carry an echo in the 'alien soil' of a post-modern culture. It does not seem like a time for singing. But Nano Nagle has been there. Her song once filled the slums of Cork city – surely 'an alien soil' to one who was accustomed to the luxury of the Parisian court – and the song has endured to this day. Her human voice is stilled, but her song continues to echo in the lives of her spiritual family. Dare we allow it to fall silent in the 'alien soil' of our time and place?

Distinguishing between the external, non-permanent manifestations of vowed life, especially in the ministerial expressions of it, and the inner, essential core is one of the urgent tasks of vocation ministry in our time. Vibrant vocation ministry addresses the continuing formation needs of professed members as well as outreach to potential new candidates. For the professed among us, *Aggiornamento* and *Rinnovamento* go hand in hand, but they are not identical. We have prayed, we have discerned, we have updated, and we have responded with enthusiasm to the call of Vatican II. We have shuffled off many skins, shed much baggage and we travel lighter. But we feel diminished in many ways, uncertain about what steps to take regarding 'the vocation crisis' as it affects us and the future song of Nano. We acknowledge it. This is part of our truth. Denial of reality is never helpful. Like our founder, we are meant to be socially aware, reading the contemporary culture with eyes of faith, refusing to be deterred by obstacles: 'There is nothing in my power that I shan't endeavour to do.'[9]

Apart from the fact that a changed and changing church has opened up new and challenging avenues where prospective candidates for religious life can serve the Gospel and make a difference (as lay missionaries, as chaplains in hospitals and colleges, as pastoral ministers in dioceses, as theologians, writers, journalists, spiritual directors and more) there is widespread confusion about the relevance of consecrated, vowed life, especially in its ministerial dimensions. A few decades ago the confusion was constellated around the relevance of contemplative religious life. In an era when ministerial Religious were highly visible through their work in schools, colleges and social services, scarcely anyone questioned their relevance to church and society. But people questioned the relevance of enclosed monastic life because, of its nature, it was less visible. People wondered what contemplatives did all day. Today the situation is reversed. Vocations to the contemplative life have not suffered anything like the decline known in the congregations of ministerial religious. The visible nature of Christian ministry in education, healthcare and social service was guaranteed by the visibility of large institutions staffed largely by members of apostolic religious congregations. With the disappearance of these institutions and of accompanying large conventual dwellings, ministerial religious life has hit a 'crisis of visibility'. Two challenges follow from this: the first challenge is at the existential level and the second is at the level of communication.

Challenge at the Existential Level

To say that religious life is not needed in our era, simply because the State has assumed responsibility for education and healthcare and social services in the Western world, is to lead to false conclusions about the *Why* of consecrated life. It reduces it to some kind of glorified social service – a kind of NGO that is needed only for a time, dependent on social circumstances. It denies the very essence of consecrated life as a prophetic and covenantal life-form. In the case of Presentation, it denies the founding vision of one who said: 'my views are not for one object only'.[10] Presentation ministry today continues in multiple forms across the globe, depending on how the Spirit leads a response to current need. Most often that ministry will be on the margins in some sense or other, not simply because we follow in our founder's steps, but because prophecy belongs on the margins. Its task is to proclaim the Word of God in the here and now, tailored to a particular situation, in a particular place or culture, addressing a specific need. But the essence of consecrated life is not determined by ministry or defined by it. The essence of Presentation is neither defined nor determined by what we do or do not do. It resides at the ontological level of identity. This is not to denigrate ministry or to deny its importance. Ministry is essential to the life-form which is consecrated apostolic life. But it is important to note that total, lifelong consecration of a person to God through vows of celibacy, poverty and obedience has a prophetic value beyond calculation, and Nano embraced this particular gospel path after years of discernment. It is equally important to note that her compassionate vision and outreach were not confined to any one category of person or to any one ministry:

> If I could be of any service ... in any part of the globe I would willingly do all in my power.[11]

She set up schools for the poor of Cork city; she took responsibility for educating her pupils in the proscribed Catholic faith; she visited the poor in their homes; she cared for the sick and dressed their wounds; she sent out young missionaries to the West Indies; she cared for the city's ladies of the night; she dreamed of building a refuge for the elderly homeless which was completed after her death. Her vision was wide as the world. To say that Nano Nagle was primarily 'about education' or 'about the street children' or 'about the West Indian mission' is to do her no favours. She was primarily and consistently 'about the gospel', as her biographer, Sr Mary Pius O'Farrell, has emphasised again and again.[12] The Gospel was Nano's preoccupation and her focus. From this came her passion for justice, for healing, for liberation, for 'any service ... in any part of the globe'. Touching into the depth and the breadth of her gospel vision and translating it into our present cultural milieu is part of today's challenge for all who walk in her shoes. This is where the rubber of the evolving charism hits the road. A charism does not exist nor does it evolve in a vacuum. It is incarnated in real people who wrestle with real problems and seek a compassionate response. It is not afraid of the kind of questions which provoke unease, even discomfort, questions like the following:

> To what aspect or dimension of the Christian mystery does Presentation give witness? And what is the significance of this Gospel witness in our time?

Theological engagement with such questions is a sine qua non for all who take seriously their place as consecrated persons living out their baptismal calling in a prophetic manner. This is where the threads of continuity reach back into the founding story and forward into that future which is currently beyond view. In the light of Vatican II's re-emphasising of the call to holiness of *all* baptised persons, why should anyone consider vowed life with all the sacrifice entailed? If the blueprint for *all* the baptised is the following of Jesus, what is special about the call to religious life? Is there anything distinctive about it? The question of the identity of vowed life within the context of the baptismal call needs continued exploration and clarification. Stated otherwise, it means identifying and explaining what it could mean to exemplify 'a particular exegesis of the Gospel' in today's world.[13] This is a work of theological exploration. Even if one thinks that the answer is obvious, because the essence of vowed life has not changed, a new language is needed to express that reality in a way that does not distinguish between 'categories of holiness' in the Church. If all baptised Christians are called to the perfection of holiness, one calling is not more holy or better than another. The essentials of Christian life have not changed. Neither have the essentials of consecrated life as a particular exegesis of the Gospel. But there is work to be done by individuals and groups in the Christian community – in parish, in school, in the social media – in teasing out the implications of this for religious communities and for today's Church. If the relevance of consecrated life is at the level of the prophetic and of signification, there is theological mining to be done.

To identify, in light of the Gospel and of the bequeathed spirit of Nano among us, the particular dimension of the Christian mystery to which Presentation bears witness today, is a great part of the existential challenge. There is enormous work to be done at the level of signification if the prophetic Presentation song is to be interpreted and sung in our time. It may not/will not be the exact same song that Nano sang. It cannot be, because we are in a very different place. But the basic melody will be recognisable. Perhaps a harmony line or a descant, a base line or a chorus may be added. But the essentials of the song remain the same. An image that helps one to get to grips with this is that of the dawn chorus. We will have listened to this and marvelled at the way the chorus grows from the first faltering note, then responses echoing, the chorus growing until it swells into a glorious morning song, a wake-up call to creation. Nano sang the opening note. Others joined in ... then others and again others, over the years and in various places, until the chorus echoed across the globe. The contribution of each Presentation Sister and of each member of the Presentation family to that chorus is and has been vital.

Challenge at the Level of Communication

The second great challenge is that of communicating, humbly and truthfully, in as many ways as possible, what consecrated life is about and how it is experienced.[14] This means finding a new language to capture the meaning and value of religious consecration and of the vows of celibacy, poverty and obedience. Pope Francis makes this plea:

> Those who work with young people cannot limit themselves to saying things that are too ordered and structured like a treaty, because these things fly over their heads. A new language is needed, a new way of saying things ...[15]

Finding the new language is one thing; using that language in and through appropriate channels is another. Ironically, it seems that contemplative orders are much better at making use of social media than their counterparts in ministerial religious life. The reasons for this merit serious investigation.

Some Practical Implications

So what are some of the implications? Firstly, I want to stress that these are simply my own personal reflections on the issue. They are meant to generate reflection and dialogue and discernment around the future of consecrated life in its many manifestations. Investing in the future of the evolving charism of Nano may involve, among other things, the following:

> › *A Work of Witness:* There is the fundamental and ongoing task of kindling the prophetic fire within ourselves, of paying attention to the Word in the temple within each of us where God dwells. In that space we will be able to identify strains of the song, to hear it in our hearts, to sing our version of it and to become an authentic version of it. Immediacy to God and social marginality – this is the eschatological sign that defines us, the essence of our prophetic calling. Witnessing to the power of this may be the best kind of 'praying for vocations', the best kind of advertisement, especially if it is joyful. Again we are reminded by Pope Francis that
>
>> consecrated life will not flourish as a result of brilliant vocation programs, but because the young people we meet find us attractive, because they see us as men and women who are happy![16]

Following the Spirit's call within each of us and among us as community may sound easy, but it is a life's work requiring discipline, passion and perseverance. Sometimes it is easier to listen to the counter-song of the world which says that consecrated life has had its day, that Presentation charism is no longer relevant and that we should be resigned to dying out gracefully. Apart from the fact that such suicidal thinking seems out of tune with the Gospel and with the spirit of Nano Nagle, it gives an excuse for doing nothing, for evading the truth as well as the task.

› *A Work of Discovery:* The second vital task is theological engagement with our present reality and with our charismatic roots. Uncovering the riches of our heritage, revealing the wonder of the Presentation story, articulating a theology and a spirituality of Presentation for our time – this, too, will be a sine qua non for continuing the song. It is urgently needed, and it is the responsibility of this generation of Presentation Sisters and those who share their spirit to address it. Only by a serious commitment by individuals and communities to theological engagement with the question of who we are (as distinct from what we do) can solid foundations be laid for vocation ministry into the future and for a space within which the charism of Nano can continue to evolve.

› *A Work of Proclamation/Communication:* This will involve communication at the macro and micro levels, the creative use of digital media, social media and the printed word, websites, public lectures, addresses, symposia, conversations. It will also demand that each of us be aware of our sphere of influence. Each of us is privileged with a sphere, not confined to our immediate environs, where we connect with people through friendship, family, ministries, and personal history. This is our given vineyard, where bonds of trust have been established with many people. Nano Nagle used her sphere of influence to converse and to invite. Among her early companions were her own cousins, Nagles and O'Connells. We may presume that she invited them. Why do we not invite? Jesus invited his chosen Twelve, Nano invited her earliest companions. We are in good company if we acknowledge our sphere of influence in this globalised world and use it creatively for the Kingdom. If we take the courage to sing one note, others may join in.

› *A Work of Collaboration/Communion:* 'One Spirit has been given to us all to drink' (1 Cor 12:13). In looking towards God's future in this global age, we join in collaboration with all who are inspired by Nano and with Presentation co-workers across the planet. It makes good gospel sense to work together, sharing life and resources, singing the same Presentation Song in differing keys and varying tempi. At a very practical level, collaboration will reduce financial burdens. Serious commitment to vocation ministry will cost money. Theological engagement with the roots of who we are as vowed persons, of the prophetic dimensions of Religious Life in Church and society, will require funding for appropriate continuing formation of all members, irrespective of age or assignment. If the so-called 'vocation crisis' may have its roots in and among us in our communities, as many believe, as well as 'out there' in the wider church, this needs urgent addressing. If the salt has lost its taste, it needs renewing. While vocation ministry is essentially part of the ministry of every Christian, it is especially the responsibility of those vowed members appointed specifically to that task. These people need to be supported, encouraged and given all the assistance they need for their work. Their assignment must be full time, well resourced, and not just a 'token ministry', as has frequently been the case. It goes without saying that they must be adequately funded.

The development of user-friendly websites, literature, flyers, posters, conferences, discernment days or weekends, programmes on radio and television – this will require investment of time, expertise and money. It may even require major fundraising drives, which in themselves generate publicity. It all depends on how we value the song that is given us to sing.

Conclusion

In summary, we have no valid reason for thinking that the song must stop with us, or that the gift of a vocation to follow in Nano's footsteps is not a priceless treasure for Church and society, as well as for the person chosen. If it is treasured at the present time by those who are called, it will surely shine with a visible glow into the future. The force of outside factors, hostile or otherwise, will not prevail if the inner fire is burning. The primary task – and it is a continuing task – is that of kindling the original fire within and among us. Fire, of its nature, is expansive and self-promoting. But this does not exonerate us from investing time and resources in a communications strategy appropriate to our current age.

In the strengthening of our resolve to ensure the continuation of the Presentation song, we are invited to embrace the new and the untried. We do not know what shape or form the Presentation way will take in the future or how the charism will continue to evolve. All we know is that it will be different. It will bear the hallmark of newness. There will be continuity with the past and discontinuity too, as with all evolution. Because the Presentation charism is a living and particular refraction of the Gospel, it is dynamic. It is also enfleshed. It does not exist apart from persons. If those to whom it is entrusted fail to treasure it, prayer to the Lord of the harvest for new members will ring hollow. If, however, we believe with Nano that the Presentation song is really worth singing for the sake of the Church and the world, and that 'His [God's] divine hand will uphold us'[17] we will, like her, invest in the future version of that song, creatively and consciously doing 'all in our power'.

Endnotes

1. Annals of South Presentation Convent, Cork.
2. Nano Nagle to Miss Fitzsimons, AL 29 April 1770, par 2, in T. J. Walsh, *Nano Nagle and the Presentation Sisters* (Dublin: M. H. Gill and Son, 1959), 349.
3. Nano Nagle to Miss Mulally, AL 31 January 1783, par 5, in Walsh, *Nano Nagle*, 367.
4. Nano Nagle to Miss Fitzsimons, AL 17 July 1769, par 3, in Walsh, *Nano Nagle*, 345.
5. Nano Nagle to Miss Fitzsimons, AL 13 May 1770, par 6, in Walsh, *Nano Nagle*, 352.
6. Pope Francis, *Apostolic Letter to Consecrated Persons. Year of Consecrated Life*. 21 November 2014.
7. Address to the Union of Religious Superiors, Rome, 25 November 2013.
8. Psalm 137: 1-5.
9. Nano Nagle to Miss Fitzsimons, AL 28 September 1770, par 4, in Walsh, *Nano Nagle*, 354.
10. Nano Nagle to Miss Fitzsimons, AL 17 July 1769, par 11, in Walsh, *Nano Nagle*, 347.
11. ibid.
12. See, for example, Sr Mary Pius O'Farrell, *Nano Nagle, Woman of the Gospel* (Monasterevin: Union of Presentation Sisters, 1996). Also, by the same author, In Praise of Nano Nagle's Spirituality (Monasterevin: Union of Presentation Sisters, 2009).
13. Pope Benedict XVI, *Verbum Domini* (2010). No 84.
14. Here the concern is primarily with vowed membership, although it will also have relevance to associate membership and others.
15. Address to Union of Religious Superiors.
16. Pope Francis, *Apostolic Letter to Consecrated Persons*.
17. Nano Nagle to Miss Fitzsimons, AL 13 May 1770, par 3, in Walsh, º, 351.

List of Contributors

Anne M. Codd PBVM PHD
A native of Wexford, Ireland, Anne joined the Presentation Sisters in 1966. After fifteen years in school ministries, her graduate studies led her into pastoral development work in a variety of settings in Ireland and internationally. She currently serves on the leadership team of Presentation Sisters in the North East Province, Ireland.

Mary L. Coloe PBVM DTHEOL
From Melbourne, Australia, Mary is an Associate Professor at the University of Divinity where she lectures in New Testament. She has authored and edited a number of books, journal articles and essays primarily on the Gospel of John. She was recently appointed by the Pontifical Council for Christian Unity to be a member of an international dialogue between Catholics and the Church/Disciples of Christ.

Bernadette Flanagan PBVM PHD
Bernadette is collaborating as co-editor with Professor László Zsolnai, University of Budapest, on *The Routledge Handbook of Spirituality and Society* (2018). She currently serves on the leadership team of the Presentation Sisters in the North East Province, Ireland.

Beth Hassel PBVM DMIN
Beth is a Presentation Sister from Staten Island, New York, and serves on the leadership team of her Congregation. She is the Director of the Center for Faith and Learning in the Office for Mission and Ministry at Villanova University, Pennsylvania. She facilitates dialogue in the areas of vocation, religious diversity, faith and reason with faculty and students. Beth teaches in the Theology and Religious Studies Department in the College of Arts and Sciences and her research is primarily in the area of spirituality and faith development.

Gloria Loya PBVM DMIN
Gloria Loya's work has been within the context of Latino Faith and

Culture. She completed the DMin at the Pacific School of Religion, Graduate Theological Union, and taught at the Jesuit School of Theology, Berkeley. Currently she serves as Vicar for Religious, Diocese of Monterey, California.

Máirín MacCarron PHD
Máirín lectures in Medieval History at the University of Sheffield, and previously held a National University of Ireland / Dr Garret FitzGerald Postdoctoral fellowship at the National University of Ireland at Galway. She worked for the Servants of the Mother of God on the canonisation cause of their founder, the Venerable Magdalen Taylor.

Catherine Nowlan-Roebuck PHD
Catherine completed her PhD at the University College Dublin School of Education, on the Irish Presentation Sisters and nineteenth-century education. She has contributed to several scholarly journals and book publications, and is currently a researcher on the Nano Nagle digital project, directed by Deirdre Raftery, University College Dublin.

Mary T. O'Brien PBVM PHD
Mary is a native of West Cork, Ireland, and has served as teacher at Second and Third Level and in administration. She is a published author and has been Communications Officer for the Irish Episcopal Conference, 2003–2008, and is currently Lecturer in Sacred Scripture at Mary Immaculate College, University of Limerick.

Anne M. O'Leary PBVM PHD
A native of West Cork, Ireland, Anne's passion straddles education, theology, Scripture and spirituality. She lectured in education at University College Cork, and Mary Immaculate College, University of Limerick; and in New Testament at St Mary's University, San Antonio, Texas – prior to serving on the Congregational Leadership Team of the Presentation Sisters (Union, 2012–present).

Margaret H. Preston PHD
Margaret is Associate Professor and Chair of the History Department at Augustana College, Sioux Falls, South Dakota. She is the author of *Charitable Words: Gentlewomen, Social Control and the Language of Charity in Nineteenth-Century Dublin* (2004) and *A Journey of Faith, Destination of Excellence: Avera McKennan Hospital's First Century of Caring* (2010).

Deirdre Raftery PHD

Deirdre is a Professor in the History of Education at University College Dublin, specializing in the history of women religious. She is an elected Fellow of the Royal Historical Society, and has been a visiting scholar at the University of Cambridge, Boston College, and the University of Oxford. Her most recent publication, edited jointly with Elizabeth M. Smyth, is *Education, Identity and Women Religious: Convents, Classrooms and Colleges* (New York and London: Routledge, 2016).

Frank Steele DPhil

Frank is a native of Cork City, Ireland. He studied at Marino Institute of Education, University College Cork, and Oxford. He served as a Christian Brother in Ireland and in Argentina. He has taught at all three levels in Ireland, was principal of a post-primary school for twenty years, and is now CEO and Dean of Studies at the Christian Leadership in Education Office, Cork. He has lectured and published on lay spirituality and on Catholic education.

Select Bibliography

References to Presentation Annals and Nano Nagle's Letters, as well as journal articles, websites and foreign language publications, are given in the chapter endnotes.

A Christian Brother, *Edmund Ignatius Rice, Founder of the Christian Brothers* (Dublin: Catholic Truth Society of Ireland, 1914).

A Presentation Sister, Mount St Michael, Staten Island, New York. *Nano Nagle* (Huntington, Indiana: Our Sunday Visitor Press, 1939).

Allen, Sr Rosario, *A Story of Love and Faith* (Cork: South Presentation Convent, 1979).

Aquinas, Thomas, Charity, *Summa Theologiae*, in 60 vols. Vol. 34, R. J. Batten OP (ed.) (London: Eyre and Spottiswoode, 1975).

_____ *Summa Theologiae: A Concise Translation*, Timothy McDermott (ed.) (Christian Classics, Notre Dame, IN: Ave Maria Press, 1997).

Baggley, J., *Festival Icons for the Christian Year* (London: Mowbray, 2000).

Barker, M., *The Gate of Heaven: The History and Symbolism of the Temple in Jerusalem* (London: SPCK, 1991).

_____ *Temple Theology: An Introduction* (London: SPCK, 2004).

Bartlett, R., *Why Can the Dead Do Such Great Things?* (Princeton, NJ: Princeton University Press, 2013).

Bass, B., and R. Riggio, *Transformational Leadership* (Mahwah, NJ: Lawrence Erlbaum, 2006).

Beale, G. K., *The Temple and the Church's Mission: A Biblical Theology of the Dwelling Place of God*. New Studies in Biblical Thought 17 (Downers Grove, IL: InterVarsity Press, 2004).

Bevans, S.B., *Models of Contextual Theology, Faith and Cultures*, Revised and Expanded Edition (Maryknoll, NY: Orbis Books, 2013).

Bowen, D., *The Protestant Crusade in Ireland, 1800–1870: A Study of Protestant-Catholic Relations between the Act of Union and Disestablishment* (Dublin: Gill and Macmillan, 1978).

Brown, L.B., *Moral Capital: Foundations of British Abolitionism* (Chapel Hill, NC: University of North Carolina Press, 2006).

Brown, P., *Through the Eye of a Needle: Wealth, the Fall of Rome and the Making of Christianity in the West, 350 to 550 AD* (Princeton, NJ: Princeton University Press, 2012).

Brown, R.E., *An Introduction to the New Testament* (New York: Doubleday, 1996).

Brunett, A.J. and P.F. Carnley (eds), *'Mary, Grace and Hope in Christ: A Joint Statement of the Anglican-Roman Catholic International Commission'* (Seattle: ARCIC, 2004).

Buby, B., *Mary of Galilee: The Marian Heritage of the Early Church*, Vol. III (New York: Alba House, 1997).

Butler, A., *Lives of the Saints* (Dublin: n.p., 1779).

Butler, A.M., *Across God's Frontiers: Catholic Sisters in the American West 1850–1920* (Chapel Hill: University of North Carolina Press, 2012).

Canny, L., *The Way of the People* (Galway: Wordsonthestreet, 2011).

Canny, N., 'Early Modern Ireland c 1500–1700', *The Oxford Illustrated History of Ireland*, R.F. Foster (ed.) (Oxford University Press, 1989).

Challoner, R., *Considerations upon Christian truths and Christian duties digested into meditations for every day of the year*, 2 vols (London: n.p., 1754).

Clarke, U., *The Ursulines in Cork 1771–1996* (Cork: Tower Books, 1996).

Coloe, M.L, *God Dwells with Us: Temple Symbolism in the Fourth Gospel* (Collegeville: Liturgical Press, 2001).

_____ (ed.), *Creation is Groaning: Biblical and Theological Perspectives* (Collegeville: Liturgical Press, 2013).

Colunga, A. and P. Turrado, *Biblia Sacra iuxta Vulgatam Clementinam Nova Editio* (Madrid: Biblioteca de Autores Cristianos, 1977).

Consedine, R., *One Page Beyond. The Life of Nano Nagle* (Victoria: Dove Publications, 1977).

_____ *Listening Journey: A Study of the Spirit and Ideals of Nano Nagle and the Presentation Sisters* (Victoria: Congregation of the PBVM, 1983).

_____ *Fire on Earth* (Victoria: Presentation Sisters, 1988).

_____ *Songs of the Journey* (Victoria: Presentation Sisters, 2001).

Consiglio, C., *Prayer in the Cave of the Heart: The Universal Call to Contemplation* (Collegeville, MN: Liturgical Press, 2009).

Corish, P.J., *The Catholic Community in the Seventeenth and Eighteenth Centuries* (Dublin: Helicon, 1981).

Cross, F.L. and E.A. Livingstone (eds), *Oxford Dictionary of the Christian Church*, Third Edition Revised (Oxford: Oxford University Press, 2005).

Crossan, J.D., *Jesus: A Revolutionary Biography* (New York: Harper Collins, 1994).

Cruise O'Brien, C., *The Great Melody: A Thematic Biography of Edmund Burke* (London: Sinclair-Stevenson, 1992, repr. 1993).

De Aviz, João Braz and José Rodríguez Carballo, *Contemplate: Year of Consecrated Life*. (Congregation for Institutes of Consecrated Life and Societies of Apostolic Life, Rome: Catholic Truth Society, 2016).

De Castro, F., *The First Biography of St John of God* (Granada: 1585). Translated from the original Spanish with commentary notes by Benedict O'Grady (Dublin: John of God Brothers, 1986).

Donlevy, A., *The Catechism of Christian Doctrine* (Dublin: James Duffy, 1848).

Donnelly, J. S. and K.M. Miller (eds), *Irish Popular Culture 1650–1850* (Dublin: Irish Academic Press, 1999).

Dulles, A., *Models of the Church* (New York: Doubleday, 1974).

Eggert, N., *Contemplative Leadership for Entrepreneurial Organizations: Paradigms, Metaphors, and Wicked Problems* (Westport, CT: Quorum Books, 1998).

Feheney, J.H.M. (ed.), *Edmund Rice and the Presentation Tradition of Education* (Dublin: Veritas Publications, 1996).

Fialka, J.J., Sisters: *Catholic Sisters and the Making of America* (New York: St Martin's Griffin, 2004).

Fitzmyer, J. A. and K. P. Donfried (eds), *Mary in the New Testament* (Mahwah, NJ: Paulist Press, 1978).

Flanagan, B., *Embracing Solitude: Women and New Monasticism* (Eugene, OR: Cascade Books, 2014).

Flannery, A. (ed.), *The Documents of Vatican II: Constitutions, Decrees, Declarations* (Dublin: Dominican Publications, 1996).

Foster, R.F. (ed.), *The Oxford Illustrated History of Ireland* (Oxford: Oxford University Press, 1989).

Frankl, V., *Man's Search for Meaning: An Introduction to Logotherapy* (Boston: Beacon Press, 2006).

Freedman, D.N. (ed.), *The Anchor Yale Bible Dictionary* Vol. II (New York: Doubleday, 1992).

Gahan, W., *Sermons and Moral Discourses for all the Sundays and Principal Festivals of the Year In Two Volumes*, Third Edition, Revised and Corrected (Dublin: Richard Coyne, 1825).

Galvin, C., *From Acorn to Oak* (Fargo, ND: Presentation Sisters, 1969).

Gambero, L., *Mary and the Fathers of the Church: The Blessed Virgin Mary in Patristic Thought*, trans. Thomas Buffer (San Francisco: Ignatius Press, 1999).

Gaventa, B. Roberts, *Mary: Glimpses of the Mother of Jesus* (Columbia: University of South Carolina Press, 1994).

Gedin, H. and J.P. Dolan (eds), *History of the Church: The Church in an age of absolutism and enlightenment* Vol. VI (New York: Crossroad, 1981).

Gillespie, R. and A. Hadfield, *The Irish Book in English, 1550–1800*, *The Oxford History of the Irish Book*, Volume III (Oxford: Oxford University Press, 2006).

Gobinet, C., *Instructions for Youth in Christian Piety* (Dublin: James Duffy & Sons, 1872).

Goodier, A., *Saints for Sinners: Nine Desolate Souls Made Strong by God* (Manchester, NH: Sophia Institute Press, 2007). Originally published (Garden City, NY: Image Books, 1959).

Gother, J., *The Spiritual Works of John Gother*, 16 vols (Dublin: Wogan and Cross, 1792).

Greenleaf, R., *Servant Leadership: A Journey into the Nature of Legitimate Power and Leadership* (Mahwah, NJ: Paulist Press, 1977).

Harrington, D., *A Woman's Will ... A Sister's Way: The McKennan Hospital Story* (Sioux Falls: np, 1961).

Hart, T., *The Four Virtues* (NY: Atria/Simon & Schuster, 2014).

Hellinckx, B., F. Simon and M. Depaepe, *The Forgotten Contribution of the Teaching Sisters* (Leuven: Leuven University Press, 2009).

Hickey, E. R., 'Rule and Constitutions of the Society of Religious Brothers 1832', *Inheritance: Collection Two* (Rome: Congregation of Christian Brothers – for private circulation, 1982).

Holmes, C.P., *The Heart Doctrine: Mystical Views of the Origin and Nature of Human Consciousness* (Kemptville, ON: Zero Point, 2010).

Hug, J.E. (ed.), *Tracing the Spirit: Communities, Social Action, and Theological Reflection* (New York: Paulist Press, 1983).

Hutch, W., *Nano Nagle: Her Life, Her Labours and Their Fruits* (Dublin: McGlashan and Gill, 1875).

Javierre, J.M., *John of God: Loco in Granada* (Seville: 2000), trans. Benedict O'Grady (Sydney: John of God Brothers, 2000).

Karolevitz, R.F., *A Commitment to Care: The First 100 Years of Sacred Heart Hospital 1897–1997* (South Dakota: Pine Hill Press, 1997).

Kasper, W., *Theology and Church* (London: SCM Press, 1989).

Kealy, M., *Dominican Education in Ireland, 1820–1930* (Dublin: Irish Academic Press, 2007).

Keogh, D., *Edmund Rice 1762–1844* (Dublin: Four Courts Press, 1996).

_____ *Edmund Rice and the First Christian Brothers* (Dublin: Four Courts Press, 2008).

_____ 'Gahan, William' in *Dictionary of Irish Biography* (Cambridge: Cambridge University Press for the Royal Irish Academy, 2009).

KilBride, C. and D. Raftery, *The Voyage Out: Infant Jesus Sisters Ireland 1909–2009* (Dublin: IJS Centenary Committee, 2009).

Lakeland, P., *Postmodernity: Christian Identity in a Fragmented Age* (Minneapolis, MN: Fortress Press, 1997).

Laskin, D., *The Children's Blizzard* (NewYork: Harper, 2005).

Leahy, M de Pazzi, 'Transcript of the Annals of South Presentation Convent, Cork 1771–1989'.

Leahy, M., *The Flower of Her Kindred* (New York: Maurice Leahy, 1944).

Lecky, W.E.H., *A History of England in the 18th century*, Vol. 1 (London: Longmans, Green and Company, 1878).

Levine, A-J. with M. M. Robbins, *A Feminist Companion to Mariology* (New York: T. & T. Clark International/Continuum, 2005).

Loya, G.I., *The Mexican-American Woman in California: Pathways Towards a Pastoral Project, Doctor of Ministry Project* (Berkeley: Pacific School of Religion, Graduate Theological Union, 1996).

McBride, I., *Eighteenth Century Ireland* (Dublin: Gill and Macmillan, 2009).

McGrath, T., *The Pastoral and Education Letters of Bishop James Doyle of Kildare and Leighlin, 1786–1834* (Dublin: Four Courts Press, 2004).

McGreevy, K., *A Century of Care ... A Journey of Faith: Avera Queen of Peace Hospital 1906–2006* (Mitchell: Avera Queen of Peace Health Services, 2006).

McGuinness, M.M., *Called to Serve: A History of Nuns in America* (NY: New York University, 2013).

Mannock, J., *The poor man's catechism*; or, the Christian doctrine explained. With short admonitions. This edition is newly revised, and much amended, by the Rev. B. McM. Dublin, MDCCXCIV. Eighteenth-Century CollectionsOnline. Gale. University College Cork.

Mann Wall, B., *Unlikely Entrepreneurs: Catholic Sisters and the Hospital Marketplace* (Columbus: Ohio State University Press, 2005).

Martin, J. (ed.), *Give us this Day: Daily Prayer for Today's Catholic* (Collegeville, MN: Liturgical Press, 2013).

Matovina, T. (ed.), *Beyond Borders, Writings of Virgilio Elizondo and Friends* (Maryknoll, NY: Orbis Books, 2000).

_____*Latino Catholicism, Transformation in America's Largest Church* (Princeton, NJ: Princeton University Press, 2012).

Milne, K., *The Irish Charter Schools 1730–1830* (Dublin: Four Courts Press, 1997).

Moody, T.W. and W.E. Vaughan, *Eighteenth-Century Ireland 1691-1800, A New History of Ireland*, Vol. IV (Oxford: Oxford University Press, 2009).

Mooney, M., *Doing What Needs To Be Done: Sisters of the Presentation of the Blessed Virgin Mary, Fargo 1882–1997* (Fargo, ND: Access Midwest, 1997).

Murphy, D., *Memoirs of Nano Nagle and the Ursuline and Presentation Orders in Ireland* (Cork: Joseph Roche, 1845).

Nolan, P., *The Irish Dames of Ypres* (New York: Benziger Brothers, 1908).

Normoyle, M.C., *Memories of Edmund Rice Printed for Private Circulation* (Dublin: Christian Brothers, 1977).

O'Dwyer, P., *Towards a History of Irish Spirituality* (Dublin: The Columba Press, 1995).

O'Farrell, M.P., *Nano Nagle: Woman of the Gospel* (Cork: Cork Publishing, 1996).

_____ *Breaking of Morn: Nano Nagle (1718–1784) & Francis Moylan (1735–1815) A Book of Documents* (Cork: Cork Publishing, 2001).

_____ *In Praise of Nano Nagle's Spirituality* (Monasterevin: Union of Presentation Sisters, 2010).

O'Flanagan, P. and C.G. Buttimer, *Cork History & Society: Interdisciplinary Essays on the History of an Irish County* (Dublin: Geography Publications, 1993).

Ó Riordáin, J. J., *Irish Catholic Spirituality: Celtic & Roman* (Dublin: The Columba Press, 1998).

Ó Súilleabháin, S. (ed.), *Miraculous Plenty: Irish Religious Folktales and Legends*, trans. W. Caulfield, Folklore Studies 20 (Dublin: Comhairle Béaloideas Éireann/An Cumann le Béaloideas Éireann, 2011).

O'Sullivan, C. M., *Hospitality in Medieval Ireland 900–1500* (Dublin: Four Courts Press, 2004).

O'Toole, A. L., *A Spiritual Profile of Edmund Ignatius Rice*, Vol. I, (Bristol: The Burleigh Press, 1984).

Ouspensky, L. and V. Lossky, *The Meaning of Icons*. Trans. G.E.H. Palmer and E. Kadloubovsky (New York: St Vladimir's Seminary Press, 1999).

Peterson, S.C. and C.A. Vaughn-Roberson, *Women with Vision: The Presentation Sisters of South Dakota, 1880–1985* (SD: University of Illinois Press, 1988).

Pettit, S. F., *The City of Cork 1700–1900* (Cork: Studio Publications, 1977).

Portilla, M.L., *Aztec Thought and Culture, a Study of the Ancient Nahuatl Mind* (Norman, OK: University of Oklahoma Press, 1963).

Preston, M. H, *A Journey of Faith, a Destination of Excellence: Avera McKennan Hospital's First Century of Caring* (Sioux Falls: Avera McKennan Hospital, 2010).

_____*Women, Philanthropy, and the Language of Charity in Nineteenth-Century Dublin* (London: Praeger, 2004).

Raftery, D. and E. Smyth (eds), *Education, Identity and Women Religious: Convents, Classrooms and Colleges* (New York and London: Routledge, 2016).

Rahner, H. (ed.), *The Parish: from Theology to Practice* (Westminster, Maryland: Newman Press, 1958).

Rahner, K. (ed.), *Encyclopedia of Theology, a Concise Sacramentum Mundi* (London: Burns and Oates, 1975).

Raughter, R.(ed.), *Religious Women and Their History: Breaking the Silence* (Dublin: Irish Academic Press, 2005).

Ricard, R., *The Spiritual Conquest of Mexico* (Berkeley, CA: University of California Press, 1982).

Rippin, A., *Muslims: Their Religious Beliefs and Practices*, 2nd ed. (London: Routledge, 2001).

Robinson, G., *Essential Judaism: A Complete Guide to Beliefs, Customs, and Rituals* (New York: Pocket Books, 2000).

Rushe, D., *Edmund Rice: The Man and his Times* (Dublin: Gill and Macmillan, 1981).

Saravia, A. (ed.), *The Popul Vuh* (Mexico: Editorial Porrua, 1971).

Schneiders, S.M., *Finding the Treasure: Locating Catholic Religious Life in a New Ecclesial and Cultural Context* (NY: Paulist Press, 2000).

_____*Selling All: Commitment, Consecrated Celibacy, and Community in Catholic Religious Life* (NY: Paulist Press, 2001).

_____*Prophets in their own Country: Women Religious Bearing Witness to the Gospel in a Troubled Church* (Maryknoll, NY: Orbis, 2011).

_____ *Buying the Field: Religious Life in a New Millennium* (NY: Paulist Press, 2013).

Schreiter, R.J., *Constructing Local Theologies* (Maryknoll, NY: Orbis Books, 1985).

Senior, D. and J. J. Collins (eds), *The New American Bible: The Catholic Study Bible* (Oxford: Oxford University Press, 2006).

_____ *The Gift of Administration: New Testament Foundations for the Vocation of Administrative Service* (Collegeville: Liturgical Press, 2015).

Sinclair, A., *Leadership for the Disillusioned: Moving Beyond Myths and Heroes to Leading That Liberates* (Crows Nest, NSW: Allen and Unwin, 2007).

Smyth, E. (ed.), *Changing Habits: Women's Religious Orders in Canada* (Montreal: Novalis Publications, 2007).

Smyth, G., *Blessed Edmund Rice 1762–1844* (New York: Christian Brothers Foundation, 2005).

Smyth, W., and K. Whelan (eds), *Common Ground: Essays on the Historical Geography of Ireland: Presented to T. Jones Hughes* (Cork: Cork University Press, 1988).

Sölle, D., *The Silent Cry: Mysticism and Resistance* (Minneapolis: Fortress Press, 2001).

Steele, F. J., *Towards a Spirituality for Lay-Folk: The Active Life in Middle English Religious Literature from the Thirteenth Century to the Fifteenth* (Lewiston NY: The Edwin Mellen Press, 1995).

Teilhard de Chardin, P., *The Heart of the Matter*, trans. René Hague (San Diego, CA: Harvest Books, 1978).

Thomas, M., *Not Words But Deeds* (Notre Dame: Dujarie, 1968).

Tillard, J-M.R., *Church of Churches, The Ecclesiology of Communion* (Collegeville, Minnesota: The Liturgical Press, 1987).

_____*A Gospel Path, the religious life* (Brussels: Lumen Vitae, 1978).

Tynan, M., *Catholic Instruction in Ireland 1720–1950* (Dublin: Four Courts Press, 1985).

Walsh, T.J., *Nano Nagle and the Presentation Sisters* (Dublin: M.H. Gill & Son, 1959).

Wergin, J.L., *Leadership in Place: How Academic Professionals Can Find Their Leadership Voice* (San Francisco, CA: Jossey-Bass, 2007).

Whelan, I., *The Bible War in Ireland: The 'Second Reformation' and the Polarization of Protestant-Catholic Relations 1800–1840* (Dublin: The Lilliput Press, 2005).

White, C. (ed.), *Early Christian Lives* (Harmondsworth: Penguin, 1998).

Index

Annals (See 'South Presentation' below)
Augustinians
   Gahan, William 95
   Grace, Patrick 119
   Rice, Fr John 124
Avera Health 76 n1, 209–211

Bachelor's Quay 34, 83
Ballygriffin 17, 20, 33–34, 56, 80, 83, 171, 191–192, 201 n10
Barré, Nicolas 156, 220
Beale, Priscilla 124
Bellew, Miss 88
Benedictines 209
   Benedictine Convent at Ypres 18, 81–82, 91 n4
   Benedictine Convent at Fontevraud 81
   Arthur, Abbess Xaveria 82
   Busch, Mildred 209
   Crowley, Kate 209
   Fletcher, Dame Josephine 81
   Goulde, Dame Ignatia 82
   Stewart, Maureen, Sr Bernard 81–82, 91 n8
Brady William O, Bishop of Sioux Falls 208
Bray, Dr, Archbishop of Cashel & Emly 98
Browne, Judith (Foundress of Brigidines) 83
Burke, Edmund 17, 29, 31 n23, 80, 178
Burke, Elizabeth (Sr Augustine) 20, 43, 70, 86, 113, 141, 219
Butler, John, Bishop of Cork 41, 43, 85, 113
Butler, Margaret (Sr Joseph) 204–205

Callaghan, Mother Clare 34–35, 68, 215
Callanan, Fr Lawrence 89, 123, 141, 142, 158
Carleton, Francis 42
Carmelites 39
Catholic Emancipation 26
Challoner, Richard, Vicar Apostolic 100

Charter Schools (see Incorporated Society)
Christian Brothers 15, 93, 102
   Hanover St 97–100
   Mount Sion Waterford 98, 101, 120, 124
Chriswell, Sr Aloysius 204
Collins, Mary Ann (Mother Angela) 20, 43, 70, 86, 113, 122, 141, 198, 219, 223
Collins, Sr Mary Denis 209
Congar, Yves 165–166, 168
Connell, Johanna 45, 141
Coppinger, Elizabeth (Mother Augustine) 40–41, 85, 131
Council of Trent 164
Cove Lane (Douglas Street) 18, 35–36, 42, 62, 70, 111, 113–114, 193–197
Curtin, Sr Kathleen 124

Dakotas (North and South) 65, 115
Dames de Saint Louis 81, 124
de Beaumont, Christophe, Archbishop of Paris 40
De la Salle (Brothers of the Christian Schools) 102
Dominicans 19, 39
Donleavy, Fr Andrew 55, 63 n3
Doyle, James, Bishop of Kildare & Leighlin 95, 97, 99–100
Drexel, Katherine 124

Elliott, Mary 120

Filles de St Joseph 89
Fitzsimons, Eleanor (Sr Angela) 19, 36–37, 39 41, 56 58, 61, 73, 85, 87, 89, 107, 110, 113, 131, 160, 192, 195, 223–224.
Fouhy, Mary 20, 43, 70, 86, 113, 141, 219
Franciscan Third Order 219

Gleason, Neil 206–207
Gould, Mrs 198
Grey Sisters 45, 101

Harper, Isabella 194
Harper, John 194
Hedge Schools 18, 28, 34, 80, 171
Hennessy, Mother Vincent 115
Hill, Br Mark 93
Hodnett, Miss 45
Hughes, Mother Mary John 203–204

Incorporated Society for Promoting English Protestant Schools in Ireland (Charter Schools) 34
Infant Jesus Sisters 156, 220
Irish Repeal Movement 30

Jansenism 79–80, 87, 89
Jesuits (Society of Jesus)
   Amiot, Stephen 82
   Austin, John 85–86
   Barron, Nicholas 86, 92 n22, 101–102, 158
   Dalas 82
   de Lubac, Henri 166
   de Nobili, Robert 179
   Doran, Patrick 20, 39, 41, 84–85, 112
   Ignatius of Loyola 67, 79, 82, 87–88, 90, 91–92 n20
   O'Halloran, James 85, 91–92 n20
   Ricci, Matteo 179

Kavanagh, Mary (Sr Ursula) 40–41, 131
Kelly, Mother Margaret 41, 113, 131, 195

Lane, Margaret 141

McAuley, Catherine 124
McCarthy, Bishop Florence 84
McCarthy, Margaret (Sr Raphael) 204, 207–208
McKennan, Helen 205
McKennan Hospital 204–205, 207
Martin, Mary 124
Meyer, Sr Joyce 210
Moylan, Bishop Francis 20, 38–41, 43, 45, 48 n30, 57, 84, 112–114, 131, 134–135, 141, 159, 195
Mulally, Teresa 19–20, 43, 45–46, 57–58, 85–86, 88, 101, 107, 111, 127, 159, 196–197, 219–220, 223–224
Mullowney Mary 122

Nagle Family
   Ann (Nano's mother) 17, 33, 68, 80, 190
   Ann (sister) 34, 55–56, 69, 83, 171, 190, 192
   David (grandfather) 29
   David (brother) 34, 39, 192, 194, 198, 219
   Elizabeth (sister) 45
   Frances (sister-in-law) 35–36
   Garret (father) 17, 29, 33, 55, 69, 80, 190, 191
   James (uncle) 30
   Joseph (uncle) 29–30, 36–37, 39, 112, 193–194
   Joseph (brother) 35–36, 39, 198–199
   Margaret (cousin) 40–41, 85, 89, 131
   Sir Richard (great-uncle) 26–27

O'Connell, Daniel 26
O'Gorman, Thomas, Bishop of Sioux Falls 204
O'Halloran, Mr 80
Oliffe, Miss 45, 86, 141, 158
Order of Hospitallers of St John of God 67, 74
Order of St Thomas de Villeneuve 45, 65, 88, 101, 220

Penal Laws 17–18, 25–30, 34, 38, 56–57, 59–60, 65, 85, 91 nn1 and 11, 107, 110–111, 119, 121–122, 127, 131, 178, 191, 194, 201 n10, 223
petites écoles 37, 84
Philpot Lane (Clarence St) 36
Poor Clares 39
Popes
   Alexander VIII 66
   Clement XIII 82–83, 90
   Clement XIV 41
   Francis 19, 155, 166, 177–178, 225, 229–230
   John XXIII 164
   John Paul II 163
   Paul VI 182
   Pius IX 133

Power, Fr John (later Bishop) 121–122
Power, Ellen 122–123
Power, Margaret 122

PACE (Presentation Affiliated Cooperative Effort) 208–209
PHS (Presentation Health Systems) 209

Presentation Communities
   Aberdeen, South Dakota 15, 76 n1, 114, 203–210
   Alaska 115
   Australia 114–115
   Bolivia 115
   Cambodia 115
   Chile 115
   South Presentation, Cork 58–59, 61–62, 69, 72, 90, 108, 126 n24, 127, 141, 147, 158, 197, 202 n31
   George's Hill, Dublin 107, 124
   Dubuque, Iowa 15, 114–115, 211 n5
   Ecuador 115
   England 114, 126 n24
   Fargo, North Dakota 81, 114, 203–204
   Fitchburg, MA 114
   Holy Land 115
   India 114–115
   Kilkenny 114–115
   Killarney 45, 90, 114
   Newburgh, NY 107
   Newfoundland 35, 114
   New York 107, 114
   New Zealand 114
   Pakistan 114, 139 n38
   Papua, New Guinea 115
   Peru 115
   Philippines 15, 114–115
   San Antonio, TX 114
   San Francisco 114, 124, 211 n5
   Scotland 115
   Slovakia 115
   Tasmania 114–115
   Waterford 114, 119–126 n24
   Zambia 115
   Zimbabwe 115
Protestant Society for the Promotion of Christian Knowledge 34

Relief Acts 30
Rice, Edmund Ignatius 93–94, 98–102, 119–126 n29
Robbins, Mrs Ann 195
Roche, Fr James 192
Roche, Thomas 107, 198
Rule and Constitutions 65–66, 71, 123

St Finbarr's Church 20, 62
St Ledger, Mrs 120
Schillebeeckx, Edward 166
Second Vatican Council 163–169, 208, 226, 228

Sergent, Mother Magdalene 124, 126 n24
Shortall, Fr Patrick 41
Sisters (Institute) of Charitable Instruction of the Sacred Heart of Jesus 18, 20, 38, 43, 45–46, 79, 85–86, 89, 100–102, 107, 141, 157, 218
Sisters of the Visitation 19, 40–41, 115
Sleyne, Dr John, Bishop of Cork 80
Society of Friends (Quakers) 94

Tierney, Margaret 120
Tobin, Anastasia 45, 141
Troy, Dr John Thomas, Archbishop of Dublin 39

Ursulines 20, 35, 39–46, 56–57, 60, 74, 79, 82–85, 102, 107, 110, 112–113, 131, 159, 190–197, 199, 219, 223

Waters, George 194–195
Welbig, Sr Lynn Marie 209
Wild Geese 26
Williamite Wars 25